RWANDAN
WOMEN
RISING

RWANDAN WOMEN RISING

Swanee Hunt

FOREWORD BY JIMMY CARTER

Duke University Press | Durham and London | 2017

Library of Congress Cataloging-in-Publication Data
Names: Hunt, Swanee.
Title: Rwandan women rising / Swanee Hunt.
Description: Durham : Duke University Press, 2017. |
Includes bibliographical references and index.
Identifiers:
LCCN 2016045798 (print)
LCCN 2016047433 (ebook)
ISBN 9780822362579 (hardcover : alk. paper)
ISBN 9780822373568 (ebook)
Subjects: LCSH: Women—Political activity—Rwanda. | Women
and democracy—Rwanda. | Rwanda—History—Civil War,
1994—Atrocities. | Rwanda—History—Civil War, 1994—Personal
narratives. | Rwanda—Politics and government—1994–
Classification: LCC HQ1236.5.R95 H86 2017 (print) |
LCC HQ1236.5.R95 (ebook) | DDC 320.082/0967571—dc23
LC record available at https://lccn.loc.gov/2016045798

Unless otherwise noted, photos by Swanee Hunt Alternatives.

Cover art: Photos by author.

Women understand most the importance of peace.

In conflicts, women are the ones hurt most,
so each will participate in the recovery some way.

Look at the key institutions in our country today.

Women are providing leadership.

There's no way you can talk about the transformation of society
unless that group is involved.

Much as we want to benefit from this process,
we also want to be a part of it.

There's no way you can avoid 55 percent of a population
and think they'll be just recipients.

We have to be agents of peace.

We can't just have peace delivered to us on a plate.

ALOISEA INYUMBA
1964–2012

CONTENTS

Major Historical Events and the
Rise of Women's Leadership

11th–19th centuries: Rwanda organized into kingdoms. Feudal structure, with general distinctions between farmers (Hutu), herders (Tutsi), and hunter-gatherers (Twa).

Late 1800s: Tutsi King Kigeri Rwabugiri establishes unified state with centralized military.

1885: Berlin Conference divides Africa, giving the region of Rwanda to Germany.

1890: Rwanda and Burundi (Ruanda-Urundi) becomes part of German East Africa.

1895–1931: Nyirayuhi V Kanjogera is Queen Mother, then regent, during the reign of her son.

1916: During World War I, Allies capture German East Africa. Belgians occupy the region.

1923: League of Nations grants Belgium mandate. It rules Rwanda and Burundi through Tutsi kings.

1933: Belgian census categorizes population based on height, shape of nose, and color of eyes. Colonists issue identity cards distinguishing Rwandans as Tutsi (15 percent), Hutu (80 percent), or Twa (1 percent).

1957: Hutus issue manifesto calling for a voice proportionate to their presence.

1959: Hutu Power movement, self-described as "social revolution." Some 150,000 Tutsis flee to neighboring states following ethnic violence.

1961: Rwanda proclaimed a republic, amid rising nationalism and Africa's rejection of colonialism.

1962: Independence from Belgium. New president Gregoire Kayibanda is Hutu. Many Tutsi families flee the country.

1964: Madeleine Ayinkamiye appointed minister of social affairs and public health, becoming first-ever woman in a cabinet position in Rwanda.

1965: First woman elected to Parliament, A. Mukakayange.

1973: Military coup led by Major General Juvénal Habyarimana ousts President Gregoire Kayibanda. Powerful clan connected to Habyarimana's wife rises to influence as Agathe becomes first lady.

1973: Continued ethnic violence. Tutsi students purged from universities; quotas restrict Tutsi employment.

1986: Pioneering activists create first Rwandan women's organization, Réseau des Femmes Oeuvrant pour le Développement Rural (Women's Network for Rural Development).

1986: Rwandan exiles, largely Tutsi, living in Uganda form the Rwandan Patriotic Front (RPF), with political chapters throughout the diaspora.

1990: The RPF invades Rwanda, fighting in opposition to Habyarimana's government. Militant Hutu youth organize into Interahamwe paramilitaries.

1991: Adoption of new constitution and end of one-party political system. President Habyarimana's ruling Mouvement Révolutionnaire National pour le Développement (MRND) continues to dominate, but other parties emerge and some of their representatives are appointed to government.

1992: President Habyarimana creates new Ministry of Family and Women's Development.

1992: Women activists hold first-ever public demonstration, the Women's March for Peace, calling for talks and protesting the arrest of Tutsi women, whom the government accuse of being part of the RPF because of their ethnicity.

1992: Activists create Pro-Femmes Twese Hamwe, which will become the country's largest network of women's rights organizations.

1993: Agathe Uwilingiyimana becomes the country's first female prime minister, and only the third ever in Africa. She is targeted politically and physically throughout her career.

August 1993: President Habyarimana and the RPF sign the Arusha Accords, which mandate a power-sharing government. The United Nations deploys 2,500 troops to oversee implementation.

April 6, 1994: Habyarimana dies when his plane is shot down as it comes in for a landing in Kigali.

April 7, 1994: House-to-house killings of Tutsi and moderate Hutu politicians by the Forces Armées Rwandaises and allied Interahamwe. Prime Minister Uwilingiyimana, a Hutu in the political opposition, her husband, and their children murdered at their home.

April 21, 1994: United Nations Security Council passes a resolution for the withdrawal of all but 270 UN troops, in the wake of the killing of ten Belgian peacekeepers. Violence spirals.

April–July 1994: In one hundred days, 800,000 killed. Two million flee fearing retribution, most crossing into eastern Congo.

July 1994: Rwandan Patriotic Front captures the capital, Kigali.

November 1994: United Nations establishes International Criminal Tribunal for Rwanda (ICTR), in Arusha, Tanzania.

November 1994: Transitional National Assembly first session; members of Parliament sworn in.

1995: Rwandan delegation at Fourth World Conference on Women in Beijing. A watershed for the budding women's movement.

1996: Genocide Law categorizes offenses and sentences for crimes committed during the genocide. Following riveting testimony from women who were sexually tortured, final law classifies rape among the gravest offenses.

1996: Countrywide women's councils elevate female perspectives in governing and social policy making.

1996–1997: More than a million Rwandans who fled fearing RPF revenge return.

September 2, 1998: First case decided for ICTR and first person ever tried for rape as a crime of genocide. Jean-Paul Akayesu found guilty. The prosecution relied on testimonies of women from Taba, where Akayesu was mayor.

1999: Extensive advocacy by women in Parliament and civil society. Government adopts Inheritance Law so husbands and fathers can pass on property to their wives and daughters.

2000: Countrywide gacaca courts, grassroots justice process, designed to try hundreds of thousands accused of role in genocide.

2001: Children's Rights Law emerges—collaboration between women in Parliament and civil society.

2001: Some 35 percent of newly elected gacaca judges are women.

2002: Gacaca courts begin.

August 2003: New constitution promulgated after consultation led by a commission of twelve drafters, three of whom are women. Enshrines equality between ethnic groups and between men and women. Women must hold at least 30 percent of government decision-making posts.

September 2003: First postgenocide parliamentary election. Women win 48 percent of seats.

2005: Land reform requires legally married couples to jointly register property.

2008: Parliament approves Gender-Based Violence Law. Mandates strict punishments for all sexual violence, including domestic abuse.

2008: Female members of Parliament now in women-only seats vie in general election. First country in the world with female majority, at 56 percent.

2009: Nine-year basic education policy makes primary school plus three years accessible to all. Particular push for girls.

2013: Women in Parliament rate soars to 64 percent when major political parties put forth equal numbers of female and male candidates.

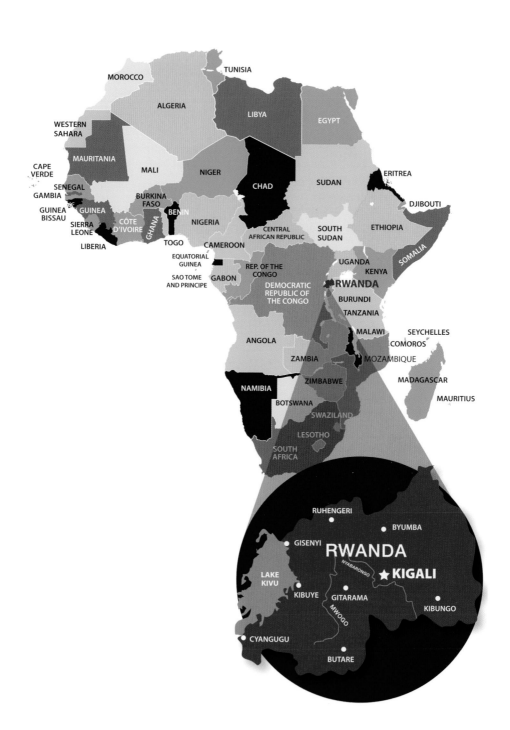

KEY TERMS

AVEGA	Association des Veuves de Génocide, a group founded by widows whose husbands were killed during the genocide
BDF	Business Development Fund
CEDAW	Convention on the Elimination of All Forms of Discrimination Against Women
FAR	Forces Armées Rwandaises, the armed forces of the Habyarimana government prior to 1994 (also referred to as ex-FAR)
FAWE	Forum for African Women Educationalists, a group whose Rwanda chapter founded girls' schools focused on sciences
FDLR	Democratic Forces for the Liberation of Rwanda, a militia based in the Democratic Republic of Congo led by some of the perpetrators of the Rwandan genocide
FFRP	Forum des Femmes Rwandaises Parlementaires, the women's caucus in Parliament
Gacaca	grassroots, community-based justice system
GBV	gender-based violence
ICTR	International Criminal Tribunal for Rwanda, headquartered in Arusha, Tanzania

Ingando	"solidarity camps" in which soon-to-be-released prisoners, demobilized soldiers, students, and others participate prior to integrating into their new community
Interahamwe	Hutu paramilitary organization backed by the Rwandan government in power during the genocide
MIGEPROF	Ministry of Gender and Family Promotion, which has existed (with slight variations in name) since 1992
MRND	Mouvement Révolutionnaire National pour le Développement, political party of President Juvénal Habyarimana
NGO	non-governmental organization
Pro-Femmes	shortened form of Pro-Femmes Twese Hamwe, an umbrella organization linking women's promotion groups countrywide
Réseau des Femmes	shortened form of Réseau des Femmes Oeuvrant pour le Développement Rural, a women's network for rural development, founded in the late 1980s
RPF	Rwandan Patriotic Front
SEVOTA	Solidarité pour l'Epanouissement des Veuves et des Orphelins visant le Travail et l'Auto-promotion, which translates to Solidarity for the Blooming of the Widows and the Orphans Aiming at Work and Self-Promotion
UNICEF	United Nations Children's Fund

BIOGRAPHIES OF SPEAKERS

Preferred name capitalized.

AGNES Mukabaranga is a private lawyer who served in the transitional parliament from 1994 to 2012.

AIMABLE Nibishaka was an advisor at the Ministry of Gender and Family Promotion before being elected to Parliament in 2003, where he served until his death in 2011.

Aisa KIRABO Kacyira trained as a veterinarian and devoted her early career to working in farming communities before being elected to Parliament, and then became mayor of Kigali. She serves as deputy executive director of UN HABITAT.

ALICE Urusaro Karekezi is an activist and lecturer with a background in law. She spearheaded campaigns during the first trials at the International Criminal Tribunal for Rwanda and was an outspoken advocate for women giving testimony.

Aloisea INYUMBA was an influential member of the RPF in exile and served as the commissioner of finance. After 1994 she held numerous leadership posts, including minister of gender, head of the National Unity and Reconciliation Commission, governor, and senator. She died in 2012.

ALOYSIE Cyanzaire led the gacaca process when it began in 2000 and then became chief justice of the Supreme Court from 2003 to 2011, where she organized the country's judicial reform.

ALPHONSINE Mukarugema was a secondary school teacher, headmistress, and women's council member in southern Rwanda. In 2003 she was elected to Parliament, where she continues to serve.

ALPHONSINE Niyigena is a businesswoman who serves on several corporate boards and is a mentor to the students at her Universal Beauty Academy.

ANGELINA Muganza was minister of gender and women's development from 1999 to 2002 and has continued in public service since then.

ANITA Asiimwe is a physician specializing in public health, with a passion for children. She served as state minister of public health and is now the head of clinical services at Rwanda University Teaching Hospitals.

ANNE MARIE Musabyemungu is an activist who played an instrumental role in convincing Rwandan rebels fighting in Congo to come home, starting with her husband. She went on to serve as a member of Parliament.

ANNONCIATA Nyirabajiwabo, a devout Catholic and a widow due to the 1994 genocide, helped create a support network of women in her church to care for each other, including wives with husbands in prison.

APOPHIA Batamuliza enlisted in the RPF when she was twenty-six years old and living in Rwanda. She was demobilized in 2004 and works for the army reserve.

ATHANASIE Kabagwira is a sociologist dedicated to the promotion of women's equality and equity. She has been an activist in Rwanda since the late 1980s.

BEATRICE Mukabaranga trained as a botanist and science teacher, worked in education, and then served as a senator until 2009. She chaired the Rwanda chapter of the Forum for African Women Educationalists (FAWE) and continues to be an active member.

Bernard MAKUZA is a politician who served as prime minister from 2000 to 2011 and is president of the Senate. He was a senior advisor to Agathe Uwilingiyimana, who became prime minister in 1993 and was assassinated on the first day of the genocide.

BERTHILDE Niyibaho is an entrepreneur and founder of BN Producers, a company specializing in mushrooms.

CAROLE Karemera is an artist, an art activist, and a mother. She grew up in Belgium, visited Rwanda in 1996 as a college student, then moved there a few years later.

CHANTAL Kayitesi is a nurse who joined with many other widows after the genocide to create AVEGA, the Association for Widows of the Genocide.

CHRISTINE Tuyisenge became a lawyer to advocate for the rights of women and children especially, a passion she put into practice as a member of Haguruka and with the National Women Council.

CHRISTOPHE Bazivamo is an agriculture specialist and member of the East African Legislative Assembly, representing Rwanda.

CHRISTOPHER Kayumba is a columnist and senior lecturer at the University of Rwanda who has a PhD in peace and development research. He wrote the 2010 book *Understanding High Presence of Women in Rwanda's Parliament.*

"CLAUDINE" became an activist in the 1980s and remains one today.

CONNIE Bwiza Sekamana joined the transitional parliament in 1999 and was reelected three times as an MP for the RPF.

DIDIER G. Sagashya was a key player in the country's implementation of land reform, holding senior posts at the National Land Centre and then with the Rwanda Natural Resources Authority.

DINAH Musindarwezo is a gender specialist who heads the Pan-African women's rights organization FEMNET.

DOMITILLA Mukantaganzwa is a lawyer who served on the twelve-person commission that drafted Rwanda's constitution and led the National Service of Gacaca Courts for nearly a decade until it closed in 2012.

ELISEE Rutagambwa is a Catholic priest and headmaster of Saint Ignatius High School. Father Elisee received his PhD from Boston College, where he wrote his dissertation on the historical role of women in Rwanda.

Emmanuel GASANA is inspector general for the Rwandan National Police, based in Kigali.

EMMANUEL Rutangusa is a Catholic priest who completed seminary in Kenya and returned to his native Rwanda in 1995 to serve in the Nyumba Parish. He is completing his doctorate at Rivier Catholic University in New Hampshire.

ESTHER Mbabazi became RwandAir's first female Rwandan pilot at age twenty-four, achieving her lifelong dream. She is also a mentor to young Rwandans.

FATUMA Ndangiza has held many government posts since she returned to Rwanda in 1994, including the National Unity and Reconciliation Commission, which she led for nearly eight years. She is deputy CEO of the Rwanda Governance Board.

FELIX Muramutsa is a researcher in psychosocial issues who served as the board chair for the women and children's rights group Haguruka.

FLORENCE Kamili Kayiraba is a gender and grassroots democracy activist and served in various elected posts in local government, including mayor.

"GISELLE" attended one of the government's "reeducation" camps before starting university.

GODELIEVE Mukasarasi is a counselor who specializes in trauma and founded the group SEVOTA to support women who had survived rape during the genocide, especially those who had children as a result of their attack.

"GRACE" is an activist for women's rights from rural Rwanda. Eager to fight against impunity for rapists on behalf of many women like her who survived rape, she went to the International Criminal Tribunal in Tanzania to give testimony in the case against Jean-Paul Akayesu.

IMMACULEE Ingabire is a journalist by training and an activist by conviction. Her reporting was instrumental in bringing to light the stories of women who survived rape during the genocide.

INNOCENT Bulindi is CEO of the Business Development Fund, who has a keen interest in promoting financial inclusion for women and small business owners. He started his finance career in banking and telecoms.

ISABELLE Kalihangabo is a lawyer and former judge now serving in the Ministry of Justice. She studied law at University of Rwanda and Queen Mary University of London and was involved in Rwanda's postgenocide legal reforms, including in devising Kinyarwanda language legal terminology.

JANE Abatoni Gatete is a senior trauma counselor and founding member of Rwandan Association of Trauma Counselors, which she has led since 1998.

JANE Umutoni studies women's economic inclusion and is an assistant lecturer affiliated with the Centre for Gender Studies at the University of Rwanda.

JANET Nkubana, the cofounder with her sister Joy of the company Gahaya Links, felt inspired by her background in arts to preserve and modernize Rwandan handicrafts and work to empower the women who make them.

Jeanne d'Arc GAKUBA is vice president of the Senate. She started her political career on the women's council and quickly rose to become vice mayor of Kigali.

JEANNE D'ARC Kanakuze, a longtime activist, was a cofounder of the umbrella organization Pro-Femmes Twese Hamwe and the national leader of the Girl Scouts.

JEANNE D'ARC Mukasekuru is an activist for her community, Rwanda's indigenous population known as the potters, and a mother of two.

JEANNETTE Kagame is first lady of Rwanda and head of the Imbuto Foundation, which, among its many programs, focuses on health and education programs for women and girls.

John MUTAMBA has carved out a niche as a rare, long-committed male advocate for women's rights. He consults for UN Women, among other international agencies.

JOSEPHINE Dusabimana lives in the lakeside town of Kibuye, in western Rwanda, where she farms and takes care of her five children and dozen grandchildren.

JOY Mukanyange served as ambassador to Kenya and Tanzania, among other posts with the Ministry of Foreign Affairs. She consults on projects related to women, peace, and security and is active in several civil society groups.

JOY Ndungutse is cofounder of Gahaya Links, a company she created with her sister Janet, that focuses on creating jobs and changing the lives of rural women.

JUDITH Kanakuze was an activist known especially for spearheading the law against gender-based violence that passed in 2008. She founded the early women's group Réseau des Femmes and served on the constitution drafting commission and in Parliament. She died in 2010.

JULIE Uwamwiza's career has long focused on economic empowerment of rural women. Her first job was with one of the country's earliest women's rights groups, Duterimbere.

JUSTINE Mbabazi is a gender specialist and rights activist who has worked as a legal advisor in postconflict countries across Africa and Asia. She closely consulted on numerous gender-equalizing reforms in her native Rwanda.

JUSTINE Uvuza is a gender and legal scholar who received her PhD from Newcastle University, where she wrote her dissertation on the experiences of Rwandan female leaders balancing family and political responsibilities.

LOUISE Mushikiwabo has been a member of President Kagame's cabinet since she returned to Rwanda in 2008, serving first as minister of information, and since 2009 as minister of foreign affairs.

MAMA DIANE and her mother are the only members of their family who survived the 1994 genocide. A survivor of rape, she chose to tell her story during the gacaca process. She's a member of a local reconciliation organization in the town of Taba.

MAMA MADINA is passionate about the education of her children. She decided to give testimony during the gacaca trials as a woman who had been raped by her neighbors, because she felt it was important for the rebuilding of society.

MAMA REBECCA, aka Jeanne d'Arc Mukarunyange, is a woman who loved the army from childhood. She's a reservist and feels the army is the main commitment in her life.

"MARIE CLAIRE" was elected to serve as a judge in a grassroots tribunal after the genocide.

MARIE Mukantabana was directing the National Insurance Company when she was tapped to become minister of gender and then vice president of the Senate. A member of the RPF, she chaired the RPF Women's League.

MARIE THERESE Mukamulisa is a Supreme Court justice who started her legal career in the private sector and civil society. She was one of three women on the twelve-person constitutional drafting commission.

MARY Balikungeri became an activist during the antiapartheid movement and founded the Rwandan Women's Network in 1997.

MATHILDE Mukantabana was a history professor in her adoptive home of California when she was tapped to serve as Rwandan ambassador to the United States. She has been an active organizer among the diaspora for many years.

NADINE Niyitegeka graduated from the Akilah Institute for Women in 2013 and since then has served as a development and recruitment associate for Rwanda's first all-female college.

ODA Gasinzigwa is a gender expert who has long focused her career on women's empowerment. An expert in monitoring and evaluation, she serves as minister for gender and family promotion.

ODETTE Nyiramilimo is a physician, health activist, and long-serving senator. She is a member of the East African Legislative Assembly.

Oswald SAMVURA is a longtime activist promoting women's participation, primarily through the women's development group Seruka. He formerly worked with the Ministry of Gender and Family Promotion.

PATRICIA Hajabakiga led the Ministry for State, Lands, and Environment for ten years, first as permanent secretary and then as state minister, and now serves as a member of the East African Legislative Assembly.

Paul KAGAME is president of Rwanda. He grew up in a Ugandan refugee camp; later, as a general he led the RPF, which returned to the country and ended the 1994 genocide.

Paul RUTAYISIRE is a professor of modern African and Rwandan histories and the director of the Center for Conflict Management at the University of Rwanda.

Protais MUSONI was deputy secretary-general of the RPF and served as a cabinet minister.

RICHARD Masozera is a physician by training and a long-serving officer in the Rwandan Defense Forces and the government. He married Aloisea Inyumba in 1996, and they have two children.

"ROBERT" served as a judge during the grassroots justice process called gacaca.

ROSE Kabuye enlisted in the RPF while the group was organizing in exile and is the highest-ranking woman to serve. She retired in 2003 as a lieutenant colonel and has held civilian leadership positions, such as mayor of Kigali and member of Parliament.

ROSE Mukantabana trained as a lawyer and was the first woman elected to serve as president of the Chamber of Deputies, the lower house of Rwanda's Parliament.

SISTER JUVENAL is a nun with the Benebikira congregation and the headmistress of the girls-only Maranyundo secondary school in Nyamata.

SPECIOSE Mukandutiye is a member of Parliament and served as president of the women's caucus from 2007 to 2009.

SUZANNE Ruboneka, cocreator of Pro-Femmes in the early 1990s, is a women's rights activist who has devoted her career to promoting a culture of peace in the Great Lakes region of Africa.

THERESE Bishagara is a senator and molecular biologist by training, who was appointed to lead the Kigali Health Institute when it opened in 1996, and stayed until 2004. She is a founding member of the Rwanda chapter of the Forum for African Women Educationalists (FAWE).

VESTINE is an orphan of the genocide who became the caregiver for her younger sisters. Facing rejection from the family of the man who raped and impregnated her during the genocide, she spoke out during gacaca to establish the truth about the crimes and her daughter's birth.

Wellars GASAMAGERA was a long-serving senator and before that a governor. He now heads the Rwanda Management Institute.

WINNIE Byanyima, a Ugandan diplomat and politician, took the helm of Oxfam International in 2013. She was an idolized elder sister and mentor to many Rwandan women as they started to organize.

ZAINA Nyiramatama founded the women's and children's rights group Haguruka to be a Rwandan UNICEF. She served as head of the National Commission of Children from 2011 until 2015, when she was appointed African Union Special Representative to Chad.

After 1994, women participated in elections not just as voters but as candidates too.

The world itself is now dominated by a new spirit. Peoples
more numerous and more politically aware are craving, and
now demanding, their place in the sun—not just for the
benefit of their own physical condition, but for basic human
rights. The passion for freedom is on the rise.

—INAUGURAL ADDRESS, JANUARY 20, 1977

Swanee Hunt's *Rwandan Women Rising* describes a remarkable example
of the spirit referred to in this epigraph. She not only captures Rwandan
women's stories of rebirth after the unspeakable hundred-day genocide of
1994—she actually shows us how they survived this cataclysm to become
catalysts for the most impressive transformation in all of Africa. And
importantly, she reveals these lessons through the voices of the women
themselves. Her interviews paint detailed pictures of the obstacles they
had to overcome, as well as their many small victories that gradually led
to enormous wins for the whole society.

At the Carter Center, which Rosalynn and I launched after my presidency, we have worked for democracy and development in more than
140 countries, many of them torn by violence and conflict. Through
this work, we learned that when women are actively involved, countries
are more likely to embrace human rights in practical ways. We've seen
how the inclusion of women and girls enables nations to end bloodshed,
achieve stability, and sustain the growth that usually follows.

We saw this illustrated in a different nation that I visited in 1978, when
I made the first presidential visit to sub-Saharan Africa. It was no accident
that I chose Liberia, given its founding by freed American slaves. Two years

later, disaster struck: the president and his entire cabinet were assassinated, and a terrible civil war ensued. Rosalynn and I visited frequently as the country descended into brutal ruin. Finally, we watched women launch a campaign that forced a brutal warlord into exile and shaped a peace deal that included democratic elections. The winner was Ellen Johnson Sirleaf, Africa's first elected female president and one of two Liberian women awarded the Nobel medal for peace.

We chose the slogan Empower Men and Women Together as we helped Liberians establish rural justice systems. This was not about helping women and girls; it was about making the entire society more fair and just. It became evident very quickly that greater involvement of women in community decision making was benefiting all citizens.

In 1995, at the time of our Liberia experience but on the other side of the continent, Rwanda was reeling from the genocidal slaughter of about 800,000 Tutsis by Hutus. The Tutsi-led troops that stopped the carnage had pursued the genocidal Hutus all the way into Zaire (later named the Democratic Republic of Congo). Along the way, the ranks of those fleeing swelled to a million with other Hutus fearing retribution.

Rosalynn and I visited the enormous refugee camp in Goma, just across the Rwandan border in the DRC. In this book, Anne Marie Musabyemungu, who had fled the country after the genocide, talks about the hideous health conditions of that camp, which we witnessed firsthand. It was impossible to secure the periphery, or create any semblance of security for those inside the camp, or for those outside.

What I remember most vividly about that camp is that violence against women and girls was rampant. That didn't have to be. But the realization that haunts me is how, when we convened presidents from the region, they made agreements that could have helped their countries stabilize and prevent disasters like that camp. Instead, even as there had been little appetite for intervening in the genocide, we received no support for those meetings from the international community. With no coherent force to hold it back, rape, not as a sexual act but as a weapon of war, exploded in eastern Congo. Bottles, sticks, and bayonets were used to rape women—in that one act mutilating them for life.

Our inadequate peace process is where Ambassador Hunt's story begins. Five years after our thwarted efforts, she began her close association with the women of Rwanda. In these pages we hear the heartbeat of that society. We listen to the mothers. We hear from politicians and businesswomen. We watch those running the local reconciliation courts that were at the grass roots of society. We follow their halting advances at the helm in hamlets and in the capital. We explore how Rwanda has become the standard bearer in female political representation: 64 percent of the seats in Parliament, not to mention half the cabinet and half the Supreme Court.

Both Liberia and Rwanda are contending with a host of problems, and it is a modern miracle that they haven't fallen back into war. Instead, Rwandan women in particular have set a high standard for stemming gender-based violence, which has been a major concern for our center in the past several years. Recently, Swanee and I have aligned as partners on confronting the purchasing of the bodies of women and girls by focusing on the brothel owners, pimps, and buyers—the men who fuel the market. Stopping that abuse is integral to the theme of my recent book, *A Call to Action: Women, Religion, Violence, and Power.*

Since I came to know Swanee Hunt in the early 1990s, we've crossed paths on different continents and across decades as we've worked together on free elections, against corruption, toward independent media, and for decent health conditions. At the heart of our work, we're fueled by our shared Southern roots and evangelical heritage. I have taught Bible lessons for more than seventy years, and as a former minister of pastoral care, Swanee holds convictions similar to mine. It's no secret that we both have found it impossible to square our religious faith with current stances of the Southern Baptist Convention. Rosalynn and I broke with our church denomination in part over its interpretation that scripture insists that women should be submissive to their husbands, and inferior to men in the eyes of God. We have found solace in the biblical injunction that in Christ Jesus there is no difference between Jew and Gentile, slave and free—or man and woman.

When we discard the creed of men's power over women, we make room for God's power of redemption. I was deeply moved by the story in these pages of Annonciata Nyirabajiwabo, a survivor of genocide joining with other Catholic mothers who were wives of imprisoned perpetrators of the terrible crime. Together preparing meals for the inmates, they were the embodiment of Jesus's parable in the Gospel of Matthew. "There the righteous ask the king, When did we see you hungry and feed you, in prison and visit you? And the king answers, When you did it to the least of these, you did it to me."

Over the years, I have taken pride in watching Swanee fight for recognition of the fact that true security must be inclusive. She argues that we underestimate the importance of not only women's wisdom, but also their knowledge and ability to lead.

Along those lines, in what seems like a modern parable, I remember telling Swanee about our visit to Zimbabwe to honor the Farmer of the Year. After we presented his award, I wanted to see his fields, but the farmer objected. Finally he agreed. I walked alongside him, with Rosalynn and his wife behind. We reached a fine crop of corn. "What kind of seed do you use?" I asked. He hesitated, then looked behind him for the answer. "And when do you apply fertilizer?" Again, he turned to his wife, the actual farmer.

To return to Rwanda and Liberia, it's worth noting that the United States has a lot to learn from those countries. Liberia has a woman as president, and Rwanda has an overwhelming majority of women in its Parliament. Women hold fewer than 20 percent of the seats in our own Congress.

On every continent, there are countries where a dramatic increase in women's influence has led to a peaceful foreign policy, higher education levels, longer life expectancy, safer streets, even cleaner water. These gains aren't coincidental.

So we're left to ask ourselves, what forces can we exert that will elevate women's status and utilize their capacity? In Rwanda, there has been a powerful blend of a pull from the top and a push up from the grass roots. In Liberia and Rwanda, the reforms have emerged out of war. Our challenge is to have them emerge peacefully.

PLAINS, GEORGIA
MAY 2, 2016

Over the past two decades, the eyes of the world have been riveted on a small state in the vast interior of Africa. Before the 1994 genocide, precious few Westerners had heard of Rwanda, home of three intermarried groups: Tutsi, Hutu, and Twa.

In the spring of 1994, we—individuals like me, a member of the innocuously named "international community"—watched from the sidelines as group turned on group in a horrific slaughter. Our gaze was a combined expression of horror, fascination, and the despair of knowing we had to help but not knowing how. As we waited to intervene, Rwanda was literally decimated: 10 percent of the population butchered. As one Rwandese diplomat commented, wryly, "Rwanda was rescued by Rwandans."

Killing squads went door to door, hill by hill, on the hunt for those they deemed "cockroaches." The offense of the targeted citizens was being classified by ID cards as members of one of the country's small minorities—the Tutsi. In a mere one hundred days, nearly one million people were killed, many by neighbors, even family members.

As the *genocidaires* fled over the border to Congo in July 1994, Rwanda lay in ruins: churches and schools turned into massacre sites, roadsides turned into open graves. Those who witnessed the horrors and managed to survive faced the tormenting task of rebuilding when every semblance of normality had vanished.

Hundreds of conversations I've had over the past sixteen years reveal an untold tale. Laden with personal burdens but driven by an ethic of responsibility, women stepped forward. In villages, mothers made sure bodies were buried. One initiated a countrywide adoption program that found homes for nearly 100,000 children whose parents were murdered. The stories of Rwandan women are awe inspiring in their passion and startling in their pragmatism.

The people around me were women, says Father **EMMANUEL**, a newly ordained priest who had lost his family in the genocide. His first posting after seminary was to a rural parish. Their church had been burned, then bulldozed, with hundreds of desperate people inside. *Women helped me reconstruct the parish, physically and in terms of the community. The way I saw it, men were more affected by the violence, even though I think women suffered more. Afterward, men couldn't do much. Women saw that they had no alternative.*

As chaos cracked open the culture, women were no longer confined to holding positions of influence solely in their homes. Given the urgent needs pressing all around them, they expanded their leadership at a revolutionary pace. Still, this wasn't a feminist uprising by design.

We didn't immediately think of creating an organization. **CHANTAL** was a founding member of a widows' organization I visited in 2001, now one of the most influential civil society groups in the country. *Most women in our group were housewives who hadn't had much schooling. We met because we needed to meet, to listen and understand each other. We needed to think things through together . . . like how we would provide for our children.*

With a strong pull from the new president, Paul Kagame, women pushed for female-friendly policies and prominent positions in the government, led initiatives to cope with the traumatic aftermath of genocide, and established businesses in the extremely fragile economy. Many who had found their voices at the national level returned to their rural communities to encourage more women to vie for public office.

In 2003, the first election since the genocide, women won 48.8 percent of seats in the lower house of Parliament, far surpassing the newly mandated 30 percent quota. In 2008 they took an even larger stride, securing 56 percent of seats and becoming the first parliament in history—anywhere in the world—with a female majority. Their gains weren't only political; across society, women took up influential roles.

One of the greatest names among Rwandan women—or men, for that matter—is Aloisea Inyumba. Our friendship began in July 2000, when I first came to Kigali to speak at a women's conference hosted by the Amer-

Aloisea Inyumba, 1964–2012.

ican embassy. As gender minister, she seemed to be an organizing force at that meeting of Women as Partners for Peace, with representatives from several neighboring countries. I was struck by how comfortable she was in her skin and the deference others seemed to grant her.

At the end of the conference, Inyumba (as she was known by followers throughout East Africa) took me to see President Kagame on my way to the airport. A year earlier, he had publicly expressed sensitivity to the economic and social benefits of gender equality, so I wasn't surprised as he and I exchanged similar views about how women shift not only the internal policies and practices of a country, but also how it is perceived from outside. "Make women the new face of Rwanda," I encouraged.

Humbly soft-spoken, Inyumba had grown up impoverished in a Ugandan refugee camp, her father killed as he and his wife, pregnant with her, fled an earlier Rwandan genocide that broke out in 1959 when the country was on the verge of its independence. In exile, Inyumba was a trusted friend of Paul Kagame. While he and Fred Rwigema organized the Rwandan Patriotic Front to reclaim a place in their native country, she mobilized Rwandans worldwide, collecting financial support for the far-outnumbered rebels.

After the last shots were fired, given her reputation for frugality and honesty, Aloisea Inyumba became a key player in the postgenocide restoration. It was over this urgent work that she and I bonded—as mothers with a mission. I had a young daughter, and she had a young daughter, but we also felt responsible for distressed children beyond our own. Kagame had asked Inyumba to serve as head of the crucial National Unity and Reconciliation Commission. Creating her own role, she was spending day after day crisscrossing rutted roads to villages throughout the country. There, she encouraged the broken to talk about, act out, or compose songs describing the impossible gore they had witnessed, the family who had been slaughtered, the homes that were no more.

When Inyumba introduced us, President Kagame asked me to help women advance in public and social spheres. My primary contribution to this bold Rwandan experiment has been to equip their women leaders. As the founder of the Women and Public Policy Program at Harvard's Kennedy School of Government and the Washington, DC–based Institute for Inclusive Security, I've taught and supported the leadership development of several hundred Rwandan women in settings inside and outside their country. In addition, Inclusive Security opened an office in Kigali for two years, from which our staff assisted the women in Parliament as they developed a strategic plan to promote their agenda for social change and stability.

Although she was revered by her people, **INYUMBA** once said to me, *I spoke in Rwanda before we met, but it was at Harvard—in the training weeks with you—that I found my voice.* I'm sure my friend had no idea that she, in turn, helped me find mine.

.   .   .

This work is personal. I'm approaching the idea of documenting women's leadership in Rwanda from the perspective of having worked with women leaders in sixty countries for more than two decades. Though my career has been segmented, my work has always been related.

For many years in Colorado I focused on public education, homelessness, race relations, mental health, and low-income community development. Subsequently (in the mid-1990s) as U.S. ambassador to Austria, I oversaw a complicated embassy of five hundred employees, many working across imploded postcommunist economies of central and eastern Europe. I made more than twenty trips across that region, finding pockets of strength within frail societies.

Among those, some countries were much more than frail. The tragic, dramatic collapse was, of course, Yugoslavia, where my husband, Charles Ansbacher, became the principal guest conductor of the symphony and I, well, I did whatever the situation seemed to require. Sometimes that meant meeting with unheeded women leaders in rooms with no heat or electricity; I chronicled their work with video interviews and journal entries that became a newspaper series and two books. Sometimes it was speaking on behalf of President Bill Clinton, such as at the opening of the U.S. embassy in Sarajevo. Sometimes it was hosting peace talks, and not noticing that there wasn't one female among the dozens on the negotiating teams.

In each of those situations I've become convinced that the best way to reduce suffering and to prevent, end, and stabilize conflicts is to elevate women. Turning up the volume of their voices, we amplify waves of clarion change. Out of that understanding a network of thousands of leaders from scores of conflicts has grown Women Waging Peace, now part of Inclusive Security mentioned above. In capitals all over the world, we are connecting these leaders to policy makers who badly need their help.

Even if there were no Aloisea Inyumba, I would be compelled to tell this story because of a simple promise. A dozen years ago, when Inyumba brought me to a widow's group in Rwanda, I met Fatima, a gaunt woman about thirty years old. Soldiers had raped her day after day until she lay unconscious, her baby on the ground at her side. Her other children were hacked to death with machetes. During the torture, she contracted AIDS. When we met, she offered me her thin, weak hand and stared intently into my eyes. Through an interpreter, she whispered, "I'm going to die soon, but will you tell others, so my story doesn't die with me?"

In the face of tiny Rwanda's desolation, lone superpower America did nothing to prevent the agony of Fatima. I was part of the U.S. security structure: a policy maker (among scores) with the ear of President Clinton, the first lady, and others. At the most personal level, failing to urge intervention, I failed as a leader.

There are many kinds of leadership, formal and informal, through position or persuasion. I know, because Rwandan women have led me, even as they've passed beyond this life. And so Inyumba remains my teacher, Fatima my conscience. This book is my promise kept to both.

WITH THANKS

A book sixteen years in the crafting has so many, many contributors, and I can touch only on a few. Those of you whose names are missing must do me one more good turn, to mentally write yourself into these acknowledgments.

The most important contributors are, of course, the generous Rwandan women who've taken me in. They've given me the greatest gift—friendship—and, as you might with a friend, found subtle ways to let me know I'm precariously close to crossing a cultural line or they'd like me to come closer. When life deals me tough times, I invariably think of them. They're unaware of how they've inspired whatever I've accomplished this last decade and a half, providing relative perspective for my own painful times.

In a more concrete way, I've depended on the synergistic help of colleagues at Inclusive Security, operating under the leadership first of Ambassador Hattie Babbitt, then the calmly talented Carla Koppell, and now a noble triumvirate of Evelyn Thornton, Jacqueline O'Neill, and Mersad Jacevic. Our board contributed not only wisdom, but also firsthand help with their impressions from a trip to Rwanda. Thank you all for offering me boosts all along the way.

There were three major phases in the writing of this book. The first was led by me, as beginning in 2000 I began to go regularly to Rwanda, building relationships, gathering information about what was happening with women there, and hosting some at Harvard and in our Washington, DC, offices.

Then to enrich our understanding at the ground level, from 2005 to 2007 Inclusive Security had a small Kigali office headed by Elizabeth

Powley with the able assistance of Elvis Gakuba, Justine Uvuza, and Ibrahim Murobafi. Elizabeth's expertise, hard work, and patience resulted in four scholarly papers on women's roles drafting legislation, decentralizing political power, defending children's rights, and strengthening their nation's new legislature. Her research forms a basic layer of the theoretical backbone of this book. But beyond, a decade later, Powley is a repeatedly cited source for other researchers. In addition, dozens of Elizabeth's early interviews offer a snapshot of a crucial moment in this story, when Rwanda's new constitution was being developed, leading the way for women's historic gains in the 2003 parliamentary election.

The interview process has been nonstop. Thank you to our Inclusive Security staff, but also to my students at Harvard's Kennedy School of Government who conducted interviews. Jessica Gomez and others helped create order out of a chaotic mound of material. And to Nashila Somani, Jean Demmler, Barbara Brockmeyer, and Lia Poorvu, thanks for your help in the field and at home.

The third phase was this last four years, pulling from dozens of sources to construct the final manuscript. Inside Rwanda, we had great help from the Ministry of Gender and Family Promotion, especially Honorable Minister Oda Gasinzigwa, and senior advisor Judith Kazayire. Mr. Alphonse Umulisa at Rwanda's National Museum and historians Rose Marie Mukarutabana and Jean-Paul Kimonyo were more than helpful, as were translators Sophie Manzi and Muhire Enock, and transcriber Jessica Lane. And as a photographer myself, I have enormous appreciation for Roopa Gogineni and Sarah Elliott's beautiful images that grace this book, as well as our internal organizer par excellence, Peggy Wang.

In these acknowledgments, Gisela Fosado at Duke University Press deserves her own space for giving me space to finish this book. Duke also, for letting me use material I already wrote for *Foreign Affairs*, the *Boston Globe*, *National Geographic*, and the *Daily Beast* to commemorate the twentieth anniversary of the genocide.

Bless her, Amy Sysyn was by my side during the last year of the project's remarkably long gestation, even counting how many times I lazily relied on "stunning" and "staggering" within each hundred pages. Likewise, a troop of my friends read and offered conceptual and granular suggestions for the manuscript, especially Catherine Heaton, Jim Laurie,

Jim Smith, Carol Edgar, Marie O'Reilly, and Sister Ann Fox. Thank you (I think) for hundreds of edits. With his extraordinary level of experience and sensitivity, Michael Fairbanks was in a class by himself, and we took to heart every suggestion.

I say "we," because when I was about halfway through this process my husband and thought partner of twenty-five years was diagnosed with a brain tumor, then died a year later. My grief was profound, and even though *Rising* was my fourth book, I wondered if I would, or could, finish it. Into my life, and into this project, stepped Laura Heaton, one of the most perceptive, industrious, talented, tolerant, and insistent people I've ever known. Laura is a specialist in East Africa who has lived and worked throughout the region. We worked hand in glove for three years, first sifting through the trove of interviews out of which my outline had emerged. Then inside the country much more than I could be, Laura followed leads from one story to another. As she added new marrow to the backbone, the form not only filled out but became a shape of unexpected angles and graceful curves. It's hard to imagine a future without Laura upside down in a yoga pose on the deck of our mountain ranch, or traipsing down to the kitchen for another cup of tea in our Cambridge home.

Speaking of home, somehow to say thanks to Charles is so expected that I almost didn't write it. But I will, so I can tell this story: At the Kigali airport, the last time I left Rwanda, I sat in the lounge with my friend Odette Nyiramilimo. "I haven't said it yet," she said. "But I'm so sorry about your loss of Charles."

Tears began to flow down my cheeks, then I remembered. "This feels so wrong. You lost something like seventy family members, right?"

"One hundred twenty," she corrected me. "But you can grieve. Every death is the same."

I actually don't believe that. We can, and must, compare pain. Rwandan women have survived loss I'll never comprehend. Having lost my partner in the middle of writing this book, I can imagine the effort it took for them to meet with me, much less open their stories to a stranger. And so I'll end where I began, with my appreciation for the women of Rwanda.

Cornfield consultation with Inyumba.

Rwandan Women Rising memorializes the resurrection of women from victims to leaders helping their country emerge from chaos. Unflinching and intertwined stories detail gruesome brutality and loss. But their raw experiences become the alchemy for grit, determination, and courage to help reconstruct a nation.

There is a strong theme of humility and generosity in the overall style of Rwandan women. At the grass roots, they've organized around common problems of poverty, shelter, health, and equality. Then, rather than driven by political ambition, they are drawn into the public sphere to protect their families and construct a new society.

Restoring their country means caring for one another as well, with trailblazing pragmatism as consensus builders and collaborators. They forgive when reconciliation defies imagination. They mentor when their own needs cry out for attention. They break a world record when seasoned legislators give up quota-ensured seats to run in the general contest, allowing a new wave to enter politics.

The five parts that follow capture the voices of some ninety pioneering women who grew from humble origins into these positions of political and social leadership. Telling the story of their resilience, savvy, and commitment was a hope expressed by **INYUMBA** numerous times during our twelve-year friendship, before her death in 2012 sent shockwaves across the world of her admirers.

There are so many women like me in Rwanda, who have done good work, my unwitting mentor told me. *Maybe others could learn from what we've gone through in such a short time, and just emerging from conflict too. If you look at the tremendous effort, the work that has been done by the grassroots communities—these stories need to be heard.*

Inyumba went on to say that when she traveled abroad she initially assumed everyone knew about *the good work being done by Rwandan women. But hardly anybody knows. . . .*

Many of her colleagues, like **JUSTINE M.**, have joined her in urging us to collect their stories. *We work extremely hard, but we don't know how to document our work. We don't know how to put it on paper so that our process can be a model. And the challenge we have now is to offer something to our sisters in Burundi and Congo—because they're at the beginning.*

It's no surprise to most who know Rwandan women that they've contributed to this book in order to help others. But these aren't helpers who remain behind the scenes of history. Through their accounts they are coauthors of astonishing and restorative tales. The narrative their voices create includes lessons in shared power, inclusivity, and transparency. And the trajectory of these women who rise from tragedy to influence is not the story of their personal ascension. It's the story of a country's redemption.

· · ·

It would be simplistic to assert that the genocide was a war on women waged by men. On the other hand, not to see dramatic female/male differences in this story requires fat blinders. The evidence: more than 94 percent of people accused of participating in the genocide were male.[1]

That's not to say that any one man is pathologically aggressive, or that no women are. But the experience of Taba in 1994 was repeated across the country. The town, an hour-long bus ride from Kigali, is at the end of a long dirt road that extends into the bush. Women there discovered that when men, including their neighbors, were in a group, they were capable of unimaginable sexual assault. One woman was raped by six men until she lost consciousness. Another was gang raped in the village square as neighbors looked on. Another was held as a sex slave by her neighbor. Two were teenagers, one married. One became pregnant by a rapist.

In the accompanying photograph here, they joke as they pose for a photo shoot. They're excited to have their pictures taken, laughing, swap-

United by the unspeakable, they heal together.

ping clothes, like girlfriends of any age. But they have been particularly bonded by years they've spent together, preparing to testify in local and international courts.

So what's the lesson in this photograph? If the Rwandan conflict was gendered, so has been the recovery. New studies of war zones worldwide reveal consistent differences between how women as a group behave and are regarded compared to men as a group. Likewise, researchers have documented the gulf between women's positive impact at the peace table and the cramped space into which they're welcomed. It seems extremely difficult for policy makers and military leaders, even those who are believers, to break the dense, heavy mold of the security sector and foreign policy traditions. But individuals' reluctance and systemic recalcitrance only underscore the timeliness of this book.

The findings, qualitative and quantitative, are in: it's important to have women in large numbers in peace talks, reconciliation work, and new government structures after a war. Grannies, mothers, wives, aunties— generally the primary caregivers—have enormous motivation to create stability for their family members. Former vice president of the Rwandan Senate **MARIE** extends that family emphasis to the crafting of public policy: *As mothers, they can understand people's problems; they can be more patient.* But she adds, *As leaders, women understand better because they're level headed.* Partly because of their caretaker roles, women in Rwanda, and worldwide, are generally seen as less threatening in hot-blooded settings. They're also assumed not to be the ones carrying AK-47s or firing mortars.

Present in a critical mass (approximately 30 percent), they have an unusual propensity to cross political and ethnic divides, whether speaking up to break parliamentary gridlock, or withholding sex until men agree to revive a moribund negotiation. More recent research has added a new twist: groups with males and females find solutions more readily than single-sex groups.

Women's power is partly in the new information they bring to the talks. The picture sketched by former parliamentarian **AGNES** is familiar to women across the world: *In Africa we deal with kids; we go to markets; we see rural poverty. Men are used to thinking about political struggle and how to get themselves into leadership. As we women are coming into leading positions, everyday life is embodied in our politics.*

But beyond their practical effectiveness, scenes of women creating the new Rwanda have sparked global interest, in part because of a mounting respect for—and hope in—the characteristics of so many (but not all) female leaders. Rather than a limitation, Joseph Nye, who ranks consistently as one of the world's most influential thinkers in international relations, sees value in the difference. In general, women contribute perspective and style that exemplify "soft power," a term Nye coined that has revolutionized the way we talk about global influence—not simply as arsenals of bombs and bullets, but also persuasion, diplomacy, and attraction.[2]

Without being carried away by the elephant in the room: the most common question of the man on the street (why always a man?) is whether males and females act and think differently because of biology or culture. We touch on that question in our epilogue, pausing for a brief look at some of the most current thinking about the mix of those two. In short, there are very significant differences between how most women act (as they focus on families and communities) compared to most men (who readily put themselves forward as leaders). And beyond, there is the perception of gender differences, which is its own force.

Understanding those differences is certainly useful. But generalizations become dangerous when we try to fit individuals into clumsy boxes we've constructed out of social roles. In high-drama situations, stereotypes may take on archetypal stature, with words like "victim" evoking unbearable sympathy and compelling a call to action for the needy, or "hero" inciting mad adulation with inspiration to emulate a champion.

Victimized and in control. Complicit and heroic. Cowardly and courageous.

Women in Rwanda, as in any conflict, were never purely one or the other. A drafter of the constitution and key promoter of grassroots justice, **DOMITILLA** captures the range of experiences: *Women were some of the first elected as judges. And they could describe what happened, because they actually witnessed the crimes. But we also have women in prison because they were involved in the genocide.*

The complicity can be distorted, however, as we look for faces and names that will stir our imagination, onto which we can hang some simple, if wrong, idea. In September 2002, I was amazed to see a *New York Times Magazine* article focusing on Pauline Nyiramasuhuko, the only woman—compared to some eighty men—being prosecuted for genocide at the International Criminal Tribunal for Rwanda.

Ten years later it was a gorgeous head shot of Beatrice, Pauline's daughter-in-law, on trial in the United States. Standing in my kitchen that Sunday morning, I marveled at the gall of the *Globe* singling out a woman for shock effect. But women aren't always left out. Sometimes they're front and center. I didn't sense that the magazine editors had an ax to grind. Yet the treatment of these two women by major media outlets revealed something more complexly gendered. Why do these stories make great copy? It's all about shock value—because directing rape and ordering massacres are not what we expect from women.

The exception proves the rule: women generally don't go around planning genocides.

On the one hand, with the media mantra "if it bleeds it leads," it's no wonder that except for their carefully placed inclusion as villains, there's a dearth of attention to women, given that it's men who spilled enough blood to fill many tomes. But like essentialism or stereotypes, near-sighted reporting carries far-reaching danger by skewing history as the story of men.

In the same vein, most mainstream coverage of the carnage (such as the film *Hotel Rwanda*) has treated women as victims of gruesome sexual violence. They were. But the popular genocide canon barely touches on women in their wisdom, perseverance, and strength. With a few notable exceptions, even scholarly research has glossed over more complicated, interchanging roles women played during the frenzied one hundred days of killings and the preparations leading up to them.[3] And almost nothing has been written about how they became experts in the rebuilding of their destroyed homeland.

The women who have inspired this book are not two-dimensional paper dolls, to be pasted onto a bucolic, if bloody, landscape in the middle of Africa. After poring over hundreds of hours of interviews, my thinking has become more healthily muddled, as I've realized there is no monolithic "women's experience" of the genocide.

One woman may fit into several categories. For example, a longtime member of the Rwandan Patriotic Front and women's rights activist, **JOY M.** brings the theoretical home. *I remember one time during a genocide commemoration, a survivor testified how a neighbor in the village hid her for two weeks—in her small house, where she kept her pots and things. Before, the neighbor didn't even know that the woman was Tutsi—it hadn't mattered to them. They were just going about their lives and suddenly they were drawn into this conflict. The neighbor didn't want her own son to know that this Tutsi was there, because the son would have killed her. So he would go out and come back and tell stories about where he'd been and how many people he'd killed, in gory details, and this woman could hear from where she was hiding.*

The shelterer is certainly a hero, but why didn't she take the next step and turn in her son? And how shall we think of the woman being hidden? Was she simply a victim crouching in the corner, or was she heroic in her determination to stay alive—possibly for the sake of her family?

Drawing this discussion together, there are three points to remember: First, despite popular portrayal, leading up to, during, and after the genocide Rwandan women were certainly not only victims. Second, depending on the situation, observers might see a woman move from one

Beatrice Munyenyezi, featured on cover of *Boston Globe Magazine*.
BY MATT KALINOWSKI

stereotype to another—for example, from hero to nurturer, perpetrator to victim. And third, those stereotypes can't really capture who these women were. Like all of us, author and readers, one woman likely had multiple and contradictory impulses and tendencies at the same time. And though this is not a theme of our book, in the intensity born of crisis, I imagine those contradictions may have plagued our protagonists.

Setting

Like the genocide itself, the recovery era is complex. At the heart of that complexity is President Paul Kagame. He is both a shaper and shaped by the remarkably progressive eight-point manifesto of the Rwandan Patriotic Front, which mandates full inclusion of all citizens in decision making.

On the other hand, there's no question that the former general holds full sway over his governing apparatus and society as a whole. Thus a common critique of this book's argument (that strong women have ascended to admirable heights and have been essential to the rebuilding their country) is that women's leadership is not actually significant because the president of the country holds so much power.

Some see the president wanting little opposition, and thus promoting what they say are weak (meaning female) officials beneath him, because he can control them more easily. Clearly, I disagree, in line with those who counter that power at the top of a pyramid does not mean that the blocks below are not strong.

Some argue, fascinatingly, that Kagame has used political might to promote the success of women because they are generally more moderate and less inclined to advocate violence. While he has not made that claim, the president has noted in interviews that women often exceed their male counterparts in terms of responsibility, diligence, and lack of egotism, qualities that are the spine of solid leadership. But going a step further, what if having more women in decision making were, in fact, also a recipe for less hunger and illiteracy—and less killing? What if a critical mass of women sitting next to men at the negotiating table, in the parliament, or in a cabinet meeting would lead to "inclusive security"? It's hard to imagine a more welcome unintended consequence of a politician's maneuvering.

Of course, political reckoning isn't multiple choice. The question is the extent to which any of these ideas are true. In what time period? Through whose lens?

No one, including the president, can answer those questions. Certainly there's enough goodwill in the country and beyond toward Paul Kagame that I feel comfortable not dealing with the question of his political standing. But also, settling such controversies is beyond the scope of this book. Instead I won't be shy pointing out the scores of women we interviewed who described the president's investment in their success. This book lets Rwandan women speak for themselves, and I won't edit out their dogmatic assertion that President Kagame was a central figure promoting their leadership.

Dancing the *intore* to celebrate and welcome visitors.

On the Ground

To tell this story, we've relied heavily on direct quotes, which relay audacious visions. They present unrelenting challenges as well as enduring achievements. My team and I have interviewed women and men serving in government posts, running businesses, and organizing civil society, as well as some working with them. Longtime Rwanda observers have offered astute insights on the country's experience specifically, or comparative knowledge from other contexts. And we've consulted with trusted advisors who suggested whom we should interview, made introductions, and helped us navigate sensitivities that are, unsurprisingly, abundant twenty years after the country's calamity.

Obviously we've wrestled with the best way to include voices of different ethnic identities. To stabilize the country, the government has mandated in the strongest terms a rejection of those distinctions that had been put to deadly use; instead, it vigorously cultivated a Rwandese identity. Still, feelings of separation do persist, as personal history—interwoven with firsthand memories of hardship, opportunity, or loss—remains a part of the individual. Often it's possible to guess ethnic identity, but I won't go there in this book unless it's necessary to a point a subject is making. I know that may be frustrating to you, the reader, but I hope you'll focus on the truth in the speakers' words.

INYUMBA, wise woman, offers this warning: *If you look at Rwanda today, the Hutu, Tutsi—there's no difference that justifies one killing another. None. There are more similarities that bring them together as people. It's about schools for their children. It's about roads. Many people are poor. It's about having clean water and a place to live. The needs of the Hutu, the needs of the Tutsi, the Twa—they're the same.* On the rare occasions I use the words "Hutu," "Tutsi," and "Twa," I've chosen the singular, rather than the Anglicized plural, in order to reinforce that those words are primarily adjectives rather than nouns describing distinct kinds of people. I also use "Rwandan" and "Rwandese" interchangeably, as the people I've interacted with have done.

We have a strong representation of every group, including those with mixed backgrounds. That said, some readers may criticize an imbalance that favors Tutsi experience—specifically those who were refugees in Uganda. It's impossible to know the precise proportion of ethnicities across the country or the government; that said, with so many Tutsi returning from exile (often with more educational opportunities), members of that minority group likely hold more high-level positions than their proportion of the population would suggest.[4] Still, describing the past two decades of female leadership, I clearly have to profile those at the heart of this movement, regardless of background. The point of this book isn't to analyze why speakers come from this background or that. In fact, I've found there are many more diverse life experiences among the leadership than the common perception holds.

In some instances, we're highlighting one story or commentary like others we've heard a dozen times. Other moments, we've sought out a woman with a narrative that stands out as unique but captures an important dynamic, even if her sphere of influence is relatively limited. That is, after all, my job—to compose the most authentic experience.

Across a span of sixteen years, my colleagues and I have conducted interviews and had conversations—directly and interpreted, in English, French, and Kinyarwanda—inside and outside the country. The soft-spoken beginnings of conversations (a characteristic particular to the women) took some getting used to for me, but as minutes rolled by, eyes began to sparkle, voices intensified, gestures became more forceful, and words began to flow. The collection of interviews we ended up with was much more than a resource for historians. It was an archive spilling over with the expected sorrow and laughter, but even more inspiring was the degree of personal, insightful revelation.

Almost ninety Rwandans are featured by name in these pages. Some appear many times; several only once. Rather than linger over who's who, I hope you'll appreciate the multiple facets of each story, described by their many contributors, in their cohesive whole. Give up on character development. It's not that kind of book.

Actually, I considered presenting just a small set of profiles so that you could trace each voice throughout the book. Instead, I opted to feature a huge chorus, whose voices, in harmony, build out this extraordinary history. There's meaning in that choice.

Ultimately, this is a story of a fascinating period of time—Rwanda's rebuilding—and its telling is in keeping with the Rwandan ideal of collective effort and collective success. That means you'll sometimes have to read carefully between the lines to understand exactly how a given speaker contributed to an achievement, accepting that the best ideas rarely originate from just one person. Even the most accomplished woman gently noted, "I was given an opportunity to . . ." before launching into her story. It's worth mentioning, because there's a beautiful humility in that formulation. We also saw how often the most color came out when a woman was talking about the achievements of her friends or of the group. Tellingly, none of those featured in these pages would ever have written this book; that would risk placing herself too close to center stage.

When the setting of an interview allowed, we had a video camera rolling, so as not to miss the body language our notebooks wouldn't always reflect. We tried to pose open-ended questions and take cues from themes our interviewees raised when describing their own work. In fact, I encouraged them to go where they would, hoping I could limit the contamination, if you will, of my assumptions.

Once we had their words, the artistic work began. For weeks every year, I had hundreds of pieces of paper, sometimes color coded with bright slashes of Sharpie highlighters, spread across every table in our home. I walked from one set to another, exploring like a miner standing above a stream, panning for gold. When I found a nugget, I marked it with sloppy asterisks. Only then could I create an outline—based on the women's narrative, not mine—stringing together the quotes.

I had a huge advantage a miner wouldn't—I could edit awkward turns of phrase that didn't reflect the expertise of nonnative English speakers. An essential step was then to review the crafted story with each person, in whichever language she or he felt most comfortable with. New details would emerge, as memories long stored away came alive on a printed page for the very first time. This was a rare collaboration that allowed us to guard personal details contributors didn't want shared and identify them as they wished, a very few times with pseudonyms, signified by placing the name in quotation marks.

Now let me be as straightforward as I can be. This isn't my story. Those who've lived it have had final say in how their experiences are represented for the world to appreciate. Instead, I'm a chronicler, a witness who sometimes had the opportunity to join in. At first, I observed. But eventually, I started actively looking—and that's where inevitable bias comes in. Each question has assumptions: "What prepared you for leadership?" presupposes that leadership can even be prepared for.

All authors bring themselves into their analysis. My given, I confess, was this: I love courage. I love Rwanda. I love women. I love the courageous Rwandan women.

Our relationships will shape my work and my spirit as long as I live.

Why This Book?

The broad purpose of this book is not to report on the progress Rwandan women have made. Not to highlight great Rwandan heroines. Nor is it only to tease apart just how women in Rwanda came to have such influence, or to see what difference it has made to have women in such a high proportion of leadership.

Since 2000, I've been collecting and studying interviews with women in this small country because of the travails but also opportunities in lands of all sizes. No country in the world will have the same combination of rough instability, uneven political structure, stable or unstable leadership, windows or limits of economic and educational conditions, or changing social expectations of women. But within every country there are opportunities.

Perhaps a nation shares only two conditions with Rwanda; it has others Rwanda doesn't that can be stirred into a mix. Whether Congo or Cambodia, the United States or United Arab Emirates, in these pages ingenious activists and politicians across the world may find not only ideas but also inspiration.

One particular clarification is critical: The most common misunderstanding about Rwandan women's progress postgenocide is that it occurred primarily because most of the males had been killed, imprisoned, or had fled, leaving a power vacuum into which females, some 70 percent of the population, needed to step. While that may have been true in the immediate aftermath of the cataclysm in some parts of the country, the larger picture is that an integrated group of factors led to women's progress. Their journey was much, much more arduous—and much, much more interesting.

In five parts broken into forty short chapters, we chart why and how women like Inyumba rose to prominent positions throughout the country, and the difference it has made to have them head so many parts of society.

Part I sets the stage by looking at women's traditional roles leading up to and immediately following the genocide. Through reflections by women and men, "Starting Places" explores how society's expectations and women's experiences in the home, in refugee camps, and in the di-

From the field
with harvest.

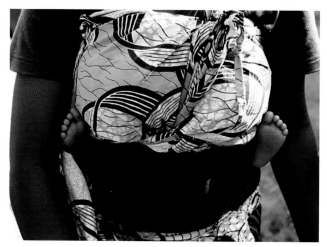

Tiny feet.

Coming forward to speak the unspeakable.

aspora farther afield refined their capabilities. The mass killing turns everything upside down, wrecks institutions, and crushes families. Women tell their stories of how and why they became involved in the calamitous struggle as military officers, survivors, or rescuers.

Part II describes how, in the aftermath of the catastrophe, women worked night and day in the rebuilding and beyond through fascinating initiatives and off-the-charts creativity. "The Path to Public Leadership" includes ten major elements that melded to support their upsurge: community organizing as a training ground, pull from the top led by the president, creation of the Ministry of Gender and Family Promotion, a pyramid of countrywide women's councils, a women's caucus in Parliament, collaborative constitution making that sought out female voices, seats

One of the most striking achievements is the stride in girls' education.
BY BOBBY SAGER

at the constitutional drafting table, the government and parliamentary quota, smart political campaigns, and the reach back to rural communities for the next crop of leaders.

From their new positions of influence, what have these women accomplished? Part III, "Bending toward Reconciliation," shows them pioneering landmark justice and encouraging reconciliation with neighbors.

In part IV, "Signposts," women are magnifying civil rights, spurring economic progress, nurturing health, and investing in the next generation of Rwandans.

After documenting these major strides, part V lays out how women are ensuring that their gains are sustained, and that ongoing challenges

A new generation with more opportunity—but with the grit?

remain at the forefront of their agenda. We also hear from young Rwandan women about how this rising generation takes stock of the progress and how they see the mantle they're inheriting. The title "Building the Road They're Walking" acknowledges that their progress must continue even as everyday life goes on.

Finally, the epilogue. My reflections draw out the significance of Rwanda's story beyond the country and debunk long-held myths about development and security, turning the lens on all of us with what I hope is a convincing call to action. And then, an unforeseen realization: in an almost inconceivable twist, Rwanda is an example of how the tragic upheaval of war can create disruption of a society, allowing for an unexpected breakthrough for women.

Women's advancement travels in a jagged line, as we've seen in Afghanistan or the Arab Spring.

But when stars align, social chaos and political expediency or progressive thinking may usher in a new era of women's leadership and girls' advancement. That this uplifting phenomenon accompanies a time generally marked by trauma, despair, dread, and pessimism is all the more remarkable. For policy makers trying to figure out their roles, and for anyone concerned about the future of our planet, this is wonderful news. Just how to help escort women to the top is another matter, but even recognizing the possibility is an important first move.

Rwanda has led the way, and we would do well to study this experience. There are always excuses to turn a blind eye: The president is too powerful. The women were uniquely toughened from years in the bush. One country's experience can't predict another's. But these are more defenses than reasons not to notice the example before us. In fact, for the sake of the elusive ideal—global security—and hundreds of millions of lives shaped by those two simple words, we must take it all in.

PART I
Starting Places

In spite of its small stature, Rwanda has owned an outsized place in public imagination. Much of its renown stems from the unutterable horrors of 1994. Images stay seared in the memory of anyone who turned on the nightly news that spring. Nauseating footage and photographs showed the torturous roadblocks, the makeshift weapons (nail-studded clubs, farm shed machetes), the heaps of bloating bodies. Because the country had plunged so far, its renewal—remarkable safety, economic swell, inspiring women—is especially awe inspiring.

So what's this book about, horror or brilliance? Every story in the pages that follow has played out behind a scrim of unimaginable fear. Yet rebirth, rather than death and destruction, is the theme here. That's because for all the words written about Rwanda, missing from understanding about this immense turnaround is a careful look at just how dynamic, determined female leaders came into central roles in all facets of the restoration of their country. With innate and learned intelligence, they've been both playwrights and players in the unfolding of a new Rwanda. Like a patchwork quilt that covered continents, women have assumed all sorts of individual roles without being able to necessarily see a pattern, much less the whole.

Those roles have ranged from the expected to the improbable. Several years before the genocide, **JANET** moved from the refugee camp in western Uganda where she had been raised to find a job in the capital, Kampala. That's where she was recruited to join the struggle of Tutsi to return to the country from which they had been driven over the decades by Hutu extremists. Her words tell not only her personal story, but also a story of many of the women of Rwanda.

It was before '90 when I came to really understand. The Rwandan Patriotic Front was organizing itself in Uganda and other countries where Rwandans had sought refuge. Someone would come see you, knowing you're Rwandan, and tell you what was happening, and how they wanted to go home. (I was approached by Ambassador Zephyr [Mutanguha], who lived in my neighbor-

hood.) So we belonged to a particular cell, where we contributed and attended meetings to hear news from the front line.

We worked so hard—sometimes all night in someone's garage, collecting materials, organizing, putting together dry ration (roasted maize) for the soldiers to carry in their pockets. There was so much night work, my marriage was collapsing.

Personal sacrifices came in many forms. My father loved his cows, but he sold one to contribute to the struggle. Sometimes he would pray at night, saying, "God, we want you to weaken the opposite side; we want our children to win, and then we'll go back home." Then my mother would say, "Let's pray for the children who are on the front line." So, even if women couldn't give money, prayer was very important for them. Yes, we can be proud that every woman contributed in one way or the other.

Notions and narratives about gender in Rwanda, however shaped by selective memory, are an important backdrop to understanding how women wrote their future scripts. They've been spectacular at garnering allies over the past two decades, but as with the other aspects of Rwanda's history—in fact, every country's history—society's traditional views are complex and contradictory. Some cultural practices exalt women as household managers and doting mothers at the same time that others undercut their authority or make them dangerously vulnerable.

That past has an especially complicated place in Rwanda today. For more than a decade after the genocide, the government enforced a moratorium on teaching Rwandan history in schools, because of the way skewed lessons had been used to foment ethnic tension and rationalize violence. "History became a space to tell stories of hate and division . . . a home for propaganda," says Karen Murphy of the Holocaust-spawned Facing History and Ourselves, which helped develop a new curriculum with the Rwandan Ministry of Education and partners.

There are no more credible historians than those whose everyday lives are creating the history. Speakers weave in and out of the pages of this book—as the narrative progresses from precolonial stability, to colonists' greed, on to social injustice, hateful oppression, then blistering perdition, exhausting emergence, now new stability, and, finally, what future? The line is never so straight: moving forward, sideways, backward, these

A women's movement with a distinctly Rwandan flair.

speakers portray the ascent of Rwandan women and the lacy web of factors that has supported them.

There is obviously a connection to women's experience worldwide and over time as they have leaned into massive calamities and, unlike in most conflict situations globally, began immediately to take on formal posts. Yet, as in any country, these achievements became visible gradually and only as they emerged from traditional views of women.

This is the story of their rise—from the first chapter.

1 FOREMOTHERS

> RUTAYISIRE: Terms like "gender," "equality," and "human rights" are Western-derived concepts that have a basis in the individualistic system and culture of the West. Traditional Rwanda had its own context and value systems.

Figuring out Rwandan traditions prior to the arrival of the German and then Belgian colonists in the 1880s is knotty, because little from that earlier time was written down. The newcomers often misinterpreted norms, hell-bent as they were on looking through European lenses and the infamously *en vogue* "science" on ethnicity, eugenics, and "inherent" superiority. Much of our understanding of customary roles has been passed down orally and is remembered today through Kinyarwanda expressions that often come up in interviews with elders, historians, women leaders, and others.

Division of labor rather than equality characterized traditional understanding of gender. Men and women fulfilled distinct functions within family and community, so the emphasis was on harmony rather than equality. Even when the government created a national gender policy, it framed its enlightened attitude by looking back. Compared to men, "women's roles were accorded proportionate value and considered to be complementary and indispensable."[1]

Revered and Feared

JOY M. loves talking about her country—past, present, or future. *In Rwandan tradition, women had backstage power. Within the kingdom, the queen mother was one of the most influential people in the country.*

Queen Mother
Kanjogera ruled
alongside her son,
the king, from
1895 to 1931.
COURTESY OF
THE INSTITUTE OF
NATIONAL MUSEUMS
OF RWANDA

For centuries before the colonists arrived, women were feared and revered. Tutsi monarchs ruled Rwanda as a kingdom arranged in a hierarchy of chiefdoms. The German colonial administration, which lasted until after World War I, made the most of the power of the *mwami*, or king, and the chiefs that governed hill by hill countrywide. Men in the royal family and their ilk occupied nearly all top positions, but some esteemed women held high-ranking roles behind the scenes. Most significantly, a Tutsi king was never crowned alone. He shared authority with his mother or a stepmother. If the heir was young when he assumed the throne, the queen mother governed the kingdom.

Rwanda's history, passed on orally and often spun into illustrative or cautionary proverbs, includes queen mothers and female chiefs who ruled ruthlessly. Most infamous was Kanjogera, who became queen mother in 1895 alongside King Rutarindwa, born to another of her late husband's wives. Within a year of her husband's death, Kanjogera and her brother conspired to kill the new king and install her own teenage son on the throne. They would rule until 1931, more than a decade into the Belgian era. It was during this time that Belgian colonists created state-enforced political identities that institutionalized discrimination between Hutus and Tutsis based on a racialized ideology. The Belgians' depiction of Hutus as the indigenous Bantu race and Tutsis as the alien settlers sowed the seed for genocidal violence.

Divisive school lessons taught after independence described cold-blooded Kanjogera using her Hutu servants to support her spear as she lifted herself from her royal perch, the sharp point impaling their feet. Or her appetite for killing babies on a whim: supposedly the queen mother would say, "Ruhuga is thirsty"—using a pet name for her sword—and a baby would be brought before her and fed with milk just before she pressed Ruhuga into its belly. In a modern version, First Lady Agathe Habyarimana was given the nickname of Kanjogera for her clout in the Akazu group that would plan the genocide.

Some traditional Kinyarwanda sayings draw a connection between women leaders and a propensity toward violence, such as, "A domineering woman brings strife to the home" (*Uruvuze umugore ruvuga umuhoro*). Others portray women as strong (she can stop a snake from biting) but dangerous (she can take away an ability to resurrect the dead).

Certainly not all allusions to powerful women in these traditions are negative, and many people now emphasize a reverence for women. When discussing the origin of women's public leadership today, many people first describe the folktale of Ndabaga, the most famous female warrior.

Her father was a warrior protecting the king. When it was time for the elderly guard to leave his position, he didn't have a son to replace him. To save her beloved father from the death sentence expected in his situation, Ndabaga cut off her breasts. She shaved her head, and trained herself to run, jump, and shoot with a bow. Though her father was afraid when she presented herself to the king disguised as a young man, he was reassured when she competed against the boys and came out on top.

When the king eventually learned a female had put her life on the line to serve among his soldiers, he was not only astonished but also impressed, praising her bravery to protect her aged father. Her example challenged the perception that women aren't able to do a "man's job," soldiering. In fact, "Ndabaga" now refers to a desperate situation that calls for a quick wit and sacrifice. A group of female veterans bears her name.

Appreciated

CHRISTOPHE has vast appreciation for the power of women, beginning at home: *The basis of our existence is the family. Men publicly make decisions, but if you don't compromise with your wife, it won't be carried out.*

In the traditional family, the wife was honored for making the first imprint on children, instilling early values and teaching distinct expectations of girls and boys.

Motherhood and homemaking afforded women strong, unique social value, even if their influence and importance weren't openly lauded. Ambassador **JOY M.** describes the expression "Umukobwa ni nyampinga": *It means that a woman goes beyond the hills and hamlets to get married to a different clan, thereby creating new alliances for her family.*

Traditionally, you can't marry within your own clan, so marriage meant a union between two clans, who would now be relatives. In the psyche of the Rwandan there's still that idea of a woman bringing families together. Another implication of "nyampinga" is that a woman is compassionate and kind (normally) and would help even strangers.

A feud between families or clans would sometimes be resolved by exchanging brides. If she refused, they wouldn't force her, but it's not like the Western or modern tradition where you choose your partner. Wealth, influence, friendship, or assurance their daughter was going to be treated well—there were all kinds of considerations.

A new bride was given preferential treatment when she arrived at her husband's home, with in-laws fawning over her to optimize her ability to conceive. And, in glaring contrast to what in most places would be considered disgraceful, while a new baby was the goal, a woman's pleasure in the bedroom was a high priority. It's delightful to imagine aunts and uncles (separately) quietly tutoring soon-to-wed girls and boys in maneuvers to optimize female gratification.

Wedding day for King Mutara III and Rosalie Gicanda.

A young wife was excused from her household work and given the family's best food to prime her body for pregnancy. *Women were seen as the receptacle of life,* explains Jesuit historian **ELISEE**. Once the baby was born, her sole focus was caring for her child while relatives took care of her.

Not only mothers but also wives were esteemed for their impact on their husbands—decision makers, thought leaders, and elders throughout the social and administrative hierarchy. They also shaped the views of their sons, who obviously would grow up to head their own families and communities. By many accounts, husbands were expected not to publicly announce a decision until they reached consensus with their wives. If the couple disagreed, family elders would weigh in.

Past shapes present. **CHRISTOPHE** was governor of Gitarama (now part of Southern Province) in central Rwanda. *When you make a decision without consulting your wife, you have to be very diplomatic—negotiate with her so that she accepts it. In the democratic process or development process it's easier if the women are closely involved; we succeeded in every policy change we wanted in part because the ladies influenced their men.*

Similarly, **JANET** draws a direct link between traditional appreciation of women and their rising influence in modern times. *When Rwandans decided to have women in positions of leadership it was because the government realized what women were worth. . . . Even during the precolonial era women's role was key. That said, women weren't given equal rights or opportunities outside of the home. Men started feeling superior, and they changed their minds about what women should be socially allowed to do.*

Subjugated

ROSE M. describes what is a drastic situation worldwide: *They said it was the husband's right to beat his wife. "Ah, he's correcting her; we shouldn't intervene." That's because there were no women in decision making, no women in Parliament, no women in government, no women. . . . Only men made those laws.*

While traditional Rwandan culture is sometimes touted—especially in today's parlance—as having been exceptional for valuing women's public influence, reality was marbled. In general, women were expected to defer to men or to provide their perspectives only through their husbands. They didn't speak in groups with men present, and girls were taught that it was polite to speak softly, or not express themselves at all in public settings. While the culture valued nonconfrontational behavior by all, the constraints on women were particularly strict. **JOY M**. notes how *even in traditional ceremonies, even at their own children's engagement—an event about the union of two families—women don't talk.* **LOUISE**'s echo is typical. *The culture didn't grasp the significance of what a successful young woman could do, and we learned to stay in the background, not to make noise about it.*

At home, practical factors limited a woman's influence and reinforced the man's having final say. Women weren't allowed to own land, the fundamental source of wealth and social standing in this overwhelmingly agrarian country. Upon death, a man's property passed to his sons or brothers, leaving wife and daughters dependent on their male relatives. A woman with children was expected to marry one of her late husband's brothers (facilitated by polygamous marriages), keeping the children and the inheritance line within the marital family. If the woman had not borne children before the husband died, or the couple divorced, the wife had no entitlement to the family's land and would return, destitute, to her parents' home to await another proposal. Further, cultural restrictions against airing family matters prevented women from disputing land ownership.

Given the high regard for motherhood, it's not surprising that a woman unable to bear children was left in a precarious position within both the family and broader community. The common curse "May you die childless" (*Uragapfa utabyaye*) is considered the worst of all insults. In a childless couple, the woman was blamed first for the infertility, and the man was free to remarry. Divorce and remarriage or taking an additional wife were also acceptable outcomes should a woman give birth only to daughters—seen as inferior to male heirs who could inherit family assets, preserve the lineage, and support elderly parents.

With this dramatic power imbalance, it's not surprising that a culture of silence long surrounded domestic sexual violence in Rwanda, where men were understood to have the right to force sex with—that is, rape—their wives. These topics were taboo (apart from the coming-of-age tutorials from aunties); a woman who spoke about her experiences or didn't conform to society's expectations about virtuous sexuality, such as by having a child outside a committed relationship, was ostracized and sometimes punished by her father or her husband's family.

Neglected

ODETTE remembers the possibility and the limits of growing up in her family, whom she would lose almost entirely in the genocide. *My parents had eighteen children. We sisters tried hard to be like boys.*

In this multidimensional look at traditional treatment of girls and women, the word "neglected" can't be avoided. Formal education, introduced under colonial rule in the early 1900s, drew a hard line between who was privileged and who wasn't, with opportunities based on newly cemented ethnicities that conveniently ignored muddling realities like intermarriage. Gender was high on the same sad list. The first schools were run by missionaries and admitted only boys.

Young Odette was up against dual challenges: a society that didn't yet see the value of women's roles beyond the home and a country that bla-

Physician and politician Odette Nyiramilimo.

tantly discriminated against citizens of her ethnicity. *In Rwandese families, when a woman is giving birth only to girls, it is very badly regarded. When I finished secondary school, I told my father I wanted to go to university. He said, "My daughter, you don't know the country we're in. You'll never be Madeleine Ayinkamiye!"* Appointed minister of social affairs in 1964, Madeleine Ayinkamiye was the first-ever female cabinet member in Rwanda (she served for about a year), and the last until 1992.

It wasn't until the 1940s that the first school to admit girls opened, with the sole focus on training nuns. (These women, the Benebikira sisters, were dauntless during the genocide and also in the rebuilding, but that comes later.) By the next decade, other girls' schools had opened, specializing in nursing and midwifery, or in the homemaking skills sought by young women preparing for marriage to elite men. The spread of Christianity further restricted the few roles women played in indigenous religion and public ceremony. And with the cementing of governance wholly dominated by men, women's standing in the colonial era was sabotaged.

Apart from the way accessibility to schools widened the chasm between women's entrenched position in the home and men's reach in pursuing various vocations, the deep power imbalance between males and females was set early. *As a boy, I was enjoying life compared to my sisters.* **EMMANUEL** recounts the memory with a chuckle, but also a nod of respect. *My mother always knew what was needed around the house, and she passed on that awareness to my sisters. I could play outside with the other boys, but my sisters were expected at home, preparing food, even making my bed.*

With a supportive father, Odette eventually broke through a series of obstructions to graduate from medical school. Many years later, she would defy her pragmatic father's prediction and rise to hold the same post as Minister Madeleine. . . . But fresh out of university and twenty-one years old, opportunities were scarce, and given stiff traditions, educated women like her were met with skepticism.

FELIX: Culturally, it wasn't easy for women to move beyond family responsibilities. With the arrival of formal schooling, you'd find them as teachers or nurses, but very few politicians. Their involvement just wasn't a priority for society at the time, so there wasn't a political climate for including women—or, for that matter, any other people.

It's almost impossible for a reader—or writer—to comprehend the bravery of a woman carving her way through dense cultural mores, political structures, and a flank of power-hungry men. Leading up to the genocide, women were excluded, publicly slandered, mocked, and assaulted. Whether Hutu or Tutsi, taking an assertive stance on behalf of women's rights was not just discouraged. It could be fatal.

Holocaust survivor Viktor Frankl once said to me that the most generous inmates of Auschwitz gave their crusts of bread to the boys and younger men who hadn't tasted many of the joys of life. The best among us didn't make it, he concluded.

And so this is a reminder that the stories of many of the justice-seeking women were crushed during the genocide. Although their narratives are not preserved here, their place in history must not be an unmarked grave. The women profiled in this book walked through a path others had cleared. Those described in these pages lived to tell the tale. Many did not.

•   •   •

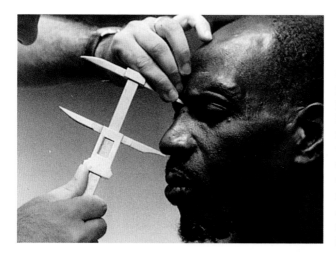

In the 1930s, colonialists used phrenology—pseudoscience based on cranial measurements—to prove Tutsi superiority. USED WITH PERMISSION FROM THE FILM *RUANDA-URUNDI* (1949) BY GÉRARD DE BOE

The 1994 genocide was the nadir of decades of violence and prejudice. The culture had traditionally distinguished between people based on wealth (cows and land) and occupations (farmers and herders). But the Belgian colonists saw these differences as dyed-in-the-wool ethnic characteristics and issued identity cards accordingly. Many Tutsi had longer, thinner noses than most Hutu, and in keeping with the idea of Caucasoid traits popular in the new biological anthropology, that facial characteristic was used as a sign of kinship with Europeans. As far as many Hutu were concerned, the small, lighter-complexioned Tutsi minority had made it to a place of privilege and then pulled the ladder up behind them.

Resentment soon metastasized into campaigns of violence targeting Tutsi. Certainly there were some abuses of power by the favored Tutsi, but their friendship with the Belgians wasn't even skin deep. Tutsi challenges to colonialism were wearing the relationship thin, plus mounting global sentiments were favoring majority rule. The Belgians switched allegiance to Hutu shortly before Rwanda's independence in 1962.

That political chaos fueled the fire. All hell broke loose. Pogroms and fierce discrimination against Tutsi started in the late 1950s, for the next two decades spurring mass migrations into neighboring countries—the largest number of exiles in dismal Ugandan camps, literally dirt poor.

Those who defied the threats and stayed faced systematic bigotry, if not outright hostility. Young people weren't always fully conscious of the

Foreign Minister Louise Mushikiwabo. BY ADAM SCOTTI

restrictions, but over time the abuses and stifling environment took a heavy toll. **LOUISE** describes herself as ambitious to travel and become a journalist. *When I was growing up here as a young girl, I had a very loving family, a large family. We had relatives from other parts of Africa, in Burundi, Congo, and Uganda, whom we didn't see very often. During high school, I started realizing something was wrong, that we couldn't easily go visit or have them come and stay with us over the summer.*

As Louise came to realize that opportunities were out of reach because of the ethnic classification on her national ID card, she almost couldn't believe it. *When I was graduating from high school, an incident woke me up. I came from my boarding school in northern Rwanda to Kigali to take a test from the school of journalism in Senegal. I took the test with some other young women and men, and even missed my graduation from high school to sit for the exam. After months, we still didn't get the results.*

Finally, right before journalism school started, we were called by this gentleman who was then head of the Rwanda Bureau of Information and Broadcasting. He told me I'd done well but couldn't go to my studies in Senegal. I asked why. "Look, there are issues. Apparently there was some cheating going on with the tests." And I said, "Well, am I cheating?" He said, "No, but I prefer you not ask me too many questions." I left, very upset. At that age, end of high school, with a little bit of a rebellious approach to things, I didn't give it the weight I should have. I was mainly upset because I'd missed my high school graduation. But that's when I realized something was deeply wrong with this country.

The government's tyrannical stance wasn't only on ethnicity. From 1975 to 1991, political opposition inside Rwanda was outlawed, and President Juvénal Habyarimana's Mouvement Révolutionnaire National pour le Développement (MRND) party ruled supreme. Under pressure from domestic critics, foreign backers, and an armed insurgency on its northern border, the government agreed to an opening of political space in 1991 and granted several new parties positions of limited influence. But behind the scenes, a radical Hutu group called Akazu, directed by the first lady's family, was keeping a tight rein and pushing an extremist agenda that included anti-Tutsi propaganda and training of cutthroat community militias.

In contrast to President Habyarimana's exclusionary policies, his government did enact some changes that cracked open a window for

Farmer and soldier Mama Rebecca.

women to pursue work previously off-limits. In 1975, two years after seizing power in a coup, the president authorized a new law enabling them to join the military. How perfect that Joan of Arc enlisted when she was seventeen. **MAMA REBECCA** (whose first name is Jeanne d'Arc) says the military was in her blood from the time she was a child. *The story of Ndabaga*—the daughter who disguised herself as a man to succeed her father in the king's guard—*was my favorite, and I wanted to be like her. So when I was finishing high school, I wanted to be among those taking up arms to defend my country.*

The army she's speaking of is the FAR (Forces Armées Rwandaises), which trained soldiers (including top officers) who would be major players in the genocide two decades later. But this didn't even cross the mind of teenaged Mama Rebecca then—or, in fact, until many years later when she would reconsider her place in Rwanda and join the new government's army reserves. No matter the leader in power, Mama Rebecca says patriotism was etched in her soul. President Habyarimana's words in the 1970s about the importance of having women enlist felt like a personal calling to her. *The president said that we could join the army, to have equality between women and men.*

Mama Rebecca had a couple more years of high school to finish, but her mind was made up. She enlisted as soon as she graduated. *I hid the decision from my mother at first. Eventually she found out, but she knew it was my decision. By then, in 1979, there were many women in the army. It was a job like others, but it was also a special feeling because I am patriotic. I also felt proud because I was proving a woman can do anything like a man.*

Whether in the military sphere of established governments or rebel movements, the kernels of female empowerment were cropping up across the continent. Other laws in Rwanda established women's rights to bank accounts and divorce. The MRND party even initiated a women's group, Urama, for such a key constituency. Urama's venomous ethnicity-tinged rhetoric was infamous, and though they faced ever-growing danger, many female activists didn't join up. In 1992, the Habyarimana government created the Ministry of Family and Women's Development, but its first head, Pauline Nyiramasuhuko, descended to ignominy as the only woman convicted of genocide by the International Criminal Tribunal for Rwanda.

Any accolades history might have bestowed on the few other promi-

Francs in 1974 featuring Hutu President Habyarimana, who took power through a coup the previous year. WITH PERMISSION FROM AUDRIUS TOMONIS

nent female political appointees, such as Minister of Justice Agnes Ntamabyariro or parliamentary Vice President Immaculee Nyirabizeyimana, are now overshadowed by their affiliation with President Habyarimana's party in 1994.

MAKUZA was part of the political opposition to the Habyarimana regime and eventually an advisor to Prime Minister Agathe Uwilingiyimana, who in 1993 became the first and so far only Rwandan woman to hold the post (and only the third in the whole of Africa). A moderate Hutu politician, Uwilingiyimana would be assassinated by the president's special forces April 7, 1994, as the violent vortex began swirling out of control.

Makuza and Uwilingiyimana both graduated in the mid-1980s from the National University of Rwanda in the southern city of Butare. Makuza explains: *In the 1970s and 1980s, slowly by slowly females started going to primary then secondary schools, and sometimes university. Prior to that, the proportion of girls in school was very small, and discriminatory policies limited the number of Tutsi girls.*

Rwandan traditional education for boys was built around values such as patriotism, integrity, dignity, political engagement, and culture. Boys learned how to hold not only a drum but also a spear and shield. *At home, girls were prepared for other roles, more hidden and quietly influential, confined to the family,* Makuza says. *But when they started going to school, things began to change.*

ODETTE was a couple of years older than Makuza and Uwilingiyimana and graduated in 1981 from Butare, which was the only college at the time. *When I arrived at university, there were about six hundred students. Only thirty-eight girls in the whole school. Then in my class of twenty at the medical school, I was the only girl. In the class before me, no girls. And the class after me, no girls. I was the seventh—the seventh—woman doctor in Rwanda. The seventh.*

There was no promotion for women to go to schools, to universities. And when I started working, there was no provision or law saying you should be given opportunities. It was you alone. And there was no cohesion among the women.

That began to change in the late 1980s. *I remember how it started. I was working here in Kigali. Some women would go to the Ivory Coast or Senegal, for example, and come back and say, "These other women, they're claiming seats in the government, in Parliament, so we should start." In West Africa, particularly, they were talking about women having banks, having their own businesses. We asked ourselves, "Why don't we also do something?" We started thinking of banking. Soon after we created the group, Duterimbere, which means "Let's go forward."*

Then when there were elections for the Parliament, women campaigned. My sister Venantie became a parliamentarian, and some others. Not many—maybe ten out of a hundred. It was just a start; you can't compare it to now. Women had to fight to have a seat, to have a say anywhere. There was no woman mayor, no governor. My sister was there because the government then wanted to show its ethnic inclusiveness.

Women were still left behind, but with the feminist movements around the world, they were saying, "We need to do something."

Inspiration also came from witnessing the hardships many impoverished Rwandans faced. Along with education and upward mobility, an ethos of social justice emerged, spurring an enthusiastic but novice and decidedly apolitical civil society. The Habyarimana government banned the organizing of any cluster faintly resembling a political party. However, gatherings of friends with overlapping professional interests laid the groundwork for the country's first women's groups—each with a specific bent: legal assistance through Haguruka, economic empowerment through Duterimbere, and more.

ATHANASIE was a sociologist who, in 1986, along with others in her field, created Rwanda's first women's group, Réseau des Femmes Oeuvrant pour le Développement Rural (Women's Network for Rural Development). With her easy recollection of historical moments, peppered with dates, and her narrow spectacles, Athanasie is reminiscent of a kind professor as she speaks. *Women educated and coming of age in the 1980s had a new idea: given what we'd seen in rural areas, we realized we had work to do on behalf of less fortunate women. We were working hard, but the problems our mothers, our sisters were facing weren't improving. Economic rights, health care, education—women generally didn't have very many rights.*

In the hills of Rwanda, we'd see day in and day out the challenges rural women faced. Much of our population depends on agriculture, so it made sense that this would be the first focus of Réseau des Femmes. We started organizing to advocate, to influence the political system, and to imagine what might improve the lives of other Rwandans. We wanted to focus on ending poverty and violence targeting women, and for women to be recognized as productive members of society.

The first meetings were held outside the chapel of Notre Dame de Citeaux in downtown Kigali, after Sunday mass. *We would gather in the garden and talk. Some in this small group of volunteers had a connection to the Dutch development group called snv, so we negotiated to have them provide us a small office. We started meeting in the evenings, although it was more difficult to move around the city at night. A Belgian lady married to a Rwandese would take us home in her husband's car.*

Women's debut in activism and public life in general turned plenty of heads. It wasn't just Rwanda. Wherever the women's movement was moving, some fellow activists shunned certain female leaders for their outspoken ways, which they considered too extreme to be effective.

But many of these pioneers felt grounded in the social expectations of women as homemakers as they juggled their activism and family duties. In fact, they saw their particular advantage in leadership stemming from their experience as mothers—a sentiment that would (and does) vex many Western feminists. So while the global women's movement may have sparked the notion that females could demand a say in public affairs, how they went about asserting their perspective had a Rwandan flair.

Prime Minister Agathe Uwilingiyimana and two of her five children, less than a year before her murder on April 7, 1994.
BY PASCAL LE SEGRETAIN (CORBIS IMAGES)

MAKUZA remembers how he and others who knew Agathe Uwilingi-yimana were impressed by her skill in playing dual roles as a rising po-litical figure—a director in the Ministry of Commerce, then minister of education, before prime minister—and mother to five young children. *Uwilingiyimana would say the principle was equality: a woman is just as capable—and can also be just as inefficient—as a man.*

I saw her every day at the office and also at her residence, because we would have meetings there sometimes. This woman—in spite of her capacity as prime minister at a very tense, difficult time politically—took care of her housework, was conscious about caring for her children. When there were visitors at the home, just like any other wife she would be the one serving the beer! I'd say, "But how do you manage all these small details?" And she'd say, "Listen, there are certain aptitudes we have, that have become reflexes for women, and just because I've become prime minister those don't go away."

Assertive attitudes like hers would directly endanger the lives of courageous, outspoken women. As civil war loomed, Hutu radicals drummed up support for their sickening, vicious cause with messages like those published in the Hutu Ten Commandments. "1. Every Hutu must know that the Tutsi woman, wherever she may be, is working for the Tutsi ethnic cause. In consequence, any Hutu is a traitor who: acquires a Tutsi wife; acquires a Tutsi concubine; acquires a Tutsi secretary or protégée. . . . 8. Hutu must stop taking pity on the Tutsi." No rank—even prime minister—could protect a moderate Hutu.

Looking back, Rwanda exemplified scholars' correlation between violence against women and interstate or intrastate conflict.[1] But those living out the situation were not observers. Seen as bucking the tradition of having influence only behind the scenes, female leaders—and Tutsi women particularly—were demonized. Rape became more common.[2] The genocide would devastate their small but brave ranks.

3 STATELESS

ROSE K.: In the back of your mind, you know you don't have a country.

Eruptions of ethnic violence in Rwanda, triggered in 1959 during what was known as the revolution (or *muyaga*—a strong and unpredictable wind), accompanied the country's independence from Belgium and abrupt transition from Tutsi to Hutu authority. As hateful anti-Tutsi rhetoric and state-sanctioned killings mounted during the following decades of political tumult, waves of families sought refuge across Rwanda's borders in neighboring Uganda, Democratic Republic of Congo, Burundi, and Tanzania, with some eventually settling in the West. An estimated 200,000 Tutsi fled just between 1959 and the early 1960s. By 1990, more than 600,000 Rwandans were living in exile, as the Habyarimana regime within their country became more radical and more abusive toward Tutsi and moderate Hutu.

JOY M. was fourteen when her family was forced to flee their home in southern Rwanda. *Christmas 1963 was bloody. Mass killings. My family fled through Burundi to Uganda, where I grew up as a refugee.*

Each time there was upheaval in Uganda—during the Amin regime [1971–79] and the Obote regime [1980–85]—Rwandans were targeted. This is what happens when you don't really belong. Even though Uganda was relatively accommodating and Rwandan refugees found it easier to integrate, being a refugee has many challenges. Lucky ones had UN travel documents because we registered with the refugee agency, but nobody wants to give a visa to somebody stateless, because they think you're seeking asylum in their country. And so you can't participate in politics. You can't really get involved in the econ-

omy. You're always vulnerable. That's what really moved the Rwandans in the diaspora.

The conditions in which the exiled communities lived were tough, whether a family lived the stressed and isolated life of an immigrant in Europe or North America, coped with being a foreigner in a country like Kenya or Congo where even the nationals struggle to get by, or faced the strain of Burundi's own forgotten bloodbaths, in which hundreds of thousands of Hutu and Tutsi were slaughtered. Their unshakable sense of otherness fostered a deep connection to the homeland, even among those born in exile. Determined that, come hell or high water, they would someday go home, parents and elders tenaciously taught their children the Kinyarwanda language and held tight to traditions.

The majority of exiles settled in Uganda, because of both its proximity and its relatively favorable refugee polices, having welcomed people displaced by other conflicts. Some families chose to live in the more multicultural capital of Kampala or settle with relatives, trying to blend in. Many more, typically less by choice than by necessity, set up their lives in refugee camps in the southern and western regions of the country.

JANET's family fled when she was still a baby. *In our area people were being killed, houses burned down, cows stolen. My older brothers left first because my father was worried they would be targeted. But the first memory I have is of life in the Ugandan camp. The number of people in the camps was overwhelming, and so many people were separated from their families because, like with my brothers, not all families were fortunate to be able to leave Rwanda together. People would track each other down just through word of mouth. It was chaotic.*

I almost died from measles. Of course we couldn't eat every day. Because we were a family of nine children, to supplement what we were getting from the UN agency my older brothers and sisters used to go to the villages to work as farm laborers or as domestic workers. No one wanted money; they were paid in food.

We were a people without a nation. I didn't dream of being who I am today, and where I am in Rwanda. I used to hear my parents talking about their country, but I couldn't imagine coming back. Still, one thing my parents instilled in us: they didn't allow us to speak other languages. That's why we now fit very well in Rwanda, because our parents remembered their roots. Whatever the case might be, wherever I would be, I would be a Rwandan.

Depending on the inferno they were fleeing or injustice they were facing, some were adamant about starting life anew. But years later, most still felt like visitors—sometimes welcome and sometime not. **ROSE K.** was a year old when her parents escaped the violence in Rwanda. *Even as young children we worked from the moment we woke up. I had two small siblings and two older with us in the camp, and my parents were struggling to take care of all of us. As young as we were, we were milking cows and searching for food. We didn't know we were underprivileged, so we had a relatively happy, although tough, life. I remember being barefoot and scared of snakes. Then as I grew up, I went to secondary school, then university—a poor refugee girl, studying with these privileged children. Their parents came to visit them once a month, but I had nobody to visit me.*

As a refugee, you're always working harder than the nationals. . . . You're not sure if you're going to get a job, so you're always thinking, "I have to do better. I have to work harder. I have to make a better life for my children and me."

In Uganda, fighting for a more secure place in their adopted home, many Rwandan refugees joined the rebellion that installed Yoweri Museveni as president in 1986, even holding principal positions in the officer corps of what became that country's army. But despite new legal protections and a path to citizenship earned through their sacrifices in the uprising, return to their homeland stayed fixed in the imagination of the diaspora. Instead of a force for integration in Uganda, the rebellion proved an impetus for those who would create the Rwandan Patriotic Front (RPF).

Prominent among the young soldiers were Fred Rwigema and Paul Kagame, who in 1987 began quietly organizing and training a Rwandan force within the Ugandan army, even as they held leadership posts in Museveni's military. Their first battle against Habyarimana's forces took place on October 1, 1990, in the northern hills that trace the border between the two countries.

From the movement's earliest days, women were active. Some got their start in the Ugandan army; many others became political cadres, spreading word among Rwandans in the diaspora, gathering financial support, and enlisting new members. While the nucleus of organizing

The intore dance honors the revered cow and emulates its horns.

was in Kampala, where many founding members attended the prestigious Makerere University, the movement—or struggle, as adherents knew it—soon went global.

JOY M. spent her teenage years in Uganda, then moved to Kenya, and to the Netherlands after university. *I was involved in organizing the diaspora way back in the 1970s and '80s. In Nairobi, we started a women's organization called Nyampinga, where we helped Rwandan refugees do handcrafts and find a market. We wanted to give these women a sense of value, so they wouldn't sink into despair.*

Because we were in a foreign land, to teach our children our culture we formed a little dance group. Years later, when I was ambassador, this group made Rwandan embassy events popular! She's seated, but Joy lifts her hands into position, arms upward with a slight curve at the elbows. The pose is reminiscent of cows' horns—a favorite theme in Rwandan music and dance, because cattle are the most revered symbol of wealth and prestige.

With a smile, she picks up the story. *It's not like you say, "I've joined a movement." Somehow, it was natural. I coordinated the Netherlands group of the Rwandan diaspora, and we tried to explain to the media what we were fighting for. I had a full-time job, but we all did our parts from where we were.*

Families hosted meetings. But big events were organized mainly in hotels in Brussels, London, Geneva, and other places. A group of elderly Rwandan refugee women in Burundi taught the young girls and boys traditional dance, plus all kinds of cultural skills like basket weaving and bead work. And when the struggle intensified in the 1990s, these women put on shows, inviting diplomats, international organizations, everybody. The younger ones, who had the contacts, did the fund-raising.

These fund-raisers happened everywhere there were Rwandans and even attracted non-Rwandans—expatriates, local officials. The diplomatic corps came. We did everything imaginable! We collected money from friends. Each of us contributed depending on our income. Everybody. If we were household help, we'd give $5, maybe over two months. My mother in Uganda pulled me aside on one of my visits to say she had sold her calf for the cause. And this was without anybody telling you. . . . We had to do it, because of this sense of being stateless and wishing to go back home.

Others, like Inyumba, were out there organizing, managing. . . . They used to come to Europe, because we had to get the international community to understand. It wasn't easy. They didn't have a lot of money, but their presence and articulation of issues was a great boost to our fund-raising efforts. We in turn supported them as much as we could.

Indeed, Aloisea Inyumba, appointed in 1988 as head of the RPF finance department, was on the road constantly to raise awareness about the struggle, collecting not only secondhand equipment and uniforms, but also funds. With her team mobilized in East Africa, she traveled to Europe, Canada, and the United States, at first with a low profile, essentially underground, but later speaking out to media and the diplomatic corps. Stories of her resourcefulness and frugality abound, including how she would collect hundreds of thousands of dollars from the Rwandan diaspora she had tracked down around the world but be dressed in threadbare clothes.

WINNIE considered Inyumba like a younger sister; the pair met when thirteen-year-old Inyumba started school in the Ugandan town where

Ambassador Joy Mukanyange.

Winnie's family lived. By the time Inyumba went to university, Winnie was already working in the capital and would have Inyumba stay at her house during school holidays. In her early impressions of the girl, Winnie noted the same qualities that would suit Inyumba so well in her activism. *Inyumba was quietly spoken but she was bright. She was very bright, original, very honest. She would say things in a polite way but that other people were afraid of saying. She stood out. She wasn't out there highly visible, not seeking the limelight, but you noticed her.*

Oh, my God, she organized a huge fund-raiser across Africa, Europe, and America! She was raising money among the Rwandese diaspora for the RPF. *And it wasn't just money but it was also for equipment, and her team worked from Senegal, down to South Africa, and up to East Africa and Egypt—all the big countries. They wouldn't give that job to anyone else! Even after, she remained the treasurer for the* RPF. *She was so trustworthy and did such a fantastic job.*

Many times she would come to see me while she was on her fund-raising mission, and she would be wearing a torn pair of sandals. And I would say, buy yourself a proper pair of shoes! You're walking all the time. And get yourself a decent dress. You don't win any points looking like that! She would laugh but just keep working.

INYUMBA herself remembered a visit to Brussels, where a large Rwandan community was relatively well off. (Almost anyone was well off compared to troops in the bush.) To her, warm shoes and coats weren't so familiar, and winter cold was even less. Seeing her shivering in her sandals and cotton dress, Paul Kagame told her to take some of the RPF money she was collecting to buy a coat. She proposed that instead she would just use his. *People have sacrificed*, she remembered thinking. *They have given us their money; they have given us their children.*

With a tangible challenger to Rwanda's ruling government gaining momentum and its military wing mounting attacks across the border, **LOUISE**, later the country's foreign minister, decided she was ready to engage. In 1990, as she finished school in Washington, DC, she realized she would be walking into the jaws of danger if she went back to her country. Instead of being shut down, she became all the more determined to be at the sharp edge of change. She found other Rwandans in the area, who met just socially at first.

My brother Lando founded the Liberal Party of Rwanda. The ambassador to the United States knew me and knew my family in Kigali, so I was scared to be seen as part of the group that was fighting his government, especially knowing that back home my family was also involved in the opposition politics. But I couldn't just sit still.

Louise helped put on fund-raising events, with traditional cooking and dancing. *Many of us were bad dancers,* she confesses. But those experiences worked their magic. *We learned songs from the old days. It was quite a wonderful experience when you think about it, because we found something that really held us together, and we got excited about the prospects of the diaspora coming back home. At that time, we weren't thinking there would be a genocide, of course.* Louise's brother would be among its first victims.

APOPHIA: How would I start? I'm not trained. How do I get there? What would I do when I got there? I had no idea what soldiers really do, but there was a will in my heart.

That enthusiasm about returning home especially animated young people in Uganda, who saw their fellow Rwandans contributing however they could, changing their life plans to dedicate themselves to liberation from the Habyarimana regime.

ROSE K. would become the highest-ranking female soldier in the RPF, retiring in 2003 as a lieutenant colonel. *We needed work, so I went with my sister and other friends to Kenya to see whether we could get teaching jobs—but that wasn't really what I wanted to do. The RPF was organizing.*

The movement leaders were quietly gathering Rwandan men in several capitals in the region, including in Nairobi, where Rose lived. *They'd be having a meeting and when we'd come in they'd change the subject. Then they'd send us away, because we weren't yet members and it was a clandestine plan. They were recruiting men to join Museveni's rebel movement, in the bush, with the aim of training a Rwandan force that would ultimately liberate our country. And they didn't think women would go to the army.*

I told them, "You know, I think you're up to something. I don't know what it is, but when I figure it out I'm going to find out where you are. I promise you, and I promise myself." In '86, Museveni stormed Kampala. There was such excitement! So many young men and women in uniform. That could be me!, I thought. Someday I'm going to liberate my country too! I have to join . . . but how am I going to do it?

I learned that there were political schools being set up to educate Ugandan soldiers about their country and teach them to be leaders. In a political school in Entebbe, I talked to the administrator, luckily a Rwandese, and told him I wanted to join. He looked at me, surprised. "This is a girl just coming out of university. Why would she want to come to the military?" He said I needed a recommendation letter from a senior member of Museveni's movement. I went to one of my professors. He too was surprised, but he gave me the letter. I took my few things and was admitted to the school. Before, I'd studied political science, but in the few weeks I spent in that school, I learned more about the politics of Uganda and other liberation wars than I learned in my three years at the university.

Among so, so many men, there were two of us girls, whom they called "intellectuals" because we had finished university. We were doing all the drills, but one day they decided we should go for real training. "Pack your things—we're taking you to western Uganda." It was a shock! This was something I'd wanted all my life, but I was getting used to this life of politics, thinking I'd be sent to teach or work in an office. "You are going to be in the military." No discussion; it was an order and that was it. We were scared—crying, in fact.

The camp was a huge training wing—maybe three thousand or four thousand recruits, mainly Rwandese and Ugandan nationals. As we got off the bus, they made us line up then said, "We're going to shave your hair." So, of course we started crying again. But they took a razor blade and shaved our heads completely. Then I knew, "This is it. I'm in. I'm a soldier. No going back." Of course, it was fascinating for these instructors, looking at these girls and boys from the university, with their clothes on hangers!

Later they took us to a girls' dormitory. We met really young girls who had dropped out of school because they loved their country. I realized, they have come to fight, they are not educated, and they are young. But we have finished university, we are educated, we are older than they are. We have to be leaders and help these girls cope. We went through this training, and after a week I really loved it. I liked the tactics and the parades. I liked everything.

During basic training, Rose came across the same men who had been recruited by the RPF in Kenya and had dismissed her aspirations. *They were shocked to see me! We became strong comrades. I was in that Ugandan army for about five years.*

October 1, 1990, was just a normal working day for me, but the senior

Lt. Col. Rose Kabuye.

Rwandan officers in the Ugandan army all knew the plan. They went to the southern border.

Word of Rose Kabuye's enlistment traveled. **APOPHIA** was twenty-two and studying accounting when she decided to leave school and enlist. *Rose encouraged us; she made us see it was possible. Definitely she was my role model; we were from the same village in Uganda, and everyone knew her. She played a big role in helping women get beyond their fear and join the army.*

Apophia had already signed up as a cadre, recruiting in refugee camps, including her own, and volunteering as a secretary for the RPF in Kampala. But when the movement's combatants clandestinely set off south toward Rwanda, Apophia felt that her place was with them. The thrill is still in her voice as she remembers. *We could see people in the street at night, and everyone was saying, "Rwandese are going home." So after five days I said, "No!" The radios had started talking about their movements, and I thought, "Will I just keep listening to this? Come what may, I'm going to do what I can."*

Apophia wanted to organize herself quietly so that friends wouldn't try to dissuade her from joining the rebels. No one in her family had been a soldier, so she didn't have the help of a brother's or father's experience as she prepared to leave the Ugandan capital. *I went into town and tried to shop, but I didn't know what I was looking for. Like how we'd get supplies on the front. I thought, "What if I buy just one pair of jeans and then want to wash them?" So I bought two pairs and wore them both at the same time, because I'd heard that soldiers didn't have room to carry anything except guns and equipment.*

I went with two friends from secondary school, and we took the bus all the way to where the soldiers were gathering. I left behind one of my pairs of jeans. Now I was wearing a uniform.

After an intensive but short basic training, Apophia deployed to the front in northern Rwanda.

Many other young Rwandans from outside the country were swept up in the movement. Now, more than two decades later, they recount with exhilaration the fervor of their commitment. When they started, of course, no one could guess where their choices would lead. While they knew either from experience, or from tales passed down, the brutality that the reigning Rwandan leaders could muster to retain control, the coming genocide was still unfathomable.

As **ROSE K.** speaks in 2009, she reexperiences her urgent resolve amid the confusion.

When the fighters left in the night, they didn't even tell me. Many other people were left behind, but I felt I had to go. Of course there were fears—you can imagine. All through the day, I was working on how I should go.

Finally, we left around 6:00 PM on buses. So many roadblocks had been put up, because the Ugandan army knew we were leaving with our guns and ammunition.

Maybe they thought I wouldn't go, because I had a baby. But I left my eleven-month-old behind. I never thought I would leave him. But I had to be part of the change, so I forgot my fears. I told friends, "I am going," not knowing who would look after him, what he would eat, what would happen if he got sick. I thought my husband would stay behind, not knowing that after some time he would also join the struggle. But my niece was at home. I didn't cry when I was leaving my baby.

With eyes now full, she recalls the lowest point.

The next morning, when I got off the bus someone told me news of our top commander: "Fred Rwigema has died." I was shocked and didn't believe it. "Why did I come? I should have stayed behind and taken care of my son. If Fred has died, this is the end of us." Again, I didn't cry. After all these years, maybe I can. But then I never cried.

Nobody was talking about it. We stayed there a week, not sure, thinking he might come. The journalists came and asked, so we lied: "He's on the front line." None of the senior officers confirmed his death; I just knew, because I never saw him.

Inyumba came twice, trying to meet with him. After ten days, I decided to say, "You know what, Inyumba? Suppose you don't ever see Fred? Is this war going to stop? Is the struggle over for us?" She realized I was telling her something. She went and cried, then came back, dried her tears, and said, "We have to continue."

The government army hit us badly, and our forces all disintegrated. Some died, others left. . . . General Kagame was somewhere trying to plan what to do. We went into the forest. They asked me to go across to Tanzania, to take care of people who were sick and needed nurses and doctors, as well as medicine.

Later, I got a message that we should move to the mountains. General Kagame decided that the few who'd survived should go there to reorganize. It was cold. It was harsh. But the struggle went on. The RPF movement brought the soldiers supplies.

Some women were nurses; some were mobilizing people, teaching. The women who were soldiers were on the front line, carrying guns like anybody else. No one said, "This is a man, this is a woman, so therefore you do these things." That said, there were men who wanted women to have a smaller role because it upset them if the woman was shot or killed—so they were always trying to protect us.

5 GENOCIDE

MATHILDE: Some were victims. But some knew what would hurt the women and brought young people to whip them in front of their children. That was the ultimate humiliation. And then, of course, many were heroes.

April 6, 1994, was a Wednesday, and **ANNONCIATA** was at home in Kigali with her husband Innocent, a soldier in Rwanda's national army. Being Tutsi and working for any of the Habyarimana government's institutions was risky, even though he'd managed to get the job. In the army, tension over the Hutu-Tutsi divide was especially rigid, now that the government and the rebel RPF were locked in a civil war. But even earlier, more than a decade before, Annonciata's husband had hidden his identity. He had used a forged ID card to enlist as a Hutu in the Rwandan army years earlier in hopes that his allegiance wouldn't be questioned.

Annonciata and Innocent were in their bedroom listening to their favorite radio station. An explosion shortly after dark echoed across the city. Soon, a heart-stopping broadcast came through. A plane carrying President Habyarimana home from a round of peace talks with the RPF had been shot from the sky and landed in flaming fragments. *My husband got up and said, "If it's true that President Habyarimana is dead, all Tutsi will be dead." Normally at that time of night, the radio played a program,* Igitaramo, *with Kinyarwanda songs. We usually listened as we were getting ready for bed. But that night, the station was playing only classical music, and there was an announcement that all Rwandans should not leave their houses, that no one should drive. And that classical music!* . . . Throughout the long night, they waited. *Of course we didn't sleep.*

Activist Athanasie Kabagwira.

The very next morning, other soldiers came to our house and said, "Do you know what has happened? Why are you just here at home?" Actually, my husband had a short vacation from work, but the soldiers began to beat him. The neighbors gathered around to watch, so the soldiers shot into the air to make people go back to their homes. Then they left with my husband. That was the last time I saw him.

For months, young men had been training to kill using farm tools. These local militias, known as Interahamwe or "people who work together," were primed. They would fight alongside the army whenever the call went out. Lists had been drawn up. Hate-filled propaganda blared on radios and in headlines, demonizing Tutsi and those who might defend against their extermination. Outspoken and savvy, Prime Minister Agathe Uwilingiyimana was singled out. She had become a prominent leader in government once the one-party system ended in 1991, but extremist literature and cartoons depicted her as promiscuous, a national threat. On the first day of the genocide, her murder in front of her home at the hands of the Presidential Guard was as much about being a highly competent woman as it was about being a prominent member of the democratic opposition.[1]

Prominent female activists were also at risk, regardless of their ethnicity. **ATHANASIE** remembers how the leader of Réseau des Femmes fled to Europe. *We had a very, very dynamic coordinator, Veneranda Nzambazamariya. She was evacuated during the genocide because she could have been killed, not because of her ethnicity but because of her ideas and her work. She was against the separation of people because they were from this or that group. She could speak to anyone, do advocacy everywhere, explain herself and her views so eloquently. In every generation there are the natural leaders, with original ideas who would die for their cause. Veneranda was one, and that's what made her a target.*

Other women, however, were at the center of the genocidal plans and directed the crimes. Pauline Nyiramasuhuko was Rwanda's first gender minister and a schoolmate of Rwanda's first lady, Agathe Habyarimana. Rising through the ranks of the president's party, Pauline was known as the city of Butare's favorite daughter. Even while holding government posts in Kigali, she kept close ties to her hometown, where her husband served as rector of National University and owned a hotel.

During the early days of the genocide, Butare was a rare bastion for the small ethnic minority. The ruling party's influence was relatively weak, and the top local official was Tutsi. On April 17, that leader was dismissed and then disappeared—and along with him, any sense of a safe haven. Two days later, the swearing-in for the new local leader became a rally to rouse citizens to take up arms. The next day, killings in the university town began. Later court documents describe how Pauline appealed to the new head of the local government for help conducting massacres nearby in her home village.

Wearing military fatigues, she usually based herself out of her husband's Hotel Ihuliro. In front, her son had set up one of the town's most monstrous roadblocks for weeding out Tutsi. "Nyiramasuhuko stood by the vehicle and told the Interahamwe to take the young girls and the women who are not old, to rape them before killing them because they had refused to marry Hutus," a witness said.

Many Tutsi refugees had crowded into the bureau of the local administrator, still in disbelief about the government's complete unwillingness to save them. Drawing on her role as a minister as well as prominent local figure, Pauline ordered the armed men, "There's still a lot of dirt at the Butare préfecture office, such as these Tutsi women, who previously were arrogant and did not want to marry Hutu men. Now it's up to you to do whatever you want with them."[2]

She distributed condoms to protect the men from AIDS.

Strong people were killing. Other strong people were dying, just like dogs. JOSEPHINE managed to keep her creative wits, even as her small town on Lake Kivu, at the western border, was drawn into the countrywide catastrophe. *I am poor. I'm not one of the society's favored people. But I could help. That gave me some strength.*

When Habyarimana died, a strict instruction came across the national radio that everyone should stay wherever they were. After three days, militias in the countryside started burning down houses belonging to Tutsi. We could see and smell the smoke. Soon the message was that everyone should hunt them.

The local authorities told Tutsi they should all gather together at churches and at the stadium. They were trying to trick them by saying they were trying to protect them. But Tutsi didn't know the strategy yet, and they started to

April 15, 1994, five thousand people were killed here. They fended off the militia by throwing stones but were overcome by grenades, guns, and machetes.

travel to those areas. The killers didn't even wait—they began killing them on the road. Authorities didn't try to stop them. Local leaders made clear that anyone caught hiding or helping Tutsi would be punished; sympathizers would be forced to kill the people they were trying to protect and then be killed themselves. *That's how we understood that the idea was to eliminate the Tutsi.*

I am Hutu, and I come from a family of Hutus, so I wasn't being targeted. One morning I was outside doing laundry. I saw a neighbor, a Tutsi, on the road. He asked where my brother-in-law lived, thinking he would go to him for protection. But I told him, "No, don't go there. Come into my house." The man he was looking for was already involved in the killing. He was working with the Interahamwe.

When he came in he wanted something to drink, but all I had was lake water. He asked if I could go buy him some beer. Along the road I saw another man I knew. I was surprised, because he was just walking down the road, and I knew he was Tutsi. "What are you doing? Don't you know they are killing Tutsi? Run to my house and hide among the bean plants!" I told him to wait, and I would be back soon.

The man at the shop was curious, because I don't usually drink Primus. I said to him, "And why not?" So he stopped bothering me. I brought the beers back to the house and the two men drank them, in my living room. I locked the door and returned to my laundry in front of the house. I didn't want to raise any suspicions.

While I was outside, my husband came home. I was nervous. I hadn't asked Fidel and Pierre to wait in our bedroom, because I wasn't sure what my husband would say. Also, I didn't want to explain everything outside, so I just told him, "Oh, you know, you have some visitors here to see you. Quick, go in and greet them." As soon as he saw, he understood. He told them, "Go! Go into our bedroom and hide." They stayed with us two weeks.

With militiamen going house to house to ferret out people in hiding and to punish accomplices, Josephine knew she needed to find a better option for protecting Fidel and Pierre. The shores of Congo were many hours away by paddleboat; still, the lake looked like the most promising escape route. But she didn't have a boat.

My father owned a wooden canoe, but my cousin used it to make money. He was a fisherman, so he wasn't able to just give it up. I had to negotiate with him. He asked whether the two men could pay him. I told him they'd left their homes with nothing. My cousin was raising some goats for me, so I said, "Let's sign a paper. I'll give you those goats, and I'll take the boat." I had to hide from my husband that I'd sold our goats, but anyway, I'd found a boat.

At that time we couldn't trust anyone. I was worried that my cousin would still give the men up to the killers. So I asked Pierre to give me a symbol to show that they'd escaped. He found a small ball in his pocket that belonged to his son. I told him, "When you're really about to depart to Congo, give this toy to my cousin so I'll know you made it to safety." Luckily my cousin came back to me with the ball.

Just days later, the killers began attacking people gathered at the town stadium. Two girls and a man who ran away in the chaos ended up at Josephine's door. *One girl told me her father had also been trying to escape. They'd been running together, but the killers caught him and then shot him. She had to keep going.*

Josephine searched for another boat to shepherd the trio to safety, but the saga with Pierre and Fidel had left her husband rattled. His mother was Tutsi, and he looked the part, even though his ID card read Hutu.

My husband said that if the killers came they wouldn't hesitate to kill him, because they were trying to get rid of all Tutsi blood. I was trying to calm him, but I started to get worried that he might give away our secret, not because he wanted to give them up but because he was so terrified.

I was really starting to lose hope. I was losing weight, not sleeping. I really felt that their entire fate was on me. What if they were discovered? It would be my fault. Then—and I think this was a divine intervention—I went down to the lake to collect some water. I walked so slowly; I was very distraught. When I got to the water I saw a small metal boat just sitting there. It belonged to my neighbor, but I knew that he was doing evil things, so I couldn't ask to use the boat. I noticed it was attached to a tree with a metal chain.

My husband said, "The only thing I'll do for you is give you a metal saw. You can try yourself to cut the chain. But if anyone—like the guy who owns that brewery over there—sees you, they'll kill you."

So I said to my children, "When it gets dark we're going down to the lake, and you're going to play in the water and sing, swim, yell." With all this noise I thought it would hide the sound. I started to saw, but it was hard to break the chain, so my kids and I took turns. Finally it broke, and we pushed the boat into the water.

April rains fell in sheets, the low clouds opening up, saturating the fields, and stirring the dirt footpaths into thick mud. One dark afternoon, a woman with a baby on her back—both of them soaked to the bone—scurried by the open door of Josephine's kitchen. She called them inside. *I told her to take off her wet things and put on this cloth of mine. I hung up her clothes to dry.*

The woman fed her baby and stayed for dinner. Just as Josephine, her husband, and the woman finished eating, two policemen pounded on the front door. One was a neighbor; the other was a stranger, and he had a gun. *When they asked, "Who is this lady?," my husband was smart. He said she was my sister-in-law. They asked to see her national ID.* The police wanted to check whether she was Tutsi. *My husband told them that she had just gotten out of the hospital after a month and didn't have anything with her.*

The police didn't buy it. *They ordered the lady and my husband to go outside. It was still raining. As soon as they stepped outside, I lay down on the floor and covered my head. I couldn't bear to hear what would happen next.*

Farmer Josephine Dusabimana.

Two shots. Josephine wailed.

Then her husband walked in. Outside, the woman and her baby died immediately, their blood mixing with the rain.

Neighbors moved the two bodies—one very small—away from the front door. *It was a crime to bury Tutsi at that time, so they just covered their bodies with dirt in our vegetable garden until after the genocide.*

Josephine's husband gave her an ultimatum. As she continues telling the story, she covers her eyes with one hand. A family arrived at their house: a man and woman with their two young children. Josephine's husband told her that if she wanted to save them, he would leave. *He told me, "It will be me who pays the price if those policemen come back."* Sensing the rift, the couple decided not to stay, fearful that they might be turned in. Josephine removes her hand but keeps her eyes closed. *I asked him, "How could you do this? The Interahamwe are close. If they're killed, it will be your fault."*

Josephine stood her ground when she met the last person she would rescue: an eleven-year-old boy. *I thought he was about eight or nine. After surviving in the forest, he looked very young . . . so frail, as though waiting for death. He didn't even move when I saw him across the garden. He was scared of me as I approached because he thought I could be a killer. Women could be killers too, or they could call the killers. But I insisted that it was safe for him to come with me. "If you stay where you are, you will be killed," I told him.*

My husband came home and said, "Your small Tutsi, he's going to be killed—I heard it in town." I asked how people knew the child was here. He didn't say, only that it would be tomorrow or the next day. The little boy got scared, but he didn't really understand. He asked me what was happening. I lied to him and said, "Tomorrow or the next day the war will end and you'll be safe." I had to lie to reassure him.

Josephine took the boy to her parents' house, telling them he was her husband's nephew. He lived out the genocide with them, and when the war came to their village, they all fled to eastern Congo.

As circumstances became even more dire, Josephine had taken more risks, devising increasingly daring plots to rescue neighbors and strangers who otherwise might have perished. *I realized, I'm just a human; these others are just humans. If I die, it doesn't matter, because all these people around me are dying.*

Meanwhile, after the probable murder of her husband Innocent on the first day of the genocide, **ANNONCIATA** realized it wasn't safe for her to stay in her home. Neighbors had seen the commotion as soldiers had taken her husband away, so she knew she needed to find somewhere else to wait out this horror—for how long, it was impossible to predict. Waves of violence had targeted Tutsi before, but Innocent's fearsome words about extermination rang in her ears. Nearly eight months pregnant, she traveled by foot to the outskirts of Kigali with their eighteen-month-old son Jean-Marie tied in a cotton wrap on her back. As the pair furtively made their way through alleyways, Annonciata prayed that they might find refuge on a quieter hill where she used to live. She had a specific hiding place in mind.

Many refugees were passing through, and many houses were abandoned. Yet I knew if I tried to hide in a house, the Interahamwe militia or the army soldiers would find us. No one would think someone could live in a dog house, so I thought maybe we would be safer there.

That's where we stayed. That small house for dogs. Sometimes I would go out at night and find some food refugees had left, especially if they had to leave in a hurry because of peril. Other times we were really hungry. That's where I gave birth to my second-born, a son. In that dog house. Alone one night, with no care. I survived there with my newborn and my small son.

When I gave birth, the child didn't cry. He didn't cry at all. But when soldiers were moving around, they saw some water coming from that shed. And then the baby cried. Everywhere else it was silent. Even the birds weren't singing. I knew, "This is the day I will die."

The soldiers found me and pulled me out. I begged them, "Please, kill me well. Don't kill me slowly. Kill me well. I died long ago. Kill me and kill this baby."

And they said, "We're not killers. We've come to save people."

On July 4, 1994, the RPF entered Kigali, now commemorated as the last day of the Rwandan genocide.

ROSE K. was in the capital that day. *On the day the war ended . . . oh my God, the chaos. From houses and the bush, people were emerging, wounded, emaciated. The streets were full of dead people. Young. Old. The survivors were disoriented. They had no family at all, no property. Of course it was good that there was no more war, no more machetes. But that day was not like a great victory.*

Unflinching memorial: classroom at Murambi Technical School, where 45,000 people were massacred, many bodies preserved as they fell.

As the RPF soldiers swept through the country, they sparked another exodus, this time of perpetrators, their families, neighbors—two million people together—who feared retribution or prosecution. They poured over Rwanda's borders, mostly west into Congo.

The spring deluge had passed, and the sun cast a harsh glare on the living, and on all that was dead and destroyed. Shadowy hiding places might have starved or suffocated their dwellers, but the uncompromising daylight portended a new, grim reality less bound by time: unbearable grieving, and inconceivable healing.

Several sites would become memorials—with piles of bones and cracked skulls so gruesome as to offend, except that to whitewash the reality is more offensive.

The Rwandan genocide was a more efficient killing machine than the Third Reich at its peak. As international policy makers read reports in the safety of their offices, unimaginable horrors were unfolding in towns like Murambi. There, tens of thousands ran for their lives to the technical school. Water and food were cut off. Throngs became too weak to resist. Weeks later, a volleyball court was built over mass graves.

The genocide created a perverse experiment as the country's social, economic, and political foundations were wiped out.

For many of those long in exile, their political mobilizing was driven by the idea of liberty—the vision of an unfettered life in their home country. But what they inherited as they "returned" to Rwanda—some for the first time in their lives—would call for all the courage they could muster. Before, and from a distance, the challenges they'd imagined didn't even come close to what they would find returning to a country utterly devastated by genocide.

Driven by survival instincts or deliberate choice, whether in Rwanda or in exile, the risks women took and sacrifices they made during this singularly horrific time would inform their leadership moving forward.

6 IMMEDIATE AFTERMATH

> **JOY M.:** It was horrendous—but for us who were coming from
> outside, the worst was the bloodstains on the streets and in
> buildings . . . wondering in which piles of corpses in churches
> and schools you would find your relatives.

Today's rise of women was embedded in this specific moment of dis-ordering crisis. Rwanda lay in ruins: churches and schools turned into massacre sites, roadsides turned into open graves. Those who managed to survive faced the herculean task of rebuilding when every semblance of normalcy had vanished.

With no running water, erratic electricity, and offices looted to the last piece of paper, the new Rwandan Patriotic Front government went to work, focusing first on the fetid cleanup and then on reestablishing political structures. They had little institutional knowledge to draw on: previous leaders had fled or been killed; new leaders had minimal governance experience. Of some 785 judges before the genocide, twenty survived. When the transitional National Assembly was created in November 1994, none of the seventy-four new members and only five staff members had participated in the prewar parliament.

Thirty years had passed since **JOY M.** had been to Rwanda. *Everyone was coming back, not necessarily to stay but to see and to look for family. In August, the corpses had been removed from the streets, but there were still bloodstains all over, and the whole city smelled of death. I think the bodies in the Holy Family Cathedral were still there. In some bloodstains you could even see the form of a body. It was really, really horrible.*

There was no public transport. One day, after my sister and I walked for

*about an hour looking for a niece we had been told was still alive, we found
a taxi. As soon as we got into his car, a young man carrying his baby pleaded
with us to let him use the taxi. The child was very sick, limp in his arms. He
must have recently come back too, because he didn't know where the hospital
was. But we didn't either. We drove all around town looking for a hospital for
the child.*

The ruling RPF's core committee shaped reconstruction through their
guiding principles—an eight-point plan prescribing unity, inclusivity,
and democracy—and the 1993 Arusha Accords, which the leaders of
the movement had a strong hand in drafting. But RPF followers were
deployed throughout the nascent government and expected to initiate
programs as they saw fit.

Several women were among those immediately appointed to leadership, not because they were women, but because they were among the
most trusted and capable.

One was **ROSE K.** *I was appointed the first mayor of Kigali. I didn't know
where to begin. We started trying to clean the city, to bury the people. It was
hard, hard, hard. I didn't have people to work with me. But slowly, slowly we
pulled in people, because how could we take over a country alone? We had
soldiers in the city, because civilians had run away from us when the previous
government told them, "They're going to kill you." So this was a deserted city
except us and survivors who needed help.*

Then there was Aloisea Inyumba, known as creative, undaunted, and
not yet thirty when named postgenocide minister for gender and social
affairs. *She made sure that those working around her were people friendly,*
says **FATUMA,** who was one of them. *Inyumba was a leader close to the
people. It was not like she was going to have this big portfolio and just sit in
her office. She was less formal and preferred to relate to people.*

*Inyumba had passion for change, a passion for women. With her back-
ground in resource mobilization for the RPF, she had this idea that women
should never be beggars. She didn't want women to see themselves as victims
but rather to be economically empowered.*

In those early days, women with unutterably painful stories would fill
the ministry daily in search of any assistance the staff could offer, from
advice, to food, to help finding some form of employment. *We realized
we couldn't do everything. We could not have staff spending ten hours each*

day listening to people's problems one by one and going to the villages to try to bring people together. It was not very strategic. We didn't have many experts on gender and women. What we did have was the will: our own—then she adds, referring to the country's top leadership—*and the political will.*

Inyumba started hosting regular meetings at the ministry with a group of activists, businesswomen, representatives of religious communities, and other opinion leaders. Together, they discussed major challenges women faced and strategies for emboldening them to take charge of rebuilding, both as a way of healing and because solutions grounded in women's own experiences would be the most sustainable. Their answer was a countrywide network of councils to elevate women's perspectives on a range of issues, such as education, health, and security. *We had women coming to us as victims, with problems we couldn't handle. They needed to see themselves as active participants, active agents of change. Whether peace building, reconciliation, or reconstructing a nation, it would depend on women. They were the majority in the society, and we knew the influential role they could play.*

At the grassroots level, too, women's leadership started out organically. They stepped forward and converted proficiencies into newly required skills: mothering meant taking in homeless children; house managing became caring for widows; cleaning expanded to construction. Traditionally, women never helped build houses. Now, they were on site, pushing wheelbarrows, hauling bricks.

Meanwhile, killings and raids by Hutu extremists continued in more remote parts of the country, and survivors felt especially vulnerable. But on an individual level, people gradually began reestablishing ties with neighbors, even those with family members implicated for crimes that marked people's lives forever.

ANNONCIATA took her two young sons to southern Rwanda, where her family and her husband's family had lived before the genocide. She learned that her parents had been killed. Innocent's parents had survived by fleeing to Burundi. Of course, she also clutched at hope that she would find Innocent himself.

Her husband wasn't there, as, deep down, she knew he wouldn't be. But looking for any family members felt more purposeful than staying still in Kigali.

Survivor Annonciata Nyirabajiwabo.

Near her in-laws, who had returned after the catastrophic one hundred days, Annonciata settled in a small village called Nyumba. Since she was a devout Catholic, the local parish was an obvious place for her to put down roots. But Nyumba's church, with its broad, brick arches and painted glass windows, had been the epicenter of murders. Its slatted walls, designed to let a breeze pass through the congregation on a humid Sunday, had become turrets for soldiers' guns, aimed inward. Church leaders reasoned that turning the building into a memorial would only freeze in time the atrocities committed there, and constructing a new place of worship would pile a financial burden on top of survival needs. So that same church once again became the center of the community. *During Sunday services, especially the time of sharing the sign of peace, shaking hands, you might find a Hutu woman next to you, and you could not fail to take her hand. So that helped us to reconcile slowly by slowly.*

After coming together, praying together, we could begin to see that we are all children of God. That's when we started to help people in prison—men and women jailed for their involvement in the genocide. *We made food for them. When we saw that they didn't have enough clothing, we brought some. We thought, there is no other way of living than to be close to one another, survivor* [targeted during the genocide] *or not.*

As in any conflict zone, tension arose between those who'd been fighting for their lives in Rwanda, and those outside through the toughest times. Some survivors resented the relatively well-off new returnees—even their ability to choose to return. Despite the hardships of refugee camp life in other countries, they had advantages—education, exposure to other cultures, or fluency in English. Also, Rwandans in exile didn't face the staggering emotional trauma that was tormenting everyone caught up in the 1994 horrors. In a country without trained psychologists, where 96 percent of children witnessed violence, having even a slight distance from daily gruesome scenes counted as an advantage.[1]

With time, some came to see the wider range of perspectives and knowledge as a blessing in disguise. For others, the divide deepened, as efforts designed for the greater good—like lighter prison sentences in exchange for truth telling—left some survivors perpetually frustrated.

BEATRICE is an education specialist who grew up in Uganda and would serve in Parliament. In 2006 she described what was then still a work in progress: to cultivate the pride of being a citizen of a unified Rwanda. *One major challenge in rebuilding the new Rwandan society is that we've called ourselves "du-Congo" or "du-Burundi." . . . Many different groups of Rwandans came back after living in the diaspora. If someone had been living in Sudan or Uganda for thirty-five years, maybe was even born there, it might be easier to relate more to those places. Some are Anglophone, some Francophone; some speak Swahili. So we had to grapple with those differences, as you can imagine. I think it's been for the better, and it's just natural. Many people from Israel have known such a thing, but it hasn't been easy. It's been tough. As people have come home, those who were always inside have said, "You came and started the war, so be quiet now."*

That reaction may seem unreasonable. But standards of reason are academic when an entire population is overwhelmed by what therapists would label post-traumatic stress.

Of course, the community of women activists—what remained of it—wasn't insulated from deep gulfs in trust. As the chaos began to subside and people had more time to reflect, differences actually became more pronounced. Some pulled back from the work; others tried to dictate who could be involved moving forward.

Rights activist **CHRISTINE,** who was born and raised in Kigali, brings in a perspective similar to Beatrice's but emphasizes that the commonalities among women eventually prevailed. Focused on just putting their lives back together and on coping with grief, they often saw how they could lean on each other. *We had different backgrounds: women who had been refugees in other countries; women who had been living here; women who went into exile after 1994, many in the Democratic Republic of Congo. It was really hard, but after analyzing our problems, we decided to work together.*

A woman with her husband in jail could say to another woman, "Please, can you stay with my child while I bring food to my husband?" These women actually lived together. They collaborated. They went together to church. They worked together in the fields and—what is it in English?—keep cattle. One was a survivor of genocide, and another's husband was in prison because he committed the genocide. So the genocide had an impact on every woman in this country. We weren't the reason for this conflict, but we all suffered in one way or another.

Initially, dramatic role changes were born of necessity, with women filling the places of men who had fled, died, or were in prison. But over the next few years, as former combatants returned, women didn't surrender their places. They had discovered power in their new skills, and they protected it in their solidarity.

PART II
The Path to Public
Leadership

When soldiers found **ANNONCIATA** with her small sons in the dog shed where she took cover from the genocidal frenzy, her moment-to-moment ordeal ended. But the sorrows she faced, now as a widow, would consume many more months and cast a shadow over years to come.

The main activity right after was burying. There was a building behind the church that had been bulldozed down with people locked inside. So we had to pull bodies out from the rubble. Some people had climbed into the ceiling of the church to hide and had been shot there. Their blood had trickled down the wall and soaked the ceiling panels.

Annonciata helped uncover corpses and wrap them in sheeting. *We had to bury people over there*, she says, pointing out the window. *It was very hard work, digging, carrying. All the latrines around here were stuffed with bodies. As some of the killers started to realize what they had done, they would say, "There are more bodies over there." Then we would have to demolish the toilet and bring the bodies out of the pit.*

Women in Nyumba who'd lived through the hell began meeting quietly in each other's homes, and Annonciata found solace in that support network, even if everyone was facing insufferable circumstances. *Some Hutu women had been married to Tutsi men, and their husbands and children had been killed. But really it was survivors (the word reserved for Tutsi). We hadn't really accepted others.*

Although she wasn't trained, Annonciata took a job as a teacher in the village primary school. Most instructors from the community either had been slain or had fled, so her literacy was prized. *As a teacher, I was going around, talking to all sorts of people—those struggling emotionally, economically. People who had killed. That's how I started to see that different people coming together was possible.*

EMMANUEL arrived fresh from seminary in Kenya. The recently ordained priest had a colossal set of challenges in front of him, from the

Mothering and marketing.

blood-stained church and the bones unearthed in his vegetable garden to a bitterly divided and fearful community. *But I found the women very faithful. They were committed to service. Also in terms of money, they're not as corruptible. You can trust them—not all of them—but more than men.*

I remember one woman who had been working so hard with me on some of the development programs and on a committee supported by the Catholic charity called Caritas. We would spend the whole day together visiting the poor, going house to house to see people's situation. Then one day I found out that she'd been arrested. She had been a leader of a militia group during the genocide, so she went to jail. She might still be there today. I never suspected. Experiences like that made me realize: in Rwanda, you can't fault everyone, you can't suspect everyone, because otherwise, who will you work with?

With time, Father Emmanuel managed to restore the safe and sacred atmosphere at the church, and attendance rose. **ANNONCIATA** was among those who came to see the church as a place where healing could begin. *We thought, "Many people died but we lived, so maybe God wanted it to be that way." We started to come back to church.*

As a young widow, I had a problem with men. They were looking me over because I was a free woman, without a husband. Even our soldiers. To be spared that harassment, I thought I could take refuge in a religious community and become a nun. I looked for advice from my priest. We started a mixed group—survivors, nonsurvivors. I became a leader, so I had to be a good example.

At that time, we realized that the majority of us were women, widows even. When it was mostly women and children, we had to sit down and reflect on our lives. Slowly by slowly we started raising our standards. Our primary worry was how to bring up the children, and how to get houses. At the time a preacher named Ismaragde Mbonyintege would come to give sermons here. I don't know how he found donors to help build new houses, but he did—for the widows of the genocide first, and those ladies with many children. We also got some sewing machines to make a small business.

Rising out of devastation, many women—even from different backgrounds—bore similarly heavy loads. Husbands or sons who had murdered and were in jail, or who had fled, fearing reprisals, weren't sharing the family's farm work. But in addition, the teeming prisons had no food, and the burden of taking prisoners something to eat weighed heavily on the women. Father **EMMANUEL** set up a plan for the prisoners. *The church would provide the sauce and some vegetables, and the women would bring some cassava from their fields. We divided into several groups so that there would be food throughout the week.*

The project was initially controversial. **ANNONCIATA** says the inmates were fearful and apprehensive. *They felt like, "How can these people whose families were killed now be bringing food for us?" But what helped us is that the group was mixed—daughters, mothers of prisoners along with survivors—so the prisoners couldn't fear.*

Sometimes even the survivors were abusing us, coming to the church and saying, "Why do you make us suffer? Why do you take food to the killers?" It was very hard for both sides. But doing this helped with reconciliation because it forced people to talk about the difficult issues.

Eventually, moved by the example set by Annonciata and the group, many others joined in. Everyday tasks—now focused on living, not dying—gave people a sense of purpose. But Father **EMMANUEL** adds his voice. *There are some women we failed to bring back to life.*

Still, **ANNONCIATA** emphasizes that the prominent, essential roles women in Nyumba took up in the early days after the massacre profoundly shaped their sense of their own capabilities. *Before, we thought everything should be asked of the man. But after, women saw that they had to wake up. There was no way to live otherwise, because men were gone. So we started to create cooperatives, working with banks; we learned how to develop ourselves; we began paying for our own health insurance; we paid our children's school fees. Now we don't depend on other people. We provide for ourselves.*

Stories like Annonciata's unfolded across the country as women confronted their lot in the aftermath.

The first postgenocide census found that 60 percent of (Tutsi) survivors were female, many suddenly heads of household and sole providers for their surviving children, other young family members, or friends they had taken in.[1] Shock was compounded by hunger and homelessness. On top of all that, by Rwandan customary law, women had no right to their husbands' or fathers' property. Families were often left without a roof over their heads or land to till. Others became squatters.

Women and girls impregnated during attacks had to choose between agonizing options: terminating a pregnancy is illegal in Rwanda, though many clandestine abortions likely took place with serious lasting health consequences. Some women abandoned babies born of rape or gave them up for adoption. Others decided to raise the children and deal with their own conflicted feelings, as well as a range of responses from family members, from support to shame.

Given the revered status of mothers in Rwandan tradition, infertility caused by sexual violence and mutilation could be devastating socially: they might never be able to marry or might be rejected by their husbands and families. Although an untold number of women suffered attacks, rape still carried a stigma against the victim, who was seen as sullied or even spoiled. Women who endured sexual slavery, in particular, were denounced for trading sex, albeit for their lives. Fear of being ostracized or even targeted again by their attacker drove many to hide their shame, making healing all the harder. On top of all this, infection with HIV had been a tactic used by genocidaires: Rwandan women's groups say the genocide continued past July 1994 as women infected with AIDS died.[2]

Millions of women led lives haunted by hidden trauma. Nightmarish flashbacks were sometimes incapacitating, but an astonishing number found the determination not only to endure but to brave the unknown. For those in the early rebuilding, stepping up wasn't intentionally avant-garde. Sometimes their progress was deliberate—driven by the clear vision and strategic foresight of key individuals—but their story also developed organically, out of sheer need in the uniquely troubled times.

CHANTAL: We'd lost our families, so we had to be each other's family.

CHANTAL didn't see herself as an activist. She was a nurse, just a month away from finishing her public health degree, when the genocide broke out. Her husband had been killed, and with a newborn son, Chantal was at first daunted, imagining how she would cope as a single mother. *Widows would meet at each other's houses and just talk about our problems. We had the same challenges, and we helped each other think about how we would survive. It was the only group you could identify with.*

In addition to providing direct help for the widows, those meetings grew into one of the country's leading advocacy groups. From the beginning, justice was a main concern for AVEGA, the Association of Widows of the Genocide. *How could we sit still after our husbands had been murdered and not push for people to be accountable?*

We didn't have an organization so much in mind at first; everything was spontaneous. We didn't even know the word "genocide." At first our association just stood for "widows of the war." But my brother called me after we wrote our bylaws. "You're not widows of the war. Your husbands were killed because of genocide." So we made the "G" in AVEGA stand for "genocide" instead of "guerre."

Who was the founder of AVEGA? Actually, we had to limit the number of founders because there were too many. We listed only fifty. Some of our members were as old as our mothers, and others as young as our sisters. Let's do everything for each other, we thought. We didn't have counseling, even though we needed it. We would just sit down and talk.

Nearly half a million children were orphaned or separated from their families during the genocide.

Some people called us discriminatory and said we were an organization of only Tutsi. But we said our members were not just Tutsi. We had Hutu women who had been married to Tutsi and their husbands had been killed; they needed this support too. And we have unique needs.

Desperately unique needs, in fact. But other groups were as despairing. An estimated 400,000 children and teens were either orphaned or separated from their families in the melee. Streets and alleys were filled with young ones trying to fend for themselves. Eventually, the government and global humanitarian groups, like UNICEF and the Red Cross, would take the lead in tracking down families or finding foster homes for these children. But first, while many shrank back from the chaos, some pressed themselves forward, organizing to find and encourage families to adopt orphans. "Each one, take one," was one refrain encouraging already strained Rwandans to open their homes and hearts to children.

FATUMA explains: *The first project I worked on was SOS Ramira. Like the meaning of kuramira—to save—our vision was to make a modest contribution to saving lives and giving comfort.* The fledgling group she started was in Byumba, a small town in the north hit hard by years of fighting. They got to work even while the genocide continued in many parts of the country. *We were a few women passionate about caring for returnees, survivors, orphans, and minors who'd lost touch with their families. Some were from the RPF side, others from the former regime side. But we didn't care where you came from—this side or that side.*

We didn't have money, so we gathered clothes, starting with our own. Some of our members were pharmacists, so they could try to get medicine. Food, Kotex for ladies, clothes for young children. We also went to orphanages and hospitals to talk to people and soothe them. That one-to-one recognition of another's humanity beyond the categories "orphan" or "refugee" may have been the most cherished gift of them all.

The government started establishing institutions and setting up ministries responsible for social affairs. Special programs for vulnerable people got started and more humanitarian groups came in. SOS Ramira turned to projects such as tailoring, carpentry, and farming to generate income.

Understandably, given the level of distrust right after the brutality ended, suspicion existed even among people committed to the well-being of others. By most accounts, women's burgeoning pregenocide activism (1980s and early 1990s) had managed to rise above the ethnic divisionism of the era, but it was fragile and tense. Organizers had been killed or fled, and those who remained or returned questioned how they could reunite as women with lives splintered into sharp-edged fragments, tossed away in opposite corners. Some believed the differences could not be overcome and that any organization prior to the genocide should be abandoned. Some even advocated for exclusion of activists who had been prominent, even if they weren't personally culpable for involvement in the genocide.

Filling out the picture more is **"CLAUDINE,"** who had been a member of one of the first women's organizations and remained in Rwanda throughout the cataclysm, protected from the targeted violence by her Hutu ethnicity. *At first everyone—even we activists—needed comfort, to talk to someone who could understand where we were coming from. At the beginning—really at the beginning, like July, August, September, October—people were very nervous, thinking more about the difference.*

A variety of dynamics could undermine unity among activists. *Everyone came back with a bit of the culture of the places where they'd been living, and we often found ourselves relating better to our own small groups. It's normal; it's human. Luckily there were a good number of women who worked hard to overcome those feelings of separation, to communicate with one another and encourage others to do the same.*

One of the most challenged groups was the pioneer Duterimbere (Go Forward), launched five years before the genocide. With an unambiguous vision of the value of women's economic independence, the group had given out small loans and run workshops on how to design successful projects and market products. At the same time, they'd taught women about their rights and legal protections as small business owners. Within its first month of operation in 1989, they approached **JULIE**, an industrious young professional, about working with them because she knew women in the rural areas they wanted to reach. Julie started out as an analyst, determining whether projects were bankable. But regardless of her talent, being Tutsi in the late 1980s meant she could never hold a leadership position during the blatant discrimination of the Habyarimana days.

She and her husband, Bonaventure, had decided to stay in Kigali despite the mounting dangers. *Since my husband was working for the Americans, we thought that if anything bad happens, we'd be safe.* Bonaventure was the U.S. development agency's most senior Rwandan staff member. The affiliation did offer some protection, such as when Bonaventure was rounded up with other Tutsis and thrown in jail. *The director was coming to check on me every day to be sure I wasn't dead.*

My husband was in prison for five months. The director appealed for Bonaventure's release on parole in March 1991. Bonaventure knew he'd be hunted down, so he went underground as soon as the April 1994 killings began.

The women's group Duterimbere might have been a casualty of the genocide: the organization's first general director was Agnes Ntamabyariro, who would serve as the country's justice minister in 1994 and later be given a life sentence for orchestrating crimes. Now in the early aftermath, would Duterimbere be tarnished by association?

Of about twenty-five staff in 1994, all but five had been killed or had fled. One of the five was Julie. She had survived by hiding at Kigali's Saint Famille cathedral, with her three children—two toddlers and an infant. *I kept thinking, "If I don't die, I'll spend my life working for women."* Just how does someone who has lived in stark survival mode hour after hour, day after day, turn outward to find others to care for? *I imagined many things I would do.*

When things quieted down, some of us thought, "What if we open our doors again and restart this good work?" We could focus on helping those lucky enough to survive, since our clients would probably need support even more so as they tried to restart their lives.

A team of four worked as volunteers for two months, until a donor gave them enough money for small salaries. Julie says some who had been with Duterimbere were embarrassed to join again, even if they weren't complicit in the killing. *This work was needed more acutely than ever, to help draw women out of their deep pit of despair. But it was difficult to get projects going again. Some said to us, "Why should I go on? I'm alone. Everyone at home has died." We said, "You have to eat. You have to work. You have to make it." We told survivors, "If you made it through the genocide, you're not supposed to die of hunger."* She adds, matter-of-factly, advice she likely gives to herself as much as to others: *When you're busy you won't think so much of those hard times.*

· · ·

Pro-Femmes Twese Hamwe, an umbrella organization for women's rights groups countrywide, was also in an identity crisis. Just two years old when the genocide broke out, Pro-Femmes had a reputation for being inclusive. The group got its start in 1992 by organizing a Women's March for Peace, which called for an end to the war through peace talks between the Hutu Power government and the RPF in exile. President Habyarimana shut down the protest, putting the police on alert to crack down on women activists if they organized in the streets.

Activist Julie Uwamwiza.

An early list of member groups in a reinvigorated Pro-Femmes.

SUZANNE had long focused on orphans, and she joined with other activists to reconstitute Pro-Femmes in late 1994, believing that the projects into which they'd poured their passion would thrive with pooled efforts and expertise. *My perspective was that Pro-Femmes had the mandate of bringing women together to reconstruct the country. After the genocide, all these women had different pasts. They didn't share the same political views, but we brought them together by saying, "We've all inherited a country that is destroyed."*

If I grew up as a refugee, I needed to be sure my children weren't refugees. If my husband was in prison, I didn't want my children to be victims. We had to look for our common interests. Whether or not we were targeted, we suffered from something we didn't plan or carry out. We needed to start working together, but it wasn't at all easy. Not at all.

There were some who said, "We won the war. We can create our own Pro-Femmes." And there were others who said, "With Pro-Femmes we need to preserve our identity, as it is known in the country, as inclusive." There were women leaders like Aloisea Inyumba, Veneranda Nzambazamariya, Jeanne d'Arc Kanakuze, myself, who said, "Are we going to divide the country?" That would mean that we'd return to the division that had been the source of so many problems. We knew we needed to put aside this history and ask ourselves who we want to be as Rwandans tomorrow, for our children. To create that, we needed to construct a new Rwanda where everyone has fundamental rights that are respected. So we started to make our plans for Beijing together.

In September 1995, almost 50,000 delegates and other civil society activists gathered in the booming Chinese capital for the Fourth World Conference on Women. The UN declaration their countries adopted—189 member states, unanimously—would be heralded as a historic moment for women's rights. "It is time for us to say here in Beijing, and the world to hear, that it is no longer acceptable to discuss women's rights as separate from human rights," First Lady Hillary Clinton would proclaim.[1]

For Rwanda, the occasion proved a chance to present a new face, **SUZANNE** remembers. *We thought that the country had to go. We had to show the world that even though many people are dead, Rwanda is not dead. We would have a government delegation, and civil society also needed to be represented.*

But the question remained: Which identity would civil society represent? Would we still be Pro-Femmes? Some said no, people don't know Pro-Femmes, and they won't know whether it was implicated in the genocide. But it was important for us to tell our story, not to destroy this foundation but to build upon it. So we had Jeanne Kanakuze from Girl Guides, I was representing Benimpuhwe, and Veneranda was from Réseau des Femmes. We started telling how Pro-Femmes got started, how it did its work in spite of difficulties with the previous government, how the new government was enabling its work and making an opening for women, no matter what their background: all were part of our collective effort.

Rwanda sent a large civil society delegation to Beijing with the support of the UN agency for women, known then as UNIFEM. *There was an impression in the world that if you were Rwandan you must be a genocidaire. We were humiliated.* But the meeting was also a watershed. *After Beijing we had to decide what to do next as a women's movement.* Activists returned from China rejuvenated. Pro-Femmes soon grew from its original thirteen member groups to twenty-eight, representing women across the country.

Action Campaign for Peace, one of Pro-Femmes' first postgenocide initiatives, raised the group's profile both domestically and internationally. **ANGELINA** was the government's minister of gender at the time and remembers the boldly unifying effect of this project. *Pro-Femmes Twese Hamwe women stepped out, staging marches to demonstrate that women don't want war. They joined together despite their differences: survivors of the genocide, women whose husbands were in prison, returnees who had been out of this country for over forty years—they came together in this umbrella organization. Together, they won the* UNESCO *prize for tolerance.* UNIFEM *and International Alert recognized our women's commitment by giving the Millennium Peace Prize to a member of Pro-Femmes.*

THERESE was also an early member. A molecular biologist heading up the new Kigali Health Institute shortly after the war, she often hones in on impact when describing the work of the various groups where she has volunteered over the years. She was serving as Pro-Femmes president when she explained how the organization recognized that more could be achieved if member groups brought what they do best to a joint effort and found partners with complementary advantages.

Women parliamentarians are helping us a lot. We also work with UNIFEM *and others to eradicate violence against women, because in Rwanda, it still exists. But we're organizing activities, all the way to the grassroots, to raise awareness. Everyone must understand that men and women for sure won't allow violence against women.*

But it's not just about a law being passed; we advocate that people take ownership of this law. It's written, but to see that this law is actually implemented, we must educate authorities in the administration, and even women. Some of them say, "The property is for my brother." They don't yet understand their rights. Then Pro-Femmes shows them they have the same rights as their brothers, the same as a man.

Whether they remained in civil society—deepening their activism and taking jobs in nongovernmental organizations—or moved into the government or private sectors, many women who went on to prominent roles credit their familiarity with grassroots organizing as foundational.

A hero and mentor of thousands worldwide, **INYUMBA** described her own trajectory, from an earnest young organizer in the early RPF days. *Before I became a minister, I gained a lot of experience working with the*

Government leader Angelina Muganza.

Rwandan communities abroad. But if I think back, I am who I am because of the background I acquired with women at the grass roots. Those in leadership positions today came from women's NGOs, from the community-based organizations, and other civil society.

With hard-won credibility, women began to formalize their influence, both by using their newfound power to push for strong female-friendly policies and by drawing on their confidence to vie for leadership positions. This crossover would create a force to be reckoned with, not only by Rwandans who feared change, but also by women in other countries, who would soon be looking to a postage-stamp nation in the middle of enormous Africa as a model.

A PULL FROM THE TOP 8

DINAH: His decision to appoint women makes all the difference, especially among older people and men who don't want to cede ground. If the president thinks a woman can lead, who are you to say she can't?

For worse—as the mass participation in the genocide demonstrated—or for better, deference toward authority has a strong place in Rwandan tradition. Historians hark back to the days of the monarchy, when the king maintained clear leadership across his vast lands through devoted chiefs. (Rwanda's borders were farther afield then, including territory now part of neighboring countries.) Such a system pleased the colonists, who further entrenched unquestioning reverence toward the top of the hierarchy. That uncritical adherence to rules from on high proved devastating in 1994, when ignorance and fear led Rwandans to take up machetes and call out their Tutsi neighbors—the order of the day. Today, the generation of up-and-coming leaders talks about the need for critical thinking in schools and for respectful but healthy questioning of rote versions of tradition. But top-down influence still holds particularly powerful sway, especially when laid out by President Kagame, or when nested in pride in Rwandan customs.

FELIX is a researcher long affiliated with the legal aid group Haguruka, which advocates for women's and children's rights. *For a while after the genocide, women found themselves suddenly heads of their households, without much extended family to help. They benefited from the political will of the government, and the leadership could see that those women, so neglected and vulnerable, were able to sustain themselves.*

The Rwandan Patriotic Front had inherited a country demolished and grieving, coffers empty and coffins full. The new leadership needed dedicated party members who'd proven to be talented managers during decades in exile. *The focus on equality of women and men is embedded within the RPF*, says **CHRISTOPHER**, a journalism professor and political pundit who has extensively studied the women's parliamentary majority.

Here, once more, there are multiple explanations for why the RPF looked for women to pull up. To begin with, many Rwandans say that women bore the brunt of the genocide and therefore deserve a prominent role in the nation's recovery. But suffering isn't competence. Being traumatized isn't a qualification for public leadership.

Political leaders in Rwanda understood the difference. Involving women in the rebuilding was less about fairness and much more about practicality. *President Kagame isn't pushing for women just for the sake of it*, Christopher says. *He's mostly interested in capable people.*

That isn't to say that promotion of women's rights didn't factor into the party's values. From early days, crafters of the RPF manifesto held equality—not explicitly between genders but of all Rwandans—in the highest regard. After years of exclusion, how could the group discount women who wanted to contribute?

Within the large number of Rwandans growing up in exile in Uganda, teenage girls and university students were influenced by women in that country's National Resistance Movement, which came to power in 1986. Female classmates of the RPF founders imagined themselves in their own burgeoning revolutionary cause. The RPF needed people like Rose and Apophia to mobilize supporters in the mountain bases in exile, enticing them to join the fight. They needed others, like Inyumba and Janet, to find money and supplies in far-flung cities and in camps where Rwandans had settled.

INYUMBA had finished her studies in social work and social administration at Uganda's prestigious Makerere University in 1987. She lived in the capital, Kampala, where many smart, ambitious Rwandans had moved after high school. *There was this kind of wave among the Rwandan youth.* She and her friends had heard about Paul Kagame and his circle. *They had plans of taking us home.*

Immediately when I finished my first degree, I didn't go to work for money.

President Paul Kagame. FROM RWANDAN PRESIDENCY

It's like I was looking for this organization. That's how I was recruited. I joined the RPF *and became a volunteer. I started with the peace education program. We had a special program in the schools tailored on three aspects: What were the problems of Rwanda, what are the causes of Rwanda's conflicts, and what were the possible solutions?*

While men, in both numbers and leadership roles, dominated the movement, Inyumba reminisced in 2011 about feeling trusted and included as her role evolved into finance commissioner for the rebels. *We had no major discussions about women's participation. Like the fact that I held a permanent role, during that time, there was no resistance. I remember one time in one of our big meetings there was an accountant who felt I shouldn't be in that position. He said, "This is just a young woman." So the president said, "What is your complaint?"* All he required, he declared, was a balance sheet and cash flow—no matter who produced it.

We used to hear about other liberation organizations in Africa. We would meet with them. You would hear about abuse, about sexual harassment, but those things never happened to me. I looked at the commanders as my brothers. It was so easy for me to hug them, you know. It's like sometimes I used to come [to the field], and we had issues of accommodation. I did not think of them really as men that could abuse me or exploit me. I just knew them as my brothers.

And this still holds up today. I look at them as my colleagues. I trust them. I love them. I can call them anytime. I can make jokes with them.

Some RPF members point out that single mothers in the pregenocide refugee camps raised many of today's male leaders. The hardships these young widows faced as a result of exclusion from their country stayed with their sons who were building the movement. As boys and then young men in exile, they knew not only persecution of Tutsi back home but also local discrimination. Bridging social divides became part of their political thinking.

Asked about his motivation for prioritizing female empowerment, President Paul **KAGAME** harkens back to being a seventeen-year-old in exile. *I was organizing for people's rights. All people. How could I exclude women's rights?* Others close to the family believe he was highly influenced by the strength of his mother and other women around him.

In exile as a child, Kagame watched how his father, who had been a prominent leader in Rwanda, struggled with the sense of defeat and bruised pride that came from having to tend his own fields once the family was in Uganda. Life in exile was full of tribulations and difficulties for all Rwandan refugees, and it was women who often took the lead in helping families survive and thrive, a fact which left a positive legacy that informed choices Kagame and other leaders made later.

First Lady **JEANNETTE** Kagame describes how her husband's belief about the value of elevating women reaches down to his core. *This is not simply a one-off policy move. It comes out of his own personal experience and convictions, and out of the* RPF's *deep-rooted belief in entrenching new social and political structures that are incompatible with injustice and many other forms of discrimination that existed in the past.*

Good leadership is important, and President Kagame has been consistent, in words and deeds, in his unwavering support to the empowerment of women. In a recent interview he told a journalist that if there was to be a struggle waged for women's emancipation, he would gladly take up arms again and join it!

The involvement of young women activists in the early years of the political movement carved out a place for their continued presence as the RPF gained influence. In October 1990, the opposition group's armed wing launched its attack in northern Rwanda and fought on until its defeat of the Habyarimana regime in July 1994, but it wasn't until the late 1990s that women's advancement became an explicit, deliberate priority for the party.

Organized as a meeting for the RPF to take stock and strategize as they created a new political structure, the 1998 Kicukiro Congress is now remembered primarily for one major shift: as a Rwandan friend put it, "That's when the president became more in charge than before."

IMMACULEE covered the meeting as a journalist. *Kicukiro Congress was to formalize the* RPF *secretariat, after coming into power, because the* RPF *at that time was really from the bush. It had been a political-military movement. But in 1998* RPF *became a political party completely separated from the army. The armed wing by then was the national army.*

It was a very confusing time, but during this meeting, many things about governance and security became more clear. It was not easy to know who is clean and who is not—who had been involved in the genocide. The RPF

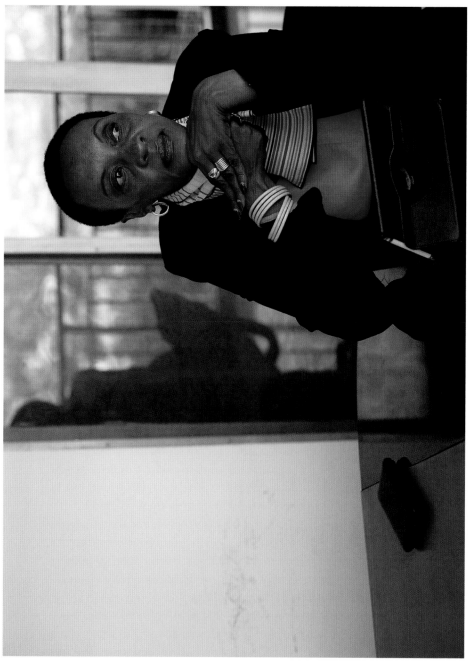

Journalist Immaculee Ingabire.

was not ready to have genocidaires with it, because the party wanted to end the culture of impunity. They didn't want perpetrators presenting themselves as innocent people and never facing justice for what they did. Still other people joined the RPF *as members and committed to the party's ideals.*

An important decision of the Kicukiro Congress was to task then-minister of gender Inyumba with creating a countrywide network of women's groups, forums that would become powerhouses for women's voices. They would have the blessing of the ruling party. (The line between party and government was purposely fuzzy for the sake of consensus politics deemed necessary because of the country's fragility.) But the women's councils would not only serve to promote RPF patriotism; they would also become a permanent forum where women could engage politically and lobby for their collective interests. And who knew where that would lead?

Several Rwandan scholars who have studied this period in the country's history point to that February meeting as the occasion when female empowerment became a central theme in Rwandan politics. Prominent female players say the pull from the country's top leaders was a major factor in the success of what, in hindsight, was the start of a movement. **ROSE K.**'s humble reflection isn't uncommon among her peers. *There's nothing special about Rwandan women. There's something special about the Rwandan government, which has encouraged women, which has brought us to the forefront. We're no better than Kenyans. We're no better than South Africans. The only thing is that our government has trusted us to be leaders, and the women have responded. Women have struggled for years to be recognized. Now we don't have to struggle; the government has said, "You're part of us, so step up."*

Women worldwide know how difficult progress can be without such an enabling political environment. Rwandan government leaders, even those spearheading programs themselves, unswervingly direct credit to the very top of the hierarchy. Almost all women leaders quickly describe how Paul Kagame has pushed gender equality internally with personal, dogmatic attention. Despite their often energetic insistence on this point, women's growth is usually not a theme of the president's speeches on the state of his country. Yet when asked, he adds what seems obvious to him: "It's an issue of rights—the rights of women too. And at the same time, it's also common sense. . . . Developing Rwanda, you cannot leave out 52 percent of the population."[1] Such clear statements have placed him squarely among prominent world leaders sensitive to the advantages of women's full participation in the society, including high-level decision making.

KIRABO served not only in Parliament but also for five years as mayor of Kigali and eventually as a provincial governor. *Our country's leadership from all corners was behind the women running for Parliament. Without that, it would be very hard. I'm happy to say that I personally have gotten great support from our leaders. We are blessed—and I say this most sincerely—that we have a wonderful leader in our president. He is so humble in his ways of working that you feel challenged to be humble by his example.*

Accolades often note Kagame's youthfulness and his readiness to entrust decisions not only to women, but also to young people, typically with more progressive, fresh viewpoints. **AGNES** was thirty-eight years old and one of eight women (of seventy-four) originally appointed to the transitional parliament right after the genocide. (Almost half the RPF delegation was female, but that percentage in the overall assembly was cut in half when other parties didn't follow suit.) During the 2003 elections, she was appointed senator. *We're lucky to have a good president. We know that many changes here are because he has the political will to change. He led a rebellion, and as the top leader his actions supporting women have been immeasurable.* The president's interest includes but goes beyond persuading women to gain skills and experience. It sends an all-important social signal to Rwandans about evolving gender norms. *Our fathers are old. But our brothers, the new generation, can be gender-balance minded.*

· · ·

Outside Rwanda, Kagame's leadership on women's progress is a beacon, according to both his promoters and detractors. While judgment varies diametrically on a wide range of stances he has taken as commander of the RPF and then president, his influence in this story is legend. Even if commentators argue about the impact of, or the political motivation behind, women's leadership, few dismiss the symbolic value of seeing so many females at the president's cabinet table, on the judiciary bench, and walking the halls of Parliament. But the trend moves far beyond symbolism into the raw practicalities of everyday life: whether organizing community trials of imprisoned neighbors, building health care clinics, or creating job programs, women have charted the course.

The prominence of First Lady Jeannette Kagame, as a force to be reckoned with in her own right, is also frequently mentioned as a signal of enlightenment in the modernizing roles for women. The abhorrent influence of former first lady Agathe Habyarimana leached into deadly policy decisions through ties to her dreaded Akazu clan, but rarely was she seen in public championing her own causes.

By contrast in every way, First Lady Kagame runs her office as a skilled policy maker, appearing on her own as well as alongside her husband to push for the issues she has selected for her portfolio—education, HIV/AIDS, youth and women, economic empowerment, and gender-based violence prevention.

JEANNETTE Kagame grew up in Burundi, where her family sought refuge. *These life experiences inevitably shaped my thinking and resolve when we came back to Rwanda. My homecoming was bittersweet and no different from that of any other Rwandan. We had all suffered many losses and knew that to leave our terrible ordeal behind, we would have to surpass ourselves. The task ahead was daunting. But beyond the tragedy, we deeply believed in the chance to build a country together, one that would care about all the people. My family became the bigger family, the Rwandan society at large.*

I had always been aware of Rwanda's turbulent postcolonial history, characterized not only by ethnic division but discrimination against women, including the denial of basic rights, such as the right to equal inheritance, which only perpetuated economic dependence. I joined several groups supporting our countrymen and countrywomen. One of the groups was the Army Wives, which addressed the needs of women who had lost their military husbands to the war.

In 1994, Madame Kagame created a foundation that focused first on orphans and women living with HIV/AIDS, many of whom had been deliberately infected when they were raped during the genocide. Among their many projects supporting vulnerable women, men, and youth, the foundation paired with the widows' group AVEGA to build homes for survivors. Madame Kagame then founded an organization called Protection and Care of Families Against HIV/AIDS to support pregnant women who were HIV-positive.

The first lady's passions are rolled into her Imbuto Foundation, as it's known today, which has gradually expanded its mission to champion peace and reconciliation initiatives and focus on the rising generation of female leaders. Imbuto, which means "seed," is perhaps best known for its scholarships to encourage girls to study science and prestigious awards to the country's top-performing students.

In the immediate aftermath of the genocide, the country's top tier of leaders wasn't insulated from the feelings of separation and mistrust that plagued local activists or communities like Annonciata's. **ODETTE** recounts how Jeannette Kagame, not yet the first lady at the time, devised a remedy. *She called the other women involved with her foundation and said, "You know, we could try to meet as women who have husbands in the cabinet, because we don't know each other. Whenever we meet at a political activity or celebration or remembrance, we even don't know who is who. Why don't we create something that will help us feel together, and maybe that will even help our men to feel like they are together." Unity Club started by having dinners, doing activities together, going to visit orphans together.* Nearly two decades later, Unity Club's membership includes more than a hundred of the most influential women in the country: all female cabinet ministers and the wives of the male ministers are invited to join for life.

Madame **JEANNETTE** is candid about the humble beginnings of the work women joined together to do. *As women, our compassionate nature and ability to multitask was tested to the limit. But our resilience and confidence grew with each success. We all learned to do things we had never attempted, and this motivated us to keep going.* The Imbuto Foundation has become a catalyst of innovative programs, finding creative ways to tackle a community's needs and then, often, passing along the project to government institutions to expand its reach.

ROSE K. describes how the first lady sets a crowning example. *She has so many programs with youth, and especially with women. She has been giving awards for highest achievers, and she doesn't sit only in Kigali. Instead, she's been moving from district to district, educating young girls and women to be leaders, with a broad range of programs reaching out to the countryside.*

First Lady Jeannette Kagame. FROM RWANDAN PRESIDENCY

She takes time to promote women, especially activities for young girls, so that they can be future leaders. Others see her doing this work and feel inspired to join, because she shows that engaging women in society is a priority.

Social change, of course, is much more complex than the leadership of any single player or an impressive power couple. Their encouragement is only one (albeit highly important) rung in women's political and legal ascent. And although this book is not about their political leadership per se, they have been key in designing and constructing the ladder.

FATUMA: We had this idea that, given the vital role Rwandan women play, if they take the lead in building bridges, it will be easier for their families and the entire society to heal.

INYUMBA was twenty-nine when, right after the genocide, she took the helm of the Ministry of Women and Family Promotion, as it was known under the emerging RPF government in 1994. Her reputation for honesty and frugality as she handled RPF finances during the struggle and her nurturing but practical character made her a natural fit for the leadership role at a time when many traumatized Rwandans were turning to the ministry for all sorts of support, from help searching for missing family members to food or advice about how to make ends meet when the breadwinner had been killed.

The first three years was just management of the aftermath of a genocide which we were not prepared for. During the war, we knew we were fighting a bad regime, a dictatorial regime. But we didn't know that the level of destruction, the level of hatred, the level of badness had gone to that level.

Then we realized that whether you're Hutu or a Tutsi or a Twa, the problems were the same: People were talking about health. They were talking about poverty. They were talking about shelter. So we started organizing our women on common problems. At the very beginning we said, "We'll not talk about reconciliation right now. We'll just sit together. We'll ask, 'What is your problem? You're pregnant? Well, you need a clinic, but we don't have a clinic here, and we don't have an ambulance.'"

Inyumba would lead the ministry for nearly five years, and she would draw on the wisdom she absorbed through that role for the rest of her life.

· · ·

Even before the genocide ended, **FATUMA** joined the response team cobbled together in the northern Rwandan town of Byumba. Solidly under the control of the RPF, Byumba became a refuge for people rescued from other parts of the country. Soldiers of the RPF brought people there for medical treatment—like Annonciata, after she had given birth in the doghouse—and others, like Fatuma, volunteered to care for them.

Once the RPF took control of Kigali, Fatuma made her way to the capital to join in the reconstruction. There she began working with Inyumba's reconstituted Ministry of Women and Family Promotion, one of the many government institutions that lay literally in shambles. She remembers the early months of working beside Minister Inyumba as they reconstructed the institution relied upon by so many. For a year, the new government staff weren't paid; they were given food for sustenance. *But we were so committed.*

This ministry was really starting from scratch. There was nothing like institutional memory. We didn't have any handover, because you can imagine after genocide. . . . You know what we found in that ministry? It was mainly propaganda from the previous ruling party. It was all political. Nothing like programs on women. Nothing.

Rwanda's first ministry focused on women had been established in 1991 as part of the Habyarimana regime's moves to appear more inclusive. Its activities were geared toward providing services and benefits only to certain Rwandans, based on ethnicity. Notoriously, its minister was Pauline Nyiramasuhuko, the only woman accused of orchestrating the genocide and found guilty by the UN tribunal.

But the new Ministry of Women and Family Promotion quickly became central to restoration, its early staff working as first responders to traumatized citizens, even while creating a new institution. **INYUMBA** remembers visiting women in rural areas to find out what kind of support they needed. *The first meetings could be very difficult for me. Some meetings were very stressed, because many women would not want to talk with their neighbor. So we would say, "We came to just share tea." We wanted to introduce ourselves to each other, and that's all.*

FATUMA describes a woman she'd never met who came to her office one day. Her husband and children had all been killed. She had been living in a house in her neighborhood after her own home had been de-

Government leader Fatuma Ndangiza.

stroyed, but the owners had returned and forced her out. She described in detail to Fatuma how, with no job and no family to care for, she planned to commit suicide. The two talked through reasons to go on living. *I told her, "If you really wanted to die you wouldn't have come here and talked to me. The fact that you came shows that maybe you're changing your mind."* The next day, Fatuma found the woman a job as a street cleaner. If the street cleaner found meaning in her new responsibility, so did Fatuma, who speaks of the encounter twenty years earlier as if it were yesterday.

Working with Minister Inyumba, we had so many widows, women-headed households. So many had been raped. So many refugees returning from different places. We had about 400,000 orphans and lost children in orphanages or other centers.

So on one hand we had to focus on the traumatized and divided population, but we also needed to work on our mandate of developing policies and building an institution. And at the end of the day we found ourselves doing almost everything. So often it was difficult to draw a line between what we should and shouldn't be doing.

Although it's challenging to establish an institution from scratch, it's also exciting. You can invent, rethink. You can innovate. Of course we were eventually guided by the national policies, but the ministry was spearheading women's advancement, gender equality, organizing from grassroots to the national level, empowering women in civil society.

Fatuma admits that much of the time their team was feeling its way along as it went, designing and carrying out programs at the same time. Still, many projects of the ministry took root and grew into permanent approaches and policies.

• • •

INYUMBA talks about that progression. *Another project was the national network of women. Without a forum, women didn't have a voice. We managed to bring them together—Hutu women, Tutsi women, Twa women—talking about common issues.*

Sometimes I would go visit them with a very ambitious project. I would talk about agricultural production. And the women would tell me, "No, there are other issues." I had what I thought were priorities, but the communities would always challenge me. I would think that their issues would be justice, but they would tell me no, their issue is education—they want to build a classroom. I would propose that maybe we should have bicycles for the women to get to market, but they would say, "No, we need clean water." So I realized that these meetings were very participatory, very educating, and though it was not in a fine setting—often Inyumba would meet with women just gathered under a tree—we accomplished a lot.

She describes, with rightful pride, how the idea evolved into the current, powerful "National Women Council" that's now incorporated into the constitution, with a budget not imagined when it began as a volunteer network.

Often the ministry team devised creative ways to market new concepts, especially ones that positioned women in more powerful roles. *We set up a women's bank, but we didn't call it that. Because if we did, it would be very, very hushed—few people would feel comfortable using it. Women traditionally don't have access to the bank, so we called it a granary instead. Wives were familiar with the concept of saving after a good harvest. It's so simple. Even a poor woman feels attracted to keep, to store.*

The ministry became the standard bearer as the promotion of women developed into a deliberate priority for the government. Ministry staff members were visible throughout the country, leading workshops in gender awareness for civil servants, public school teachers, religious leaders, and political appointees. The ministry also played an influential role in budget allocation for women-friendly activities and served as key advisors and advocates alongside civil society as together they pushed for an overhaul of legal measures discriminating against women.

A women's rights advocate since she finished law school in 1997, **CHRISTINE** served as the most senior staff member of the entire tiered system of women's councils from 2008 to 2014. *Every year the National Women Council organizes a general assembly at different levels, where women evaluate their achievements and agree on new priorities to improve their lives. They create action plans on topics like education, health, jobs, or even information technology. The National Women Council also organizes meetings to explain new laws benefiting or protecting women and families, including boys and men. Because of the way women interact in their families and villages, that information moves throughout the community, including to men and boys to promote their participation in women's empowerment.*

Attorney Christine Tuyisenge.

In 2011, **INYUMBA** looked back on the ministry. *A number of the initiatives have really become the anchor of who the women are today.*

FATUMA worked in the Ministry of Gender under Inyumba until 1999 and then with Minister Angelina Muganza until 2002. She went on to head the National Unity and Reconciliation Commission. *The overarching mind-set was about getting away from victimhood, because you can be a victim for life; it's a lot about mentality.* Ghettos or shantytowns were out of the question. *We wanted these vulnerable people to be well integrated in their own communities.*

We never came with ready-made answers. Maybe that's something unique about Rwanda: flexibility and innovation. You try something, and maybe it doesn't work. Or maybe it works. If it doesn't, you sit and think.

10 COUNTRYWIDE WOMEN'S COUNCILS

GAKUBA: This is where I was raised politically.

Following Inyumba as gender minister, **ANGELINA** took up the reins five years after the mass killing ended. She worked to find a route to bring women into formal leadership positions. The tiered system of women's councils was new to Rwanda, although there was precedent in the traditional village councils, where elders made decisions. But since women weren't welcome to speak in meetings with men present, for all practical purposes they had been excluded from those deliberations.

We cannot have peace if we are not a democratic country. For women this idea developed in 1996, when we established the women's councils. Women at the grassroots level would come together and elect a steering committee for their area. Then all those steering committees selected committees for a wider area, called a cell. Then there are higher levels—sector, district, province— that form a pyramid of women's councils, all the way up to the national level.

With the RPF's long-standing ties to Uganda, many women in the new Rwandan government were drawing from models they'd seen succeed there. **WINNIE**, Ugandan parliamentarian, later UN official and NGO leader, recalls her mentee's many questions: *Inyumba asked about the strengths and weaknesses of our system and also bounced her ideas off me of how the system could be adapted for Rwanda. As a result of her enquiry and her very thoughtful approach (Inyumba was always very thoughtful), the Rwanda women's councils were more empowered, better integrated in the wider national women's rights machinery, and have been more successful.*

But while observing the successes of the women's movement in Uganda proved formative, the unprecedented needs that Rwanda's rising leaders

An oath to represent the will and the interests of her countrywomen as president of the National Women Council.

witnessed in their postgenocide communities determined how the new structure took shape. **FATUMA** describes how the councils were designed both to fill a critical gap and to place much of the onus for finding solutions at a local level. *When we analyzed women's NGOs, we found they were playing a very big role in development but also that they couldn't reach every woman, because they were limited in funding and in the capacities of the people carrying out their programs. They operated in some parts of the rural areas, but not everywhere. We also realized that women were divided. The challenge was that some had participated in committing genocide, others were victims, and some had fled either in 1994 or decades earlier and then returned. Those who went to Congo were conflicted, seeing themselves as victims, but also as fighters defending the previous genocidal regime. Then there were those in Rwanda who wanted to get involved in the rebuilding. So of course the vision of these activists was different.*

We needed a platform to unite them beyond differences, whether political affiliation, ethnic identity, home region, or class. Just Rwandan women. Once together, they could start thinking about development, becoming aware of their rights and responsibilities, and begin improving society. This is how the idea of creating a network of women's councils came up.

We created something like a think tank, where the minister, myself, a few women from Pro-Femmes, any goodwill-minded person from faith-based groups, businesswomen, would come and brainstorm what we might do. How could we promote women's empowerment? How could we focus on building our country through the inclusion of women and gender promotion, while ensuring that women didn't view themselves as victims? At first it was a discussion group, led by Minister Inyumba. She had a way of bringing people on board.

The meetings were mainly talking about the issues and what to do. Of course we had a vision of where we wanted to be, but we needed to discuss how to begin and how to address the major issues facing women. I chaired the task force to create the National Women Council. It allowed women to elect leaders who would be their voice. And most important, it would raise the confidence of women that they need to improve their status and to make a contribution at the community and national levels.

The first elections for women's council members were held in 1996 and preceded by a campaign to teach women about voting and encourage them to turn out. Working with limited finances and challenges like illiteracy, the government designed a simple process that fit the times. Everyone gathered in an open space in the community like a school, a church, or a field. Candidates stood side by side, and voters showed their support by lining up behind them. It was one of women's earliest experiences voting—and being encouraged to do so. But setting up the infrastructure was just the first step.

We realized we needed to create a critical mass in this women's movement by involving men, Fatuma continues. We needed to think about broader issues and then come up with strategies: "We want women to participate in decision making—how do we go about that? We want women to participate in economic initiatives—what are the barriers?" We'd have to change some laws and needed allies in Parliament. There we were lucky; strong women from political parties were now in the transitional parliament. Technical people from NGOs had skills for fixing these problems.

Without even intending to, the women's councils gave women a head start before the first postgenocide elections. *If we did this well, we'd be able to build organizational and advocacy capacities, so women could drive their agenda when the other levels of elected offices were created. We had to move fast, so we were strategic and inspired others. Now women were organizing themselves across all levels of government.*

Local leaders quickly saw the value of situating themselves not just as representatives of women but as trusted spokespeople for their communities at large. **ANGELINA** says that citizens generally accepted that expanded role. *Because these women's councils were born well before the elections, women were prepared to run.* But to cultivate male allies, they insisted that all people in the district, not just women, should vote on who would be deputy mayor for women.

The councils would become a megaphone, broadcasting constituent concerns. **PATRICIA** talked in 2002 about the significance of the still new, tiered structure. *We have grassroots up to an executive level, where all women can meet to express their needs and push their views without having to go through the regular authorities or being sidelined by people above. Without that we wouldn't have representation, because if women aren't elected in a usual campaign, there is at least this deliberate way to be sure their concerns are expressed.* Of course, within a few years women would sweep into Parliament, first in seats set aside for them, and later in the general competition.

Having served five years as one of eight women in the transitional parliament, Patricia understood the tests that top women would be up against and their need to band together. *We fought for these councils—and in the constitution, being written now, we're asking for affirmative action, because we're not like in the U.S. or Canada, where women are already vocal. There you can go straight into a campaign against a man.* Right about the West's general rejection of the idea that girls should be seen but not heard, but woefully wrong about their political success, she muses, *Here we're still weak, so we're pushing to have places where women don't have to fight with men who've been there for years and are traditionally more outspoken. Women are often still shy, and even a woman voter will choose a man! We're trying to break the past imbalance.*

A year later, a parliamentary quota for women would be written into the constitution. Women would need to vie for positions, and the councils made a great practice run.

.   .   .

The women's councils are widely credited with giving a start to many of the women leaders prominent in the country today, providing them with a stage, literally, on which to speak out confidently and be noticed. Seeing **GAKUBA** seated on the wooden-paneled dais beside other Senate leadership, it's hard to imagine her as brand new to politics. But many years earlier, she prepped for her first public campaign with a three-year stint on her local women's council.

The U.S. State Department saw what Gakuba's community saw. In 2000, she was selected to join the month-long Young Leaders Forum. She visited the U.S. Capitol, shadowed a local official in Arizona (*He was in charge of what we call a sector in Rwanda*), and attended city council meetings in New Orleans (*just before Hurricane Katrina*). Those times prompted Gakuba to rethink her career. *We could see how city councils deal with local problems, because Louisiana is a poor state, and they were coping with issues like community involvement in stopping crime. I saw I could gather new ideas through my U.S. internship and think of ways to do them here in Rwanda.*

When I came back, I knew I needed to give more to my country. I thought I might be involved somehow in governance, so that I could be the link between those I most wanted to aid—rural women—and administration, helping people have more opportunities. It was just a few years after the genocide against the Tutsi, and it was important for local people to understand better what the government was planning for them.

Gakuba had returned with the inspiration to run for office, though she had no previous experience campaigning. She had been a high school teacher, then manager of a nonprofit organization. *You have to remember that this was in the aftermath of the genocide, so everyone was called on to do the maximum they could. That's why I agreed to leave my job and go where the people needed me to go.* Her husband was quickly on board; he'd done political organizing with the RPF in exile, so he understood Gakuba's drive to contribute. But her father had a different take.

Senator Jeanne d'Arc Gakuba.

At the beginning he wasn't very confident about my idea. He didn't think I could do it. But I told him I'd been thinking about it for a long time, since we were in the struggle and imagining the future Rwanda. I had caring parents, who sent me to school. Maybe I could play a role in the rebuilding.

He just kept asking me, "So are you going to leave your job? What are you going to get in return?" And I would say, "This is not a problem, Dad. My husband has a job, and the country will reward hard work in some way, though I don't know how for sure. Keeping my job in the NGO *is one thing, but saving the nation is another!" I told him I felt inspired by this work, because it's where the center of the problems are that we most need solutions.*

Finally my father supported me, especially when I was doing my public campaigning. My father had a great mind. And he was a teacher, so he saw the value of educating his daughters. He would watch my speech, see how people were reacting, then tell me what I could do better. Like a campaign strategist!

When she had first started campaigning, Gakuba aspired only to her local-level leadership. *That would be enough for me, so that I could combine my job and my family.* Just days after the votes were counted, handing Gakuba her first political win, she learned that the local body she'd been elected to serve was being reorganized. With a new government still finding its way, she was suddenly vying for a more prestigious post—Kigali City Council.

I presented my platform, and the voters gave me their confidence. Not only that: Gakuba was now unopposed for the seat of vice mayor of gender. No other female candidate had both the education and expertise to be eligible. *Even though I was the single candidate, the campaign wasn't easy, because my voice was competing with a "no" vote. And I was nervous, because I was no longer running in my small community; this was much bigger, with people I really didn't know. I needed to convince them I could do this job.*

In the span of three weeks, Gakuba went from coordinating activities at her local women's council to sitting on Kigali City Council as a vice mayor. She'd stay in this position for ten years.

The new work felt fulfilling, setting up Gakuba to make the bigger imprint that had always motivated her focus on women. *When you go see these ladies on behalf of a small, poor civil society organization, you have your action plan but little money, and then people feel like you don't have many re-sponses for them. I felt public institutions have more support to bring to these people, and I wanted to help vulnerable people get that attention.*

In 2011, Gakuba took another giant step. The capital and provinces held elections to fill twelve of the twenty-six Senate seats. Gakuba knew she was ready to compete to become the one senator elected from Kigali. *I thought about the years I'd served my city, and I put my name forward. This time I was up against eight competitors!* She prevailed.

Of course, not everyone has the intellect and charisma to climb to the height Gakuba has. So it's not accurate to imply that her life story is common, even for an ambitious woman vying for a seat on her local women's council. That's why leaders with Gakuba's success need to make space in their crowded schedules for those following behind, explaining their experiences to see which parts others can adopt or adapt.

That's one of the purposes of this book: to tease apart the overall achievements of Rwandan women, so that their sisters (as they would say) in other countries can think about which elements they might use in their own contexts. No others are going to have the same blend of char-acter, connections, and context, but they can move forward more quickly because the path has already been charted by people like Gakuba. And each election season, that path is becoming wider and more well worn.

11 CAUCUS CRUCIBLE

MARIE: When there were more women, we didn't have to shout as loud.

Pockmarked by mortar fire and with an artillery gun still mounted on its rooftop, Rwanda's parliament building is one of the capital's most prominent landmarks—and not for its ornate architecture or its history as the scene of mild-mannered lawmaking. The building's seven stories seem to rise over the city, reminiscent of a fort, as indeed it was during the war. As part of the failed Arusha peace agreement, the RPF had stationed troops here, in close range to the government forces based just a few hills away. So by the time fighting ended in July 1994, even this most sophisticated building stood in shambles.

Immediately after the slaughter, the new RPF-led government set up a transitional national assembly, with representatives from the eight main political groups (excluding those implicated in the genocide). Their first session was held in November 1994.

That day, **AGNES** was among the new members who went to a stadium for the swearing in. They needed the extra space outdoors to accommodate the audience gathered to mark this new beginning. But afterward, the new members of Parliament (MPs) moved into offices in the old parliament building, despite the rubble and broken windows, to show fellow Rwandans that the war was over. *The mood was hopeful. Of course, people were remembering all we had lost. So we had sadness on one side, while at the same time the idea of a new era.*

Political parties selected people to serve in the transitional assembly, because it was too difficult to hold elections right after genocide. The country

The Parliament building crowns one of Rwanda's thousand hills.

needed to be stabilized, especially since so many had fled. We needed to focus on peace and restarting the economy.

I believed in the manifesto of my Christian Democratic Party and its ideals. And I'd been closely following debates in the previous parliament. It was a time of reforms in everything: basic laws, parliamentary structures . . . even setting up institutions. Agnes came to the job as a Kigali lawyer in private practice.

Her profile could sound mundane, even generic. But her ability to balance public and private responsibilities was, by outside measures, astounding. Agnes was both a competent legislator and a widow with four children between the ages of six and fifteen. Just weeks before she was

Lawyer Agnes Mukabaranga.

sworn in, her husband succumbed to diabetes. During three months in hiding during the genocide, he hadn't been able to take insulin, and the disease that he had suffered from since childhood quickly overtook his health. Without her life partner, Agnes says she managed with the help of two sisters who returned from Burundi with their children. Together, they were ten people living in Agnes's house.

We had lost so many people, so much family. I kept them in mind, especially my brother who was killed, as I started to work.

An observer might see that she was credentialed, resilient, and organized—the right person for the hour. Instead, she explains why her being selected was nothing to brag about. *And truthfully, there were very few females with degrees.*

Added to her personal and professional burdens, Agnes faced gender hurdles so embedded in the ethos that they weren't obvious to most. *Even though the new government wanted women to be involved, the mind-set wasn't as it is now. We were only eight out of seventy-four in that big assembly. Plus the cultural idea was that politics wasn't for women, so we weren't used to taking the floor to give our opinions about legislation.*

As **ALPHONSINE M.** explains, necessity birthed invention. *Women in the transitional assembly had to organize; some had gone to university but had no experience serving in a parliament.* In 2014 she finished a five-year term on the executive committee of what became the legislature's most powerful internal alliance: the Forum of Rwandan Women Parliamentarians, commonly known by its French acronym FFRP, counts all female lawmakers—upper and lower houses—as members, regardless of party or ethnicity. Given that so many prominent leaders had orchestrated violence in 1994 and the years leading up to the genocide, the caucus had to overcome public mistrust of political parties and politicians in general. The FFRP was a welcome exception. Its history holds a treasury of lessons.

Two years after the swearing in, the number of women in Parliament had increased. But with fever-pitch tempers and raw trauma all around, their advancement was not a priority. Alphonsine wasn't a member of the transitional parliament yet, but she's a wealth of knowledge about that formative time, having served since 2003 when the first elected parliament came into office. *In 1996, when the caucus was formed, there were only twelve women in the Parliament* [out of seventy]. *Some had been targeted in the genocide. Others came from families just returning after years in exile—families where the husband, or the brothers, or the parents had perpetrated the genocide.*

The situation was unruly at best. *A perpetrator couldn't be in Parliament, but even if you had a family member who was one, you could have a seat.* Still, some of the situations were painfully dramatic. *There was even one woman who came to join Parliament, but when she arrived in Kigali, people started yelling, "Get that woman out of here!" They said they knew her from when she had been at a roadblock, killing people.*

It was a time in need of calm and a space in need of healing. Even as Annonciata's mixed church group was feeding prisoners of the genocide, and Chantal's AVEGA members were supporting widows regardless of ethnicity, despite gripping differences, female parliamentarians united behind one focus. Alphonsine explains: *Women and children often suffer worst from conflict. So a couple of leaders among them said, "Look at how our country has been destroyed. We need to see beyond what separates us, beyond our political parties. We're women! We must do something!"*

Women legislators had to look each other in the eye and see what we could accomplish for a Rwanda torn apart. We said, "Let's put aside our differences and move together. Okay? Pool our strength." But before FFRP really got started, there were long discussions. We needed consensus. "What are we going to defend as women?" We needed to enter debates with a common voice.

Over the two decades, the caucus's influence has risen as women pick up more seats. But beyond sheer numbers, FFRP has a reputation for being extraordinarily collaborative: a style, and a deeply held principle, that has allowed them to push policies beyond the culture's comfort zone, taking cues from activists and constituents. As it has elsewhere in the world, the formation of this caucus has not only increased women's impact on the political process; this is where not only ideas but also hearts have joined to create what the women call a sisterhood. Over the years, **AGNES** has watched the internal evolution, even as the broader external impact of the forum took hold.

As one of the pioneers of this caucus, I can talk about the slow steps. It's amazing how things changed. At the beginning, we focused on solidarity among ourselves, on being an example of unity and reconciliation. We used to talk about our families, but even when the subject was cooking, we asked how we could be less timid when addressing people. We were shy. We were new. We were few.

Many of the legislative achievements protecting women's and children's rights would owe considerable credit to FFRP for design and advocacy. *Of course, as members of the legislative branch, we had to struggle so that all the discriminatory laws could be either amended or replaced.*

Then, with several years of experience behind them, FFRP members began to take a more intentional approach to their work, mapping out persistent challenges that communities, and women especially, faced. In 2005, under the leadership of Judith Kanakuze, the caucus adopted a five-year strategic plan with policies, laws, programs, and practices that would ensure gender equity. The launch of the plan was marked by a celebratory social event, with stage, podium, and microphone. As she announced the end of their formal planning, Judith stood tall in her long-skirted beige suit—an African-Western hybrid befitting the composition of her audiences. Other speakers wore handsome finery, including flowing and colorful *imishanana* dresses, and grins all around.

Although FFRP's membership is exclusively parliamentarians, the forum's link to community-based organizations is strong, with the term "partner" used often. Activists say their advocacy is easier with the caucus as a bridge between civil society and the rest of the legislature. Although all parliamentarians say female advancement is vital, women are eight times more likely than men to actually be in touch with women's organizations.[1]

In the early days, resistance could come from anywhere and everywhere—a problem women worldwide grapple with as they begin to see their influence rise. Whether exclusion is packaged in outright dismissive and rude acts, through sly political ploys to confine their roles, or reflected in a structural glass ceiling, the ultimate effect is the same: women must beat the odds to keep up with men in terms of careers, income, and social freedom.

Still, given the obstacles they faced, solidarity in the FFRP was a matter of both strategic value and communal grounding. Its success is a source of unbridled pride, apparent even in **AGNES**'s graciously understated reflection. *The caucus worked. Now we sisters have a channel to express ourselves. What a blessing! I can say with humility that as far as Parliament is concerned, when I look back, I've played a part, a small part, in the history of this country.*

History, yes. But for generations to come, as well—in her country and across the world.

JUSTINE M.: You have to engage people, so that they own the process.

In 1994, women by necessity had stepped into a maelstrom, taking on new roles they hadn't imagined they'd play and piecing back together their shattered communities. Now, a decade after the wildest turbulence, that progress needed to be preserved and expanded. A new constitution would be more powerful than any other legal structure.

Groundwork was in place for women to play an influential role in creating the new law of the land. In some cases, that was because of political developments: President Kagame had appointed women to influential posts, and political parties had named some female members to the transitional national assembly, where they formed the women's caucus. In other cases, the influence of civil society—generally a more welcome space for women's leadership—had increased under the new government. These parallel streams would prove a mighty force.

From the end of the war until 2003, the country was governed for the most part by a combination of provisional laws drawn from its pregenocide (1991) constitution, the failed Arusha Accords, and a series of rulings enacted by the interim parliament. With the end of the transition phase nearing, the government created a twelve-member panel tasked with drawing up Rwanda's new constitution. Three of the drafters were women.

When the Legal and Constitutional Commission was formed, **MARIE THERESE** headed a national network of grassroots development groups. *It was July 2000. I was executive secretary and legal advisor for this um-*

brella civil society organization, and I'm a lawyer, of course. There were many candidates for the commission. Judith Kanakuze was also a member of civil society—I think we were chosen because of those connections.

Marie Therese and Judith were joined by Domitilla, another lawyer. The nine men were primarily from political groups, with one from the army.

A genocide survivor and widow, **JUDITH** came to the commission as an activist and gender expert well known across the country, who had held leadership positions in several women's right groups. Although she would go on to shepherd landmark legislation during multiple terms in Parliament, her contribution to the constitution remains a pillar of her legacy. (She died in 2010 after a long illness.) In 2003, just after passage of the constitution, she talked about the perspective she brought to its creation. *My goal was to emphasize gender. The whole group became very quickly gender sensitive, including our commission president, Tito Rutaremara. It was very easy to push these ideas. After a while, we all had the same sensitivity.*

It seemed that everyone involved in the process recognized the historic nature of the occasion, as they crafted a guiding document that would shift the country's foundational systems away from division, exclusion, and the long-entrenched despotic style. From activists and religious leaders eager for clear limits to the powers of the central government, to rural residents seeking a path for development, to women's rights advocates who saw the chance to address long-standing discrimination, constitution making was a watershed moment.

Each of the eight political parties included since the genocide in the unity government sent a representative to the commission. But by all accounts, the ruling RPF was in control of how the process unfolded and the substance included in the founding document. The leadership of the party saw the new constitution as an integral step as it established order and sustainable peace. In reaction to the previous government's unchecked extremism, the RPF was highly motivated to protect minority rights, no matter which party was in control. But given the country's history of exclusion and the raw wounds of 1994, the RPF-led government also greatly prized a collaborative approach.

Supreme Court Justice Marie Therese Mukamulisa.

Commissioners and their advisors traveled the country seeking input from citizens. **MARIE THERESE** vividly remembers this initial consultation, which went on for six months. *The conversations varied depending on the participants—if it was an academic group or an advocacy group. But even people at the grass roots knew what they wanted. For instance, they would say, "We don't want those politicians who come and divide us for their own interests, then leave us fighting among ourselves."*

It was a political decision to do this collaborative process—we saw it as a validation of our work. We had delegates meeting with the Rwandan diaspora of countries in Europe, in the U.S.A. But South Africa, with Nelson Mandela as president, was especially valuable. They also had the Truth and Reconciliation Commission, so their situation was a bit similar. I was among a group who went to meet with some who had drafted their constitution, and also with groups advocating for that process. They did their consultations in a different way, but it was a model.

In South Africa, in the early 1990s, public input had been funneled through elected representatives from each political party, who met in a series of forums. That country faced a colossal, tight knot of challenges, as Rwanda would several years later: while one major party might have had the power (through public support, military superiority, or self-professed moral authority) to write the constitution alone, an inclusive process was essential for generating buy-in, allaying fears, safeguarding internal stability, and ultimately creating a document that would last.

In Rwanda, the government opted for direct consultations. The commission's team crisscrossed the country, venturing far from the few paved roads into the folds of lush hills and farmlands to distribute tens of thousands of questionnaires and hold group discussions, eventually involving an estimated 300,000 Rwandans. Marie Therese recalls: *We asked people's views on topics like human rights, the death penalty, marriage, monogamy versus polygamy. Questions like these stirred up controversy. Because of our history, political parties needed to change the way they approached people, not inciting violence. That was a major challenge before and during the genocide, so it was very much on the minds of many people.*

In November 2002, the commission convened a national convention to introduce and debate the draft constitution. Ahead of the forum, representatives were selected to serve in a new caucus that would strategize and advocate for women's interests throughout the review process.

JOY M., who has held many positions of responsibility since that time, reaches back. *One of the most fulfilling moments of my career was when I served as president of a national women's organization that brought together leaders from all walks of life—political, civil society, business, etc.—to address the issues facing our country at that time. We got women to speak as one voice in the constitution-making process, which contributed greatly to the gender equality guarantees enshrined in the constitution.*

Such a collective approach was unprecedented. The country's first constitution, in 1962, had been entirely the work of colonial officials, with only limited input from "native experts." After that, a major feature of the revised charter, completed in 1978, was the abolition of political parties, shutting out discordant voices to give unchallenged authority to Habyarimana's regime and ultimately their atrocious plan to exterminate the Tutsi. Even the last pregenocide constitution, created in 1991, was written with a commission process that disenfranchised the population. *They didn't do this kind of consultation like we did,* **MARIE THERESE** remembers. *So when we were moving around the country, people were pleased. They wanted to give their input, and they felt invested. Sometimes they raised so many questions, and we had to try to help them understand. You know, to comprehend the constitution you have to understand some of the guiding principles.* That was difficult to do countrywide, where literacy rates were dramatically low and the vast majority of people had never been asked their opinion on such matters.

You have to first understand what a constitution is! We organized so many meetings with different groups. Then after the first draft, we invited some representatives again, and we showed them what we had designed based on their input. It was challenging. Some people wanted a lot of details, and there were differences of opinion. The first draft was good, but often there was too much detail, probably because it was the result of this major consultation. Still, after revising and condensing, the main principles were maintained.

Particular effort was made to solicit the input of women. Civil society groups, working closely with the female caucus in Parliament and the Ministry of Gender, offered feedback on certain elements, but they also were key to organizing women who were not typically politically engaged. *We organized meetings with women alone, because when they're with men, they hesitate to ask questions or offer up ideas.*

It wasn't an odd idea, since the women's councils, from village to national strata, had been created for the same reason. Once they were in comfortable spaces, the dynamic changed dramatically, Marie Therese explained. *They were very eager to be involved.*

KIRABO: Women were rising to positions of power well before
the constitution came into effect, but it was a key factor. We didn't
have to go on struggling as individuals but could reflect together
about where to go as a country.

Given the value of inclusion in the new Rwandan government, moving
from a draft to a new constitution was intensely complicated. Women
would be vital to that process, and the existence of the women's caucus
in Parliament turned out to be a godsend.

As it grew, the effects of the parliamentary women's forum had crept
across the country, spreading throughout economic strata and seeping
into professional spheres. **MARIE THERESE** ruminates on her time as one
of the three female commissioners on the crucial constitution drafting
team, who began their work five years after the birth of the caucus: *Our
role during the drafting was easier because* FFRP *had paved the way, sensitiz-
ing the public about the need for women's equality.*

While Marie Therese can commend the drafters' final arrival with a
phrase like "paved the way," **AGNES** describes the trailblazing itself. After the public consultation, but before the public vote, the constitution
needed to be approved by the transitional national assembly. She offers
an unvarnished backstory about the tough maneuvering in which indom-
itable MPs have become expert.

*Since I'd practiced as a lawyer for a long time, I could talk about what we
should do when it came to practical things.* With so few attorneys left alive,
Agnes was one of the parliamentary leaders reviewing drafts. *For instance, it was very important to refer in the preamble to the* UN *Convention to*

Eliminate All Forms of Discrimination against Women. (By ratifying CEDAW, Rwanda joined 187 UN member states—all except Iran, Somalia, Sudan, South Sudan, two small Pacific Island nations, and the United States.)

But when the commission presented the draft to the Parliament for approval, it was a real fight. We advocates in the assembly formed a common front to explain the importance of women's representation and why it should be captured in the constitution. Like having seats set aside for women.

The question was how many seats; what would be fair? Agnes was among those pushing for an even split. *I personally experienced how difficult that was to get through! We pushed, but the men refused. "No parity in terms of one man, one woman," they said. It was really, really hard, but at least 30 percent was accepted.* It was a groundbreaking triumph: twenty-four out of eighty seats of the lower chamber were set aside for women, chosen by members of women's councils. This was the first essential step in Rwanda's world-renowned political advancement.

In addition, there would be a general election for the other 70 percent. That contest would be decided by "proportional representation," a model used in most democracies (although not in the United States). In this system, a legislator is chosen not individually, but as part of her party's candidate list. That said, each candidate still needs to campaign, to represent the group's policies. Campaigning builds momentum for the party overall, and everyone on the list needs to do her part as a member of the team. And finally, being out there and being winsome is important, since voters may choose a party precisely to help a favorite candidate win a seat.

Proportional representation can be a way of excluding or including women. Each party makes a list of candidates with the same number of spots as the entire Parliament. If the party wins 50 percent of the vote, the top half of its list goes into Parliament. Someone at the top is a shoo-in if the party receives any votes at all; but the last candidate won't take office unless the party sweeps. So one further element is to be sure women are distributed across the list, or even alternately with men.

Though reflecting back six years, **AGNES** still is impassioned as she explains, *We women MPs and ministers kept up the fight, saying, "If the 30 percent of women are put at the bottom of the list, it won't work."*

Ultimately, a rule on even distribution of women on party lists didn't end up in the constitution. *I'm telling you, it was hard.*

A place of their own: Parliament.

Of course politics is filled with moments of compromise that may feel like failure, but the insistence of the female MPs no doubt was a force that moved the needle on the whole idea of women being fairly represented. The tussle shifted to the individual political groups themselves. *Back then, parties were happy to put women at the bottom of their list. Even though I was a vice president in the Parliament, I had to struggle within my party.*

In the end, thanks to political figures like Agnes, many parties, including the RPF, would adopt the policy of distributing women throughout their lists. That nudge was the second far-reaching shift.

· · ·

On May 26, 2003, the constitution was overwhelmingly approved by a countrywide vote, with 93 percent in favor.

JUDITH recalled the morning of the referendum. *The voting was supposed to begin at 7:00. I woke up early and went to the polling place in my area. There I saw women who had come much earlier. Voting was supposed* *to be in hiding, but there was no money from the constitutional commission to create that confidentiality, so women brought their traditional cloth to make walls for people to cast their ballots in secret. A high percentage of the voters were women. They were also the ones counting the votes.*

The experience was formative for Judith. She had seen her primary aim—women's equality—gain traction. *Our constitution established the principle that women must be in decision-making institutions. That's what encouraged me to campaign to become a member of Parliament.*

With the pull of Marie Therese, Judith, and Domitilla on the drafting commission, and legislators like Agnes pushing from the inside, Rwanda's new constitution would promote equality between women and men and mandate women's continued public participation. Twenty years after the genocide, when she lost most of her family members and despaired of ever having a future in her own country, **MARIE THERESE** sits in her office at the Supreme Court, where she's now a justice. She seems contented remembering these stories, with her bright red judge's robe and window looking out over the capital behind her.

Article 9 was fundamental, the cornerstone. It talks about preventing genocide and promoting national unity and reconciliation, equal sharing of power, and equality between men and women. She pauses, and a smile broadens across her face as she nods toward the pocket-sized Rwandan constitution open on her lap. *That part is very special for women. We were proud that this idea passed through the Parliament, ensuring that women are granted at least 30 percent of posts across all the government. Yes, this really was a success.*

That 30 percent requirement applies across the board, from the president's cabinet to courts and elected and appointed positions at every level. (It's a key element illustrated in the diagram on page 148.) The requirement was an intrepid experiment, to see if a quota might carve out a policy-making space in which women could, and would, bring their own knowledge, perspective, skill, and style.

Among other gender-equalizing provisions, the constitution calls for the creation of a Gender Monitoring Office to supervise efforts toward equality and submit recommendations for inclusivity. The document also holds onto guarantees promoted during the transition, creating the National Human Rights Commission, as well as the National Unity and

Reconciliation Commission. The Constitution also enshrines laddered women's councils designed by the Ministry of Gender.

We wanted to create a constitution that wouldn't simply be a piece of paper but instead a guide that would positively affect Rwandans in their everyday lives, says Marie Therese. That was always on our minds. Since I'm a lawyer, the section about human rights was especially interesting. I feel proud of the way we included the provision about promoting women and about power sharing. Those were principles always missing before, and it's from those that you can evaluate the efficacy of a document. We're a postgenocide country, so we needed to strongly consider the past—as we look to the future.

Looking to the future has turned out to be shaping the future, not only in Marie Therese's own small country, but also far beyond. Today, students worldwide raise their hands when asked what country has the largest number of women in a parliament. Their counterintuitive answer was born when Rwandans came in droves to the polls to approve a constitution that heralded their belief in the power of women.

14 THE QUOTA

KAGAME: Of course the danger is that I may end up with only women in my cabinet [laughs] and forget the other balance.

As a world-renowned game changer, the gender quota is important enough to deserve its own focus in this book.

Despite the hard, even dangerous, work that women's rights catalysts undertook in the late 1980s and early 1990s, the number of women represented in the pregenocide government was abysmal. Starting from independence in 1962, only sixteen women ever served in Parliament, and they were often sidelined as just one or two female voices in the whole chamber.[1] And those in office were often taunted about their so-called manipulative femininity or tainted as power-hungry operatives of President Habyarimana's inner circle.

Throughout the mid- to late 1990s, as Rwanda was devolving into killing, then emerging from chaos, increasingly strong civil society groups across Africa were pressing governments to adopt quotas to ensure that women would be involved in decision making, despite the cultural barriers they had to surmount.[2]

There were plenty of variations on the theme. A quota could mandate that women fill a portion (as low as 10 percent) of seats in the Parliament, cabinet, or other parts of government. That quota (or sometimes a guideline) could be a rule of an electoral commission, a constitutional requirement, a political party norm, or simply a commitment by a person with authority. Women like Agnes had become wise to how a party could game the quota, relegating women to the bottom of their candidate list, as opposed to "zippering" it—alternating between women and men—to ensure females an equal shot. These systems created a floor, but not a ceiling, for women's participation.

Female members of the constitutional drafting commission and in Parliament point out that Rwanda's focus on inclusion owes much to the RPF members' earlier exposure to Uganda's gender equality promotion while living in exile. In 1989, that country was reserving one female seat from each district, resulting in a minimum of 14 percent in Parliament. Men and women in the RPF also watched carefully as Nelson Mandela's powerful African National Congress became the new leading party in postapartheid South Africa; women there won 26 percent of seats in Parliament in their first democratic elections, only days before the Rwandan slaughter began.

Seven years later, when the concept of a quota for women came into play in Rwanda during the drafting of the constitution, the country already had experience with women in leadership roles. But activists saw the chance to expand women's involvement and ensure it wouldn't slip if political will shifted. Fundamentally, this quota would be a tool to launch women into leadership, giving them the chance to prove their value as political equals while the culture caught up.

There was discussion about parity, the ideal, but you don't start social change like that. **DOMITILLA** served on the constitutional drafting commission alongside Judith and Marie Therese. *You have to go more slowly. Do something, then give people time to get used to it. You have to be progressive, but also manage the shock.*

The quota was about numbers, but it was also about much more.

It's really important to have provisions like the quota in the constitution so that we can stipulate, we can push, we can make it mandatory for each step in the life of this country to have women participating.

We put it in, first of all, because women are equal to men. They're different, but when it comes to studying, working, rights, they are equal. The big challenge was our culture. Parents think when they have a boy and a girl, they have to educate the boy.

But also, the idea of the quota was necessary because women were not so sure of themselves. You know, they think public life is for men and not women. So it was important for the constitution to make it mandatory that whatever you're planning, you have to think about women. With time, people will get used to seeing women involved.

Typical of many Rwandans, fifteen years later Domitilla sees the cultural change already in action. *Now when I'm advertising a job, I have female and male candidates. It wasn't always that way, so it's good to have a legal basis, which is binding. Now women can say, "This is our right. This is our part. Here we are!"—and no one disputes it.*

But some did dispute it. **MARIE THERESE** adds her perspective as one of the constitution drafters. Since Rwandans had seen women taking on important public roles after the carnage, it wouldn't be a stretch, she thought, to reinforce their progress through tools like a quota. But thorny questions came up during the community consultations.

I remember one time, maybe in the outskirts of Kigali, some people said, "Okay, these things promoting women's rights are good, but we have to be careful not to confuse their rights with a kind of revolution."

Some people would say women have a role to play and have capacity, but it would be bad if they stopped acting like women and forgot their responsibilities as mothers and sisters. I remember one man saying he supports giving rights to women, but he'll be alarmed if the next night he sees his young daughter going out wearing a short skirt, not obeying their household rules because she's now free.

In the end, at one meeting some elders described how in the precolonial period women played an important role in governing, although behind the husband; so on the outside it looked like a man, as king or chief, was ruling, but really the hand of a woman was very influential.

The sentiment was that it's good for women to be educated, to have opportunities, but we have to also consider our society. The positive parts of our culture need to be promoted at the same time. It wasn't controversy really—more like an awareness of our culture.

That balancing act would be a constant feature of women's rise.

·   ·   ·

Four months after the May 2003 constitutional referendum, Rwanda held its first parliamentary election since the butchery. Female candidates and voters turned out in a big way, and women won 48.8 percent of the seats in the lower house of Parliament, far surpassing the newly mandated 30 percent.

The first women's council elections (1996) gave women early experience campaigning and voting ahead of the first postgenocide national elections (2003), when women took 48 percent of seats in Parliament—far surpassing their 30 percent mandate.

Rwanda is replete with examples of women who got their start at local levels and have risen through the ranks. An example is **ALPHONSINE M.**, who that year moved to Kigali from southern Rwanda. The women's council had selected her for a place in the 30 percent of set-aside seats. *The women in my province said, "Here we have our sister who is a teacher, who has been district mayor, who we know well in different roles." So women from my province decided to send me to Parliament to represent them there.*

Not all women used reserved seats. When she ran for district mayor, **FLORENCE** had been a member of her local women's council, like Alphonsine.[3] *If I had passed through the women's ballot, it would have been easy for me, because the competition would have been less. There were very few women and many of them were timid and would not stand against men* *for election.* On the general ballot, she would be facing off against men, many of whom had previously been in public service. *But I felt it would be unfair to run on the women's ballot because I had the potential for standing in the general competition.* She could leave the woman's slot for a candidate who was, in her words, *a bit shy.*

Beyond her personal story, Florence has a broad sense of the challenges for women in politics. *In many African countries, women fear it. It's true that historically, many women have lacked the education qualifications, but even those with qualifications prefer working in an office, a bank, in different institutions rather than going into politics.*

It isn't easy. You have to tell your community what you are going to do and how productive you're going to be. You cite your experience, when you performed such and such a duty. But women are afraid to market themselves.

KIRABO, for one, has mastered that delicate balance and gracefully stepped forward into the public arena. Straightforward and confident, she speaks with more thoughtful intensity than one might expect from a veterinarian. She was a member of a women's council in 2003 when her family's home province was selecting its female representatives in the first election under the new constitution. Working closely with local government and civil society—while doctoring cattle and goats—made her a likely choice. *The farmers sent me to Parliament. But even after we have the numbers, it's one thing to be elected and another to be effective and efficient.*

To her point about being effective and efficient: after three years in Parliament, Kirabo ran for mayor of Kigali and won. In 2007 she talked about how ideas to embolden women were working. *I've got a lady vice mayor, Jeanne d'Arc Gakuba, and a man vice mayor, so our executive group is 60 percent female. This affirmative action at our level gives a chance to women who wouldn't be politically assertive or strong enough to go through the party system. At the end of the day, given the women's caucus in Parliament and all the capacity building, I see us coming to a point where we may not need to have affirmative action, because women will be strong enough to prove themselves.*

Similarly, **JUSTINE M.**, a gender specialist and activist, offers a candid take on the excitement and sense of opportunity that accompanied the creation of the quota. *We were at the forefront of bringing gender equality* *to our new society. If we sat back until we totally understood the concept, it wasn't going to work. There was no time to wait.*

And we did it! Women did it! We influenced the constitution making. Before we knew it, we had a massive number of women in the Parliament. It counted just that we would be in the room; the rest we'd pick up when we got there. Do all men understand politics? No. But they're there. Now it matters that we're there, because we learn by doing.

15 PIONEERING IN PARLIAMENT

JUSTINE M.: The representatives didn't understand what they'd gotten into, but they knew their presence counted.

In 2008, women worldwide broke out the champagne as their sisters in Rwanda secured 56 percent of Parliament's seats, creating the first parliament in history, anywhere in the world, with a female majority.

ALPHONSINE M. explains the astute strategy she and her fellow MPs devised to expand their influence (illustrated on page 148). With a five-year term behind her, she wagered she was ready to vie against men. *In 2008 I presented myself as a general candidate. I knew at the level of the women's council I wouldn't have a problem being reelected. But I wanted to leave that place for another woman, who would have the boost of the council. I would run at the level of the political party. Then we would win twice.*

Not everyone had to give up her set-aside seat. Each person could decide. But many of us thought that to mobilize women it was important to get others to take our places. Many of the other representatives from 2003 did the same.

We haven't had trouble finding a large enough pool to draw from to replace ourselves. Women in local positions are there. They are conscientious, and I think they've been encouraged by seeing the women who came before them. "Yes. I could do that too," they say.

This wasn't the only strategy leading to parliamentary results that riveted the world's attention. During the transition (and before the new constitution), the ruling RPF consistently appointed women to nearly 50 percent of the seats it controlled, but other political parties lagged. A decade later, female representation vaulted to 64 percent of the lower house, not only because of the quota, but also because political parties began placing women prominently on their candidate lists. Most influentially, the RPF (no doubt with the approval, if not requirement, of President Kagame) mandated that its list be not only 50 percent women but eventually zippered with female and male candidates in alternating order.

These numbers represent an inspiring cultural development. **LOUISE** returned to Rwanda in 2008 after years in Washington, DC. *I was mesmerized by rallies where they were getting ready. I hadn't ever seen Rwandan women actually campaigning, let alone doing so with all their energy, with so much passion, and outdoing men.*

You think, "That's just politics." But how does a woman stand in front of a crowd and brag about things she's done, and talk about what she plans to do? I couldn't believe it. And the positive and tacit support you saw in men when some of these women would come out and say, "Look, I've made a big difference: I've sheltered orphans. I'm very active in the school in my neighborhood. I can do this for my community." You'd see smiles on men's faces. Louise, in turn, grins as she describes men's literal and figurative nods of approval as women started stepping up for elections.

As for the male legislators, some may have been supportive of the large increase in women taking what had been mostly the men's seats, but many say this goodwill wasn't the norm. In fact, that may be an understatement. *We need women to try to change these guys who aren't peacemakers and point them in the right direction,* says **CHRISTOPHE**. He was helping set up the first-ever National Electoral Commission, encouraging all the country's potential voters to feel they had a stake. *Sometimes when you say "gender," people think only about women. But we won't progress if we don't consider men, who generally are the source of problems. If you don't cater to their biases and insecurities, they'll even bring up new troubles.*

I used to say to women I was working with, "You're more than half the population! Why don't you go and each change one man? Then you can't fail! It's not easy to change your own man—you have to accept him as he is—but you can easily change another man. So that's a strategy!"

If the men didn't really get it, they had to act like they did as the women had evolved into such a large and mostly unified group. As their numbers soared and they sought out male allies for innovative legislation that they would champion together, they found that men's resistance

How They Rose

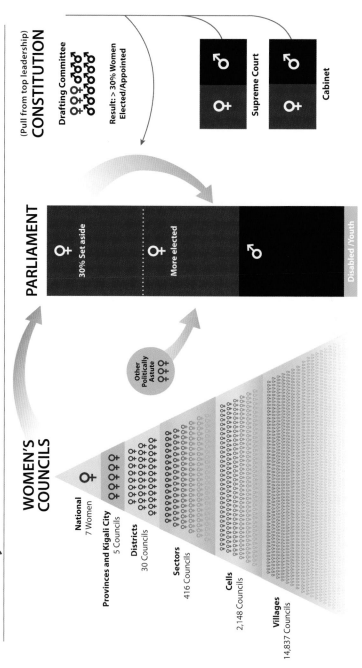

This schematic shows the general flow of women into higher office. The **purple arrows** represent a trend that has steadily evolved:

- Women's councils created (1996)
- Constitution drafted and promulgated, >30% women across government (2003)
- Parliamentary results beyond 30% seats set aside for women (2003 - 48%; 2008 - 56%; 2013 - 64%)

WOMEN'S COUNCILS

National
7 Women

Provinces and Kigali City
5 Councils

Districts
30 Councils

Sectors
416 Councils

Cells
2,148 Councils

Villages
14,837 Councils

Other Politically Astute

PARLIAMENT

30% Set aside

More elected

Disabled /Youth

CONSTITUTION
(Pull from top leadership)

Drafting Committee

Result: > 30% Women Elected/Appointed

Supreme Court

Cabinet

softened. Instead of a face-to-face standoff, they could work side by side. To wit: at the reception celebrating the launch of the strategic plan for the women's caucus, a tall and large senator shook hands with honored guests, offering his hand and his name, then adding, as the coup de grace, "and I'm gender sensitive," as if those words were embossed on his business card.

The victories weren't all about gender, but about the health of the fledgling political process as well. **GASAMAGERA,** a senator from 2003 to 2011, says he found the increasing presence of women had a transformative effect on how the Parliament did business. *Diversity—both men and women in Parliament—contributes to the overall quality of the process. In our plenary sessions, women are outperforming men. We're talking on and on about ideas, but women are tenaciously sticking to their points. They're determined, and they're a real added value.*[1] Many became convinced of what Gasamagera asserted. *When it comes to advocacy, we'd better send a woman, because I might talk about abstract things, but they express it in a more practical way.*[2]

Now, with colleagues expressing appreciation, women's caucus leaders were quick to see the need and advantage of reaching out to men to promote and sustain gender equality. They began to form alliances with their brothers. Senator Gasamagera's comment is so familiar that it tends toward a cliché: *As you'd expect, when it comes to children, women are more resolute than we are.* Women used those stereotypes—groan-evoking as they are to gender academics and activists—to assert their leadership. At a tactical level, they understood that their work would be most potent and long lasting when all parliamentarians shared their priorities, even if they were labeled "women's issues."

Awareness of these dynamics wouldn't come automatically. It took an open mind and clear thinking to win over doubters and cultivate alliances. In 2009, FFRP President **JUDITH** referred back to the caucus's comprehensive strategic plan, of which most women policy makers in other countries could only dream. It included, she said, working alongside men: *I can't be—and my colleagues can't be—on all the committees, so we're developing training for our whole Parliament, with specific tools for gender analysis not only in our budget, but also in different policies and laws.*

Pushing their agenda, women refused to push alone. Instead, they formed partnerships with the willing and made projects of the skeptics. With this strategy, over time they would come away with marvelous victories, while building a strong case for making gender integral to Rwandan politics. In coming years, male MPs would join their female colleagues in a parliamentary triumph that became a gold standard for women's safety.

Former MP **CONNIE** offers a smart observation about women parliamentarians' approach, informed by her tenure as a representative of the RPF. *When we're in the Parliament, we can vote the way we want to vote. We don't go into party-think. If there's a bill—let's say the budget—we look at it as a national issue, irrespective of the political parties we come from. We may be in the same political party and divided with our ideas. Your opinion, mine—there's no problem, so long as it's an opinion along constructive lines, wanting things to be better.*

But when it comes to the women's caucus, we unify. We don't think of our parties, but the challenges that surround us as women. In fact, formal research bears out Connie's comments. Excluding the women chosen to fill the 30 percent female set-aside seats, 64 percent of women elected through the general ballot rate their party interests as very important. That compares to 83 percent of men.[3]

These women leaders' desire to keep their sights on the larger good may be the most important lesson they've brought to their country. That wider focus turns on the personal humility and stoicism demanded by Rwandan culture, which discourages individuals from taking credit for positive change.

When the world today looks at this tremendous tale of female advancement, the spotlight is on women's record-breaking representation in Parliament. But rather than being starstruck by media attention and invitations to international conferences as they became a national force and global icons, female MPs would radiate a broad and diffused glow that reached not only ahead, but also back—home.

ALPHONSINE M.: Now we had our sisters coming up.

To secure their sway at the national level, women leaders rooted in the upper echelons needed a strategy to bring along the country as a whole. There was no shortage of possible tactics. Trying out a new ballot system? Playing off the restructuring of the political administration? Coaching a chorus of rural candidates to move onto the stage? They took on all three.

The most promising chances for change would be local elections, from village to district, in 1999, 2001, and 2006. Paradoxically, it was the social and political devastation of the genocide that allowed government and nongovernment groups an opening for complicated constructs and changes, many benefiting women.

In one experiment, each voter received three separate ballots: for women, youth, and general (mostly male) groups. The fact that the system was too intricate to last beyond a few years is probably testament to how hard the designers were working to thread the needle between fair gender representation and an equal say for all.

A different and permanent change was a massive administrative shuffle just before the 2006 elections to devolve power from central to local government. The theory was that governance would become more efficient, physically closer to people, and therefore more in tune with their needs. Statistics tell the story: Suddenly there were thirty districts instead of 106 countrywide, and they became the new seat of power. Women had more than 30 percent of high-level local positions, although only a measly 6 percent of the top: the mayorships. But the picture was brighter than it might appear since women were 83 percent of the vice

Taking governance closer to the people has given women a chance to move into leadership.

mayors for "social affairs," and their responsibilities increased as the number of districts shrank, widening their constituent base.

Decentralization usually means more room for people excluded from a top-down, male-oriented system. In Rwanda, as in many developing nations, a university degree is needed for national office, but in villages even literacy isn't required—a boon for women who are often savvy but unschooled. As an added plus, the demands of local office are part time, compared to full time for national; women could try out politics as they managed their homes and worked the family farm.

With novelty comes uncertainty. Shortly after the 2006 elections, **BEATRICE** considers the potential she saw in the new structures. *Rwanda is an excellent laboratory. We sometimes feel we're dreaming, because about three months ago they told us to go out to the provinces and districts and tell them we're going to decentralize. The complaint was that the national administration hadn't reached the rural services at the grass roots.*

So we ministers of local government and parliamentarians worked around the clock on this experiment of grassroots public administration. Soon they announced on the radio that the new administration is reaching down to the districts. Our dream is that in two years' time, we'll be down to the sector level—from the county to clusters of villages. That's where the work is going to be. The ministry in the capital will deal with monitoring and policy making.

. . .

Decentralization in the mid-2000s, which created many more government jobs at the local level, made space for women. But it wasn't enough. In the same way, the constitutional quota was well and good, but it couldn't produce a political transformation alone. In fact, three years after its passage, women had gained almost none of the top local posts. Now, with more institutions in place and the central government starting to focus on local governance, female candidates needed to step up to fill local positions, putting themselves forward in a formal setting, which—except in the women's councils—was contrary to traditional Rwandan culture.

BEATRICE laid out the problem in 2006. *One worry is that many of the local women won't be part. We'll have local elections and encourage them, but some say, "I don't know administration. I don't know how to plan. I don't know how to budget." Yes, we have to advocate for implementation of the quota at the local level, but it will take time.*

The women's caucus helped coordinate a strategy for what would be the momentous 2008 election, when female parliamentarians from the 2003 cohort would give up their set-aside seats and vie for the coed places so that women less practiced and known could rise politically. That development would turn out to be crucial as women from top to bottom rungs would be able not only to pass policy measures, but also to see that they were carried out all the way down to the village level. But first the more accomplished women needed to persuade those without experience to put themselves forward.

ALPHONSINE M. was both living out and shaping a political zeitgeist when she drew on her personal story as someone who had entered low and made her way up. *Slowly by slowly, women in local positions had come to realize their capabilities by doing that work. They began to dare to think about what else they could achieve.*

Women in the transitional parliament, plus those of us first elected legisla-

tors, kept in touch with women from the grass roots. Right before the election, we went to visit them and said, "Voila! Women are capable! You should participate in the elections—and not just as voters but as candidates!"

We had the constitution backing them, plus the political will of the government, especially our president, to promote women. That gave them confidence to imagine what their future could be.

In a 2006 conversation, six years before **ODA** became minister of gender, she described from her vantage point as the chair of the National Women Council the unparalleled effect of having parliamentarians urge other women to run for local office. *They went down to the grass roots. They became the models. They explained, "You know me. You know my family. You know where I was born. You know we went to the school together. And you remember when I started how I was, you know, feeling that maybe I cannot do it. But you see now what I am doing." And that helped us a lot to give the courage to the women.*

Oda was one of the leaders on the first national secretariat of the women's councils. As part of the push to boost involvement and make the program more official, Oda and others traveled the country to recruit more women.

We encouraged them by saying, "You have a role to share and contribute." This was the first time many women had heard that message: their voices were sought after and valued. At that time there were many activities focused on reconciliation, and women especially had a deep role in that. That's when I started to really love and be moved by the work we were doing.

In an aside, Oda added how this spirit of inclusion she found in the organic women's movement stood in stark contrast to an early experience in her job search when she came back to Rwanda in 1998. She was in her late thirties, with experience working in banking, and she was a mother to three boys.

I went to one of the private banks with my cv, and the guy told me, "We're only looking for employees who have no plans to get pregnant." (He didn't want people who were going to take time off work.) I said, "You're not serious!" I think he was shocked and kind of embarrassed. He started to say, "You know, the work in the bank can be very tough, takes lots of time. . . ." Which of course I knew—I'd worked in banking!

That experience was very different from the way that I had seen the opportunities among the women who were organizing. Not only was it assumed that the women would have children, the principle of excluding people was completely counter to the tenets of the movement. Oda could see where she belonged. *I never went back to that bank, or to any bank for work for that matter! They were looking for profitability, but they were ignoring inclusiveness, which was something so important back then—and today of course too.*

Oda found her stride, moving her way up through the women's councils to various government posts, and then to the office of cabinet minister at the Ministry of Gender and Family Promotion in 2013.

The demands on female leaders can be weighty, both in stress and in time. The job is even more complex than it appears: national figures must manage up and manage down from presidential residence to earthen hut, while grassroots officials have triple duty—tending to immediate constituents, engaging with higher-level decision makers, and building bridges between the two.

Keeping those channels open is tricky. The disconnect was apparent to **MARY**, longtime head of a women's advocacy group with its office in the capital but initiatives in rural communities countrywide. She's well aware of the need for leaders to venture out and cultivate partners and successors.

In 2002, exasperation seeped into her voice. *We've been here for the last two years and are still not able to reach the constituency we want to develop.* Mary mentioned that lack of funding was one of the biggest hurdles. The postgenocide government was strapped for cash, and the international donors who were contributing to the rebuilding weren't yet interested in cultivating local leaders who might work their way into national posts. *We're trying to help women from the grass roots get involved in national leadership, get organized, form their own groups. We have a clear goal: as we train those at the elite level, we want them to go down to women at the local level and expose them to the opportunity of political life.*

Nine years later, she was much more satisfied. *The policies our Ministry of Local Government has put in place are all excellent, so now we must translate those into action. All women leaders are connected: political, nonpolitical*

Gender Minister Oda Gasinzigwa (*seated left*).

like us, and private sector. As we sit together, we can strategize about electing more women. The biggest challenges are funding, consolidating, helping newly elected women better understand their roles, promoting them in the community. We've trained all the women leaders in urban Kigali, and we're joining them with women elsewhere.

• • •

Beatrice, Oda, Mary—three voices represent countless more. The changes in Rwanda that elevated the voices of rural women were not incidental. They required vision, hard work, and perseverance.

Here's a snapshot of the impact: In only seven years—nourished by a stew of the triple-ballot experiment, constitutional quota, top government pull, women's councils, gender ministry, decentralization, role modeling, sisters' coaxing—women doubled their local representation. A virtuous circle formed. Local officials rose to higher roles, gaining influence to make decisions that helped others follow in their footsteps. As years went by, that upward flow required less and less of a push. To use an American metaphor, the glass ceiling had been cracked, and the women streamed through.

• • •

Women wouldn't have accepted genocide, even if men proposed the idea. **ALPHONSINE M.** builds on that thought. *When I entered local government, and then when I entered Parliament, it was because of that conviction.* It's a nervy assertion, that women's sharing leadership could have dodged a cataclysm, but she frames it with this explanation: *Women are sensible, and they're conscious of the problems of others. They raise children, and they know that when a war comes—when a genocide comes—it will be those children who will suffer, who will fight.* Indeed, like the women she's describing, Alphonsine does more than opine. *That's what motivated us to go back to the grass roots.*

Before the collapse of the country, although they were indispensable in family and fields, women generally had no legal protection, and their voices were heard only behind the scenes. As war brewed, they felt powerless to stop those (mostly men) who were becoming crazed by the possibility of power. Yes, in the genocide there had been a few notorious female masterminds and perpetrators, but, in general, women didn't see themselves among those steering their country into an abyss. Now they had the opportunity to be at the metaphorical—and literal—table where issues of life and death are debated and decided.

Alphonsine is one more firm voice supporting a different, fundamental point expressed by many directly and indirectly, in simpler or more complex ways: the value of gender balance is ultimately not about numbers; it's about the wisdom of seeking out people with a wide variety of perspectives, values, life stories, social roles, and other differences.

Those differences include the ease with which women (as a group) form close relationships, compared to men (as a group). Women like **KIRABO**. Although many women progressed in the direction of Alphonsine, from local to national spots, then reached back to bring up more women, Kirabo shifted in whichever direction made more sense to her at the time. She cut short her time in Parliament when she saw the government's decentralizing of authority from national to local offering a chance to lead with a different style as Kigali's mayor. A year into the job, she explained, *This is an opportunity to contribute in a way that's more tangible than legislative. I requested permission to leave Parliament to campaign for about two months. Every day people would ask, "Exactly what are you about?" "Why are you leaving Parliament?" "What would you bring to a new position?" That made me reflect much more deeply on the possible move, which I'm happy to say I've never regretted.*

Being mayor is challenging; every day has its surprises. But it's also energizing as I realize how much others in the country, at all levels, are doing. With a listening ear and the right environment, they'll pull it off.

Maybe Kirabo's experience as a veterinarian for the community reinforced her nurturing tendencies. In a barter economy, where cows or other livestock have been a measure of wealth, Kirabo served as the equivalent of a money manager. Most Rwandans are subsistence farmers, so the person who could keep one cow or three goats alive was enormously important, central to the well-being of a family. She was the protector of their sustenance. Now, as mayor, she was again central to a community. *The good news is that the process at this level is more partic-*

ipatory. As the executive, I'm not just the leader of the city—I'm part of the city. The connection is closer.

A leader has to engage people but ultimately be decisive enough to change. The cost of not making a decision is there for you to see. So you have to engage, collect all the information, but finally decide and stick by your plan. And if your decision goes wrong, you're the one responsible.

As Alphonsine is thinking about the past—how the genocide might have been prevented—and Kirabo is focusing on her responsibility to shape the present, Mayor **FLORENCE** is looking forward. Her sense of responsibility is broad as she talks about the impact—positive and negative—that she and other mayors could have on the public's inclination to keep selecting women. *For the next elections, we'll help them come up. We'll make our district a model—a marketing tool. If the five districts headed by women perform well in their first time in office, then in the next campaign we're going to get more. But if the first is a disaster, the public is going to moan, "Oh, please . . ." So we have to work hard and work as a team.*

Florence served in city government for a decade and then left because of term limits. She recently finished her master's degree and is planning to launch a local organization focused on legal rights and vocational training for the most vulnerable in her community. *I got into politics because I realized that as a businesswoman I was making money, supporting my family, but I wasn't making much difference for my community. As a woman who had a chance to study, I felt like I should be helping create our new society.*

When commended for her years of service, she nods at the compliment but immediately insists: *It wasn't just me; it was a collective duty. I'll continue my support wherever I'm needed . . . and I'm still strong.*

PART III
Bending toward
Reconciliation

"In our culture . . ." That ubiquitous phrase is often followed by an explanation, leaning toward an excuse, explaining how, although women have influence at home, they are not welcome in the public arena. The place where decisions are made that directly affect their lives is a man's sphere. Women are afforded scant political voice as that male space is guarded in one society after another.

But there's a hopeful and rather elegant pattern playing out in a few bright spots across the globe. Over decades or even centuries, women are subjugated; they somehow come forward; they lead reforms, including for their own rights and their families' well-being. Rwanda was no exception. But the lightning speed with which it moved through those stages makes the country a model well worth examining. In fact, the progress has been so fast that a reorientation is in order, to take stock of this book: where we've been, where we are, and where we're going.

The important role of women in family life couldn't save female leaders or Tutsi women in general. As Hutu extremism spread throughout the country, they were taunted and targeted. But those who had grown up in exile—mostly in Europe, North America, or other parts of Africa (in large part, Uganda)—had a significant place in Rwandans' struggle to return home.

After the carnage that ravaged the population, women were the first to begin to put the country back together. They gained confidence in their own readiness for leadership through women's councils, staged from the village to the national level. When their basic rights were established in laws promoted by the new government, several women were appointed to help draft a constitution. The progressive charter passed because of a citizen-input process, an increasingly powerful female caucus in the new legislature, and ultimately, a public referendum.

Rather than staying shackled to outdated customs, women now found freedom to move into public roles, supported by new rights, legally guaranteed. In addition to having a third of the Parliament set aside for women, a 30 percent gender quota would stretch across the entire government. Those new successes were solidified by women's alliances with men, as well as local female candidates, whom the national leaders instructed and inspired.

This advance could not have been nearly so successful without a parallel evolution, which is where this chapter picks up.

Justice and community mending had to replace endless exile, impunity for war crimes, a spirit of revenge, and deep-seated suspicion. Gender violence had to be criminalized. The economy, health, and education needed attention. In each case, led by women, the meaning of the phrase "in our culture" was transformed.

· · ·

Many Rwandans, like **CHRISTOPHE**, laud women's capacity for forgiveness with comments like, *Women think about their children, their husbands, themselves . . . of terrible things that could happen. So they're more peacemakers than men, more sensitive than men, more loving,* as if that's self-evident. But apart from individual impressions, the Imagine Coexistence Project offers a valuable third-party corroboration. This initiative of the UN refugee agency worked with local groups to repair tense community relationships and promote tolerance as "a way-station to reconciliation."[1] Although it began without a specific focus on gender, after its two-year pilot the project reported that women were more likely to be bridge builders in their communities. They found that women's groups showed particular skill in working across ethnicities and reaching out to those whom society might ostracize, such as prisoners who had already served their time.[2]

Many other outside groups, as well as internal decision makers, share that view of women having the right tone and talent for the crisis at hand. Those wanting to stanch the trauma have seen women's advantage as not only their actual bent toward crossing divides, but also others' perception of that inclination. Interpersonally, socially, and politically, reconciliation was treasure in a land stripped bare.

INYUMBA: There are those who only wanted to talk about Tutsi-Hutu differences. We said to them, "We are just one people."

JEANNE D'ARC K. remembers her dear friend and fellow activist Veneranda Nzambazamariya. *Even when times were hard, Veneranda was outspoken for peace.* In 2000, she died in a plane crash. Yet she was such a force that each year on that anniversary, activists gather to remember her devotion to equality among all, and her willingness to stake her life on that idea. During the height of the Hutu Power regime, Veneranda had been targeted for her progressive views. She was among the handful of Rwandans evacuated from Kigali in early April 1994. But within weeks of the Rwandan Patriotic Front taking control of the country, she was back, quickly becoming a central figure pressing for reconciliation.

She could organize and mobilize people to show our spirit. Jeanne says Veneranda was beloved for her open-minded, no-fuss disposition and buoyant outlook. *She would tell you the truth—people appreciated that about her. She loved Rwanda, loved the women's movement, loved music. She was very romantic actually.*

When she returned, Veneranda resumed her post as head of Réseau des Femmes, the rural development organization she had cofounded eight years earlier. The late **JUDITH** spoke of Veneranda's ability to bring together and convince people to consider ways to forge ahead—ways that seemed far-fetched so soon after the genocide. *Réseau des Femmes organized a big meeting with different organizations. She told everyone, "As women, we've been victims of war; but now we have to be actors of peace." Who was talking about peace in October '94?*

The gathering drew about a hundred participants from all over the country, including ones new to activism. Judith was the director of the women's financial empowerment organization Duterimbere. *All the refugee ladies who returned in 1994, and even some women from Burundi and Uganda, came to the meeting. The group had long, sometimes tense conversations. But we talked about how as women we have to be the solution, not the problem. Some of us were widows, others had husbands in prison, and others didn't know where their husbands were. We created a network. People exchanged addresses and made dates to get together—they were living out how women can understand one another.*

So afterward, as Réseau des Femmes talked with women in rural areas, the organization developed the idea to launch a campaign . . . but through action. That's why it's the Action Campaign for Peace. The women had to be working but thoughtful: "Which projects will actually create peace?" There were many, many orphans, so they reflected, "How can our actions with children strengthen peace?"

Pro-Femmes Twese Hamwe, which had a commission of culture and peace, and a network of twenty-eight homegrown groups, took the lead in coordinating activities countrywide. **SUZANNE** was in the inner circle. *In 1998, I was coordinator for the Action Campaign for Peace, so this awareness-raising work was in my portfolio. Our message was, "There are three categories of Rwandans, and if we don't work hard to bring them together, we'll never arrive at lasting peace.* Like Judith, Suzanne mentions the disparate groups: the survivors, the imprisoned, and the soldiers who had fled. *At first, as you can easily see, it was very difficult. Many said, "No, I can't talk with the ex-prisoners," for example. These were the challenges that our community trainings slowly addressed.* Pro-Femmes members worked with village leaders in conflict prevention and resolution, with support from international donors. Key to that was helping others open up, to talk about their experiences. *People gradually began to give their testimonies.*

It wasn't only the seasoned activists who took up causes. Local women organized protests against ongoing violence and encouraged citizens to look for commonalities among themselves, even when differences were impossible to miss.

In her small village in the south, **ANNONCIATA** credits a group called Mamas Catholiques with helping calm tensions, as they connected over

Activist Jeanne d'Arc Kanakuze.

their common faith. *The group actually started in Zaire [now Democratic Republic of Congo], because of the war there. After the genocide, the movement came this way, and it inspired us. The mothers in Congo went into the road with their rosaries and said, "Stop it! Those killing—those are our children. Those being killed—those are our children."*

So we had to do something, we as mothers, to stop the conflict in our hearts.

People were living on the edge of peril. *The survivors would gather and stay near the soldiers. One of them could go home just to get something to eat and be killed there. The militias were surprised when they found people alive. If they had the chance to kill them, they would. Even now—twenty years later—some of those intentions continue.*

Once again, the grassroots push was met with a pull from the top. *The government also insists on reconciliation, so we were involved in public programs to make those who had killed and those who were targeted work together and talk to one another.*

The most prominent government programs were designed and overseen by the National Unity and Reconciliation Commission, established in 1999. This was the government's first endeavor to spur interactions that would instill a common cause of security and give Rwandans language and space to speak about what they'd lived through. An identity based on being Rwandese rather than Tutsi, Hutu, or Twa was crucial, not only for individual healing but to foster a sense of patriotism that could encourage healthy and honest governance—sorely needed in the wake of the divisionist politics that had driven a deadly wedge through society.

When the ruling RPF party created the commission, its secretariat tapped the trusted **INYUMBA** to lead.

She was a beatific listener, and she led with great dexterity, but from behind: *We're not here to tell you the answers on reconciliation; we want your views.* That humility served her well as she launched the commission with a countrywide listening tour, accepting the staggering challenge of drawing communities back together after such pitiless violence.

After Inyumba's death, her husband, **RICHARD**, recalled her reaction to taking on such a delicate, crucial project. *At first she was overwhelmed. She'd say, "I don't even know where to start." Then she realized she needed to take direction from the people.*

Three years into that work, Inyumba sat on a sofa in her home, her face weary but with a lamplit glow. In a slow voice, she described how at night she lay in bed, in the dark, her mind and her heart groping for answers. Was she doing wrong by her young daughter as she set out, day after day, week after week, for long hours on roads almost impassable? Yet in these settings with no infrastructure, she had discovered people with profound wisdom who could guide her. Looking back, her husband sums it up. *She came to know this country in and out, every village.*

"This country" was hardly a cohesive concept. During decades leading up to the genocide, unstable groundwork had been laid in the many bouts of ethnic tension and terror. Then, in the horrible summer of 1994, the vast majority of soldiers with the previous government, including many genocidaires, fled the advancing RPF, most crossing into Congo. These combatants, along with their large families and many others who feared retaliation by the new government, mainly stayed just over the border in teeming refugee camps of eventually some two million people. Their return a couple of years later added to the upheaval inside Rwanda.

INYUMBA, in a 2011 interview, said she saw how skeptical people were about the possibilities of restructuring a sense of unity. *We conducted a kind of national grassroots consultation, and we asked three questions: Do you believe reconciliation is an option? The second was, if you believe reconciliation is the best option, what programs should we develop? And the third question, which was very important, was, what will be your personal contribution to this program?*

When I went to South Africa to look at the Truth and Reconciliation Commission, we felt that ours should be more community based. People should understand that by working together you reap the benefits as a community.

Inyumba was convinced that practical work could loosen impossibly tight psychological knots. *The peace basket is part of our peace program. It's our culture. It's building on our foundations. Everyone in this country, all the women, even my mother, knows how to weave. And so we show that other than engaging the community together, we're doing the work together, appreciating one another . . . but more importantly earning this income together.*

That is the philosophy of the peace basket: the Tutsi, Hutu, and the Twa women weaving something together; building something together. We are going to get an income, and together we are going to enjoy the benefits of our labor.

That's the message.

To move forward with everyday life, some victims coped with grief and lingering misery by avoiding those in their communities whom they feared. As Annonciata described, killings motivated by retaliation or to silence a witness had a chilling effect.

Others claimed a sense of normalcy amid their new realities by trying to ignore the deep rifts between themselves and their neighbors. Still others confronted community members they'd been pitted against during the engulfing violence. Expressions of penitence were accompanied by reparations, such as rebuilding a house or helping till the land—and asking for forgiveness.

These down-to-earth approaches, and the fragile relations and sensitivities that drove them, shaped the work of the commission. Said **INYUMBA** in 2011: *You can't look at peace in isolation of our survival. You have to bring people together for a purpose. It's not reconciliation for its own sake; it's reconciliation for the betterment of our people.*

We've been managing the aftermath of the genocide fifteen years ago, rebuilding the foundations, but really the next stage should be about building ourselves: building homes, building individuals, tapping into every opportunity in Rwanda.

Reconciliation is an engagement. . . . It's a commitment. . . . It's a day-to-day experience. It's your life.

SUZANNE: We asked the prisoners, "But how do you plan to live with the survivors, whose family members you've killed?" And you know, they said that they were afraid.

One of the longest-running Rwandan government programs is *ingando*, "solidarity camps." A stint at the camp could be months (or shorter), with days spent doing physical drills and community service, or listening to lectures on themes like history, patriotism, and reconciliation. Activities there are designed to reeducate (in the common parlance) various segments of the population: refugees (largely Hutu) returning from Congo and eventually other citizens on the cusp of a new life phase, such as starting university or taking a government job.[1]

But most pointedly, immersion in ingando was originally designed to enable the reintegration of former enemy combatants into the new government's Rwandan Patriotic Army, as well as the return of prisoners about to be released back into their communities.

As head of the National Unity and Reconciliation Commission, **IN-YUMBA** and her team oversaw the ingando camps when they first got started. *These soldiers had committed atrocities, so we organized extensive reconciliation programs before we sent them out to the communities. That included encouraging relatives to come see them.*

It was so emotional—a mother reunited with her son, a wife visiting her husband. Then we allowed the soldiers to go home for short times. It was mainly a confidence-building program.

We organized football programs for the ex-soldiers with the local communities, and we had T-shirts that said, "Reconciliation Is for All of Us." The soldiers wore these T-shirts as they went around telling their stories. We had a civic education program for them—also HIV testing, because we wanted to be sure that, with the long time they'd stayed in the bush, they were healthy.

Most of the former soldiers were in very, very bad shape. Some were wounded, so we needed to nurse them and give them medicine. Others wore tattered clothes, and we gave them clothing. Others just needed care and love. Some people didn't understand why we were kind to them. But our government was visionary; they said it's an investment for peace. Rather than fighting them in the bush, let's bring them in—treat them as ordinary citizens.

While the ingando camps were an initiative of the government, **SU- ZANNE** explained how Pro-Femmes got involved as part of its peace campaign. *The president of the republic gave an instruction that if prisoners admitted their fault and asked for forgiveness, they could be released. So we at Pro-Femmes asked ourselves the question: How will these prisoners who were involved in the genocide be received by their communities? Pro-Femmes asked the government for permission to go to the solidarity camp to speak with the prisoners. We would bring in groups of three people, one of which would be from AVEGA, the widows of the genocide.*

We went to AVEGA and asked how they had received this declaration from the president. Of course, they weren't comfortable. They said, "If prisoners are going to be released they will come and finish us." We explained, "No, the government wouldn't do this if there weren't police and other members of the community to protect you."

We encouraged these widows to come with us to the camps to begin a dialogue with the prisoners. We wanted them to think about how they would live alongside the widows.

Rwanda isn't like other places. For example, in Belgium you have the region for the Flemish, and you have a region for the Walloons. But here you have a Hutu, and right next door you have a Tutsi. A genocide survivor could be the neighbor of a genocide prisoner. There's no demarcation line in our country, so the main message of our campaign was, "First and foremost, we're all Rwandan." Before being Tutsi or Hutu, we are Rwandan.

It was essential to gradually, progressively, prepare the prisoners and the survivors for this transition. We asked them, "What are your problems?"

Ex-combatants who had fled the country but wanted to return were mostly men. Ex-prisoners who had been serving time for participating

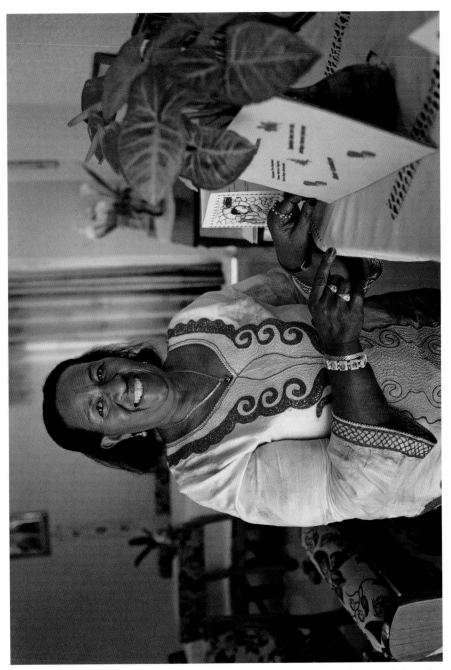

Activist Suzanne Ruboneka.

in the killings were mostly men. *We'd say, "You've left your family for two years, for ten years, and during that time many things have changed. Your wife has taken up new responsibilities in your absence. Will you accept that? In the meantime, some wives now make their own money. Many women are making their own decisions now. Can you accept that?"*

They would say to us, "Well, Pro-Femmes, you're beginning to touch upon real problems."

There were eighteen solidarity camps across the country, and Pro-Femmes sent delegations to each. *We would ask, "Is peace just a slogan? Or is peace about day-to-day living?" We asked the prisoners, "Okay, you took part in the genocide. You confessed to that, and you've asked for pardon." But the prisoners were worried about the reaction of those who had told us, "Yes, they've demanded pardon from the government, but not from the real victims." So we asked the prisoners, "Are you ready to ask forgiveness from survivors themselves?" And they asked us to accompany them.*

Some men developed homosexuality while they were in prison, so we would ask, "How will you go back to your wife? What if you've contracted HIV while in prison? Will you get tested before you sleep with your wife again?" The men were a bit shocked, but they realized that these were essential questions.

What if their wife had a child with another man? Would they accept that child? Will this child become a victim? One prisoner gave me a letter to give to his wife. He told her that he had reflected on the fact that while he was away she had another baby, and he wanted her to know that when he came home he would accept this child.

Some critics charge that ingando includes highly politicized sessions indoctrinating Rwandans to the principles of the RPF. However, many participants say their time there has been instrumental in changing attitudes. **"GISELLE,"** from the National University, describes how, through the mandatory two-month ingando camp, she met most of her closest friends. She also forged relationships with incoming students of different ethnicities and across the Anglophone-Francophone divide.

We dress the same way. We're given the same mattress, the same blanket. You may find that you're sleeping next to a survivor, with someone from northern Rwanda, or southern Rwanda. Maybe you're sleeping next to someone who has a parent in prison. But you interact. You see the humanity in the other.

• • •

Even in the male-dominated arena of national security, women have made notable contributions. From Congo, militias regrouped with the aim of returning to Rwanda to ultimately defeat the RPF, often reorganizing with the same structures and leaders who had directed the slaughter. The most hard-core among them proclaimed a chilling raison d'être: to complete their mission of eliminating the Tutsi.

The northwestern corner of the country bore the brunt of the raids, both from artillery fire and from soldiers who would slip over the border, commit massacres, then return to blend back in with the refugees. Even after most civilians returned to the country, the most militant followers of the previous regime stayed in Congo to continue the fight. Eventually, they vowed, they would return to rule the country.

Some husbands were in the Congo, but their wives in Rwanda were getting pregnant; it was clear the men were visiting. **MUSONI** headed the Ministry for Local Government when, in 2002, he hinted at a creative strategy for dealing with potential accomplices: bring them into the fold.

Women were a very big factor in security in the northwest. We set up a process of contacting them. Our first reaction could have been, "Here's somebody working with the enemy; we should deal with her as an enemy." But we said, "No, let's not take that route. Let's work with her to convince her husband to come back." Now many women have, in fact, convinced husbands and children to return, and the government will do everything possible to make sure we're fair.

The RPF took the approach that if a combatant returned from Congo and hadn't been accused of genocide, he could pass through an ingando camp. From there, he had a choice between integrating into the new Rwandan army, or demobilizing and being given support to restart life as a civilian.

That policy made a profound impression on **ANNE MARIE M.** Seated in the living room of her red brick house in Kigali—her husband's army portrait over her shoulder, and her children peeking through the door to listen—she talks about her contribution to stemming the threat from across Rwanda's border. She recounts each detail matter-of-factly, in a way that belies the impact of her grit and nerve.

Anne Marie was working for the social security agency in President Habyarimana's government when the state-led killings began in 1994.

Her husband, Jerome, had been an officer in the national army, many of whose members were conspiring with local combatants to carry out the massacres. She and her two-year-old daughter were protected from the spiraling violence by their Hutu ethnicity, but that safety made her feel vulnerable as the rebel RPF ended the catastrophe.

With her daughter, Anne Marie fled to the packed refugee camp in eastern Congo, unsure of whether the new government would retaliate against those sharing the ethnicity of the killers. Adding to the complexity and chaos was the virtual impossibility of telling a fighter apart from a civilian who, like her, joined the exodus for fear of what would come.

Two years later, facing disease and despair within the camp, Anne Marie decided to go home. Now with two small children and a third on the way, she quietly settled into a new life in Rwanda, with the help of the government. Jerome chose to stay in Congo, moving into the remote rain forest and joining the new rebel group—the Forces Démocratiques pour la Libération du Rwanda (FDLR)—spawned by the former government's soldiers, some of whom, like some civilians, were genocidaires. He eventually served as head of their notorious intelligence unit.

From the time I left the camp until 2003, I wasn't even sure if he was still alive. I lived like a widow, Anne Marie says.

In 2001 there were some [FDLR] soldiers captured near the border, but the Rwandans didn't harm them. There were as many as two thousand. I was involved in telling them to feel at ease. "Yes, you're captured, but you're home. And it's important to be good citizens. You were captured as a great enemy of the state, but we haven't killed you, because our country wants unity and peace. You must participate, and you must convince the others like you."

Anne Marie joined in this work because there was an ingando camp near her house. *I had become a teacher, and so I helped.* She had another driving motive as well. *I also wanted to see if there was anyone who could tell me if my husband was still alive.*

Then some people who were returning told me, "Yes, he's alive, and he might be at this secret FDLR camp in Congo."

Anne Marie had become involved in women's empowerment initiatives, finding inspiration in radio broadcasts about the new UN Security Council Resolution 1325, which highlighted women's roles in security. *Hearing about 1325, I felt like I could do something. That's when I started*

Activist Anne Marie Musabyemungu.

going to see those demobilized FDLR soldiers in the ingando camp. When we were together, we were at ease. They encouraged me by saying, "You can get close to fighters still in the bush."

Anne Marie set off on a treacherous mission, with the quiet support of senior Rwandan army officers: to convince fighters still in Congo to come home, starting with her husband.

She traveled to a town in eastern Congo's South Kivu province. *From Bukavu, it was five days of traveling to reach where he was in the bush—one day of driving, then four days of walking. We passed through huge forests. We slept in the forest. After four days we arrived at an FDLR camp. I was alone except for a guy I found who could show me the way.*

When we arrived, my husband wasn't there. He was deeper in. I talked with the head of the camp, who stopped me and said, "No. Stay here." There was a high-level meeting of the FDLR directors going on. Really, so many leaders. They said, "You're not going any farther. Tell us what you're doing here." Then, "If you need to talk to your husband, you can wait here. He'll come here if he decides to. You can't go further, because we don't know what you're doing." They could see that I was a Rwandese who was . . . who was not on their side, I'll just say. That I was a Rwandese for reconciliation and ending the war.

Surely in the presence of these FDLR commanders, Anne Marie couldn't make her true feelings known; if they didn't already suspect her purpose, telling them why she came would pit them against her and put her in grave danger.

But of course I told them! That was my mission. I had to explain it to them, regardless of the consequences. I'd come all the way there to reach them, and I had the great luck of finding all these high authorities together. I had to make my presence known to everyone there, so that my message would spread—my message that the people in Rwanda wanted to live peacefully together. That people in Rwanda don't want their hateful ideas. I had to tell them—it was my principal mission.

They searched for some women in their camp and had them stay with me, so they could monitor everything I was doing. Luckily, many of the leaders were from the old army in Rwanda before 1994, so we knew each other. They wanted to know, "What's the news of my wife and my children? How is Rwanda now?" They just wanted to talk. They knew I'm a woman who is brave and honest, and that if I put my mind to something, it's because I believe in it and will see it through.

I explained the new government's principles of unity and reconciliation and told them about how our new local legal system would work, what advantages the system would have, what would be the punishments. I talked to them in detail about what it would be like to put down their guns.

For two weeks I talked day and night to people eager to listen and ask questions. I started to think, "This has been my mission, to give these messages. If my husband comes or he doesn't, the mission I came to do is done."

But a moment came when some people talked to the commander. "You need to arrest that woman. She's a spy. We've talked to her, and we should kill her before her husband arrives." The top officer said, "No, just leave her until her husband comes. We'll see what he says. He may decide to kill her himself." I'm told that four times this happened. At one point the commander himself called me to his tent. "Tell me what you want to say about the situation in Rwanda," he said.

I thought, "This is my chance. I'm here in front of the commander of the FDLR, and I can tell him everything." We talked four hours. At the end he said, "You can go, but you can't keep talking about things that will demotivate our soldiers. You will be punished harshly if you continue."

When I left that meeting, I thought, "My mission has been successful if the commander himself understands that what I'm saying could cause people to demobilize."

Anne Marie also thought that if she were able to convince the top commander of the merit of her message, she would have a good chance of convincing her husband.

The people from the intelligence department had a reputation of being cruel; that's why the other soldiers said they would keep me there in the bush and leave me for my husband to take care of. He would know whether I was a spy. They were also worried about letting me go back to Rwanda, where I could say, "Here's what I saw. This is what they're doing. . . ." But I knew my husband could judge, even if the decision was a difficult one.

After two weeks, he arrived. We had one week together—that was all. During the first three days, I told him . . . everything.

The fourth day, he said that he would do what I was asking—leave these *fighters—but that we had to figure out how. He needed to think through what the Rwandese authorities wanted; since he was the head of intelligence, it would be difficult. "If we leave here, don't assume that we'll ever get to Rwanda," he warned me. Four days through the forest . . . "If they discover us, they'll kill us. But given what you've said, I can go. We'll see what we can pull off."*

Pulling it off is always hard. But you know, with soldiers, once they make a decision, they stick to it. The big decision is to leave.

The next Sunday, Anne Marie and Jerome sneaked away on foot.

With the help of God, and with the support of the high authorities of the RPF, I managed to convince my husband. Now he's chief of staff for the RPF reserves.

Anne Marie says she has done missions like this several times. She doesn't want to say how many. *Three weeks after I arrived home with my husband, I left for the forest again. The second time was for the general.* That was Paul Rwarakabije, the commander of the FDLR at the time, and the man who had asked Anne Marie to meet with him while she awaited the arrival of her husband. *He came out with 120 senior officers and soldiers and all of their equipment: weapons, radios . . . everything they had.*

In November 2003, General Rwarakabije, like Anne Marie's husband, integrated into the new national army. He now serves as the head of the prison system. *After this defection of Rwarakabije, there was an opening. These one hundred who left with the general started to talk to the others. I'm very proud that more than ten thousand FDLR soldiers defected, including a great number of officers.*

As Anne Marie and Jerome settled into normal life in Kigali, together for the first time in almost a decade, she gave birth to two more boys. But the family portrait hanging on the wall is remarkable. It features Anne Marie and Jerome surrounded by not five but eight children.

We also have three that we adopted—survivors of the genocide. They're from one family. And all their other family members were killed.

A Hutu family adopting orphan children of Tutsi? That's astoundingly common in Rwanda. It's one of a dozen ways women have healed their country, in both intimate and practical approaches as they've moved into postwar leadership.

Anne Marie herself went on to serve a five-year term in Parliament. To her, the sense of belonging she felt as she remade her life in Rwanda and took part in the country's development was astonishing. She describes how being welcomed in spite of the country's fractured past convinced her that her bold mission was worth the risk.

Can you imagine what it's like to live in a country, pay taxes, send kids to school where no one bothers them—and all the while your husband is an enemy of the state? Anne Marie is quiet for a moment, her hands folded in her lap. *That really touched me.* She put herself in danger because she intimately understood an essential, pragmatic element of Rwanda's rebuilding: to establish a peace that's not ultimately a standoff with rebels just across the border (or with neighbors next door), but a sense of shared security that enables former rivals to thrive.

19 RETHINKING RAPE

ALICE: It was as if the witness had said, "And then it was raining that night."

Well, 1994 . . . how can I say it? It wasn't a country. **DOMITILLA** was living in Rwanda until just days before the genocide broke out. The mounting dangers were clear—and grim: militias twice threw grenades into her house targeting her husband, a member of the RPF. Domitilla took their three children to Uganda in late March 1994 to settle them with family already there. She planned to come right back. *Leaving home is a very difficult decision. If you think of leaving behind your elderly parents and close friends . . . you would rather stay and die with them.* But securing her children's fate was a higher duty. *How could I live with myself if I had survived and they'd died? How could my husband and I ever live together if our children were killed?*

Her return ticket to Rwanda was booked for April 7, but travel was inconceivable a day after President Habyarimana's plane was shot down. Still, she was among the first wave of Rwandans coming home to their ravaged country three months later. Domitilla's first role was as a director at the Ministry of Social Affairs. (*We focused on burying in dignity the bodies that were everywhere.*) She then became a member of the constitution drafting commission and finally a central figure in the monumental effort to find justice for perpetrators of atrocities.

You had to look where you were. You had to look in front of you. You had to look behind you. You could find yourself fearing, "Maybe that person is a genocidaire. He might kill me."

In a country where virtually the entire population witnessed violence

For justice, it was necessary to punish but also rebuild trust in fractured communities. The first, seemingly insurmountable, step was for citizens to speak up.

committed by their countrymen, figuring out who did what to whom, then holding culprits accountable, couldn't have been more direly needed—or more difficult to do. *No one has experience with how to deal with genocide justice.*

As they did in other spheres, women leaned into the chaos and conundrums. They concurrently took on the transformation of the former regime's ordinary legal system, a new UN tribunal set up in neighboring Tanzania to deal with this genocide, and a groundbreaking local remedy to unclog prisons choked by hordes of inmates awaiting trial. Relationships among those three justice systems were rife with uncertainty.

Rwanda faced a judicial puzzle of such great weight that the future of the country hung in the balance.

For one, the inadequate existing judicial system needed to be reformed but not thrown out; it had to be shored up to be an institutional pillar when the country was stabilized. Special chambers within the existing courts would focus on crimes connected to the genocide.[1]

Second, the UN court would have international backing and status but move at glacial speed. The cost of the tribunal, stacked up against the basic needs of the people, would become obscene.

And finally, a new structure would need to be created that could confront the scope: just twenty surviving judges and hundreds of thousands of untried prisoners. The government had to find a way to optimize security while giving citizens a sense of due process and legitimacy.

That was the context into which women activists stepped. They were much more than extra eyes and ears. As women they brought not only their talents and skills, but also social roles and life experience that were different from those of the men.

Worldwide, rape was considered simply a secondary effect of war. Being aroused to kill aroused men to attack women, an unchangeable side effect of surging testosterone. After the Rwandan conflict, nongovernmental agencies, large and small, collected stories of victims. UN Special Rapporteur Rene Dengi-Segui estimated that between 250,000 and 500,000 had been raped, stating, "Rape was the rule and its absence the exception."[2] Yet at this scale, the victims were numbers, not names. Not mothers of five children, or three, or ten. Not girls whose dreams of marriage were turned inside out. Not grandmothers whose bodies were frail and easily ripped apart. Not victims who were further traumatized as they were deposed, interviewed, photographed.

Along with a change in basic attitudes, the complicated legal framework had to be reconstructed when it came to sexual violence. And for that change, activists first needed to convince fellow Rwandans, as well as the international attorneys and judges at the new UN court, that rape was a serious crime.

Change in one of the three judicial systems would likely affect the other two. If rape wasn't included in the special national chambers in Rwanda, why would it appear as a crime in the new community-based transitional process? Wouldn't the treatment of sexual assault at the UN's international tribunal in Arusha influence reform in the national laws, and vice versa?

Yet even the idea of one streamlined plan was impossible: organizations in Rwanda or outside had their own objectives. And how would individual women in Rwanda coordinate? They were constructing their platform as they were standing on it, responding to ever-changing necessities and possibilities.

For as long as we know, women around the world have been terrorized by sexual assault. Whether they meant to or not, the women of Rwanda found a way to make that violence an occasion not of retribution but of transformation. Through new laws, male domination of females was dramatically disrupted, as men accustomed to violent power over women were renamed "criminals."

To generate that shift, women had to elevate society awareness of the severity of the aggression they and their sisters had endured. That wrong needed to be brought into the open and treated with the attention it—and they—deserved.

· · ·

The nation's law had to be transformed. Soon after the genocide, police investigators who were connected to the newly reconstituted Ministry of Justice were trained and tasked with collecting testimony and evidence. Tens of thousands of people (mostly men) were arrested for participation in the rampage and jammed into prisons. In late 1995, the government convened a conference to construct a process that would both punish and rebuild trust.

But the country had an immediate need—on behalf of countless victims—to recognize the sexual violence for what it was: genocidal.

GODELIEVE stepped up. She began organizing support groups for women who had survived rape, some of whom had given birth as a result of the attack. Godelieve lived in a small town called Taba that would soon play a key role in postgenocide justice. *Women who were part of our solidarity group heard on the radio that our law would classify rape as a Category Four offense, like stealing someone's baskets or sweet potatoes. The message was that a woman was just a piece of property that could be looted.*

Those women came to me, since I was the coordinator, and said, "Did you hear the radio? Godelieve, go tell the other activists that we're very discouraged by this system that treats us like property." So I came to Kigali to speak to Pro-Femmes. Immaculee Ingabire, Veneranda Nzambazamariya, Soline Nyirahabimana, and many others demanded an audience with the Parliament and appealed to the female MPs to listen to the stories of Taba.

MAMA MADINA (which means Mother of Madina) was among those who opened her life to the world. *Of course, the very first time we talked about the attacks it was very difficult, because you relive the experience as you describe it.* That's where Godelieve's work was so critical. She understood the importance of practice, and the careful, gradual desensitization that would allow the survivors to speak their truth with confidence, and without being retraumatized each time. They also needed to be prepared for the reaction of the listeners. *The members of Parliament cried and cried as they listened to our testimonies,* Mama Madina remembers. *And later, they repeated our stories to their colleagues and to journalists.*

GODELIEVE credits women like Mama Madina for their bravery in detailing their torment. And she is grateful to women allies in Parliament for guaranteeing that the final law took their horrendous abuse into account. *The female MPs went back to Parliament and appealed to their male colleagues, who were in the majority, to ensure that the law gave special consideration to crimes targeting women.*

Advocacy and organizing for the Genocide Law was one of the first undertakings of the Forum for Rwandan Women Parliamentarians (FFRP). Its leaders recognized this unjust response to women's experiences as an opening to coordinate. They went as a group to Taba, to hear the testimonies of the women who had been assaulted. Moved by the harrowing testimonies they heard at Godelieve's center and the understanding of how women like Mama Madina continued to suffer after their nightmare ordeals, parliamentarians insisted that rape during the carnage be shifted from Category Four to Category One. **ALPHONSINE M.**'s indignant tone instantly exposes how she feels about the matter. *People before didn't see the gravity; they didn't think it was very terrible. Can you imagine? Rape was classified as if it was banal. But during the genocide, it was utilized as a war crime, which isn't at all the same as raping someone during peace time. The intention was very different.*

The women in Parliament defended this idea, and the rest of Parliament

Survivor Mama Madina.

accepted it. So a rapist was prosecuted just as someone who planned or car-
ried out the genocide.

This legal change was momentous, with consequences that reached across the country and beyond to other countries watching the difference women's higher standing made in the new Rwanda. It was also a policy that could help heal the pain of tens of thousands of individuals, their families, and their communities. Of course, even in the wake of enormous progress, there are numerous problems. Some contended that they weren't included in the initial design; without their input, procedures didn't take seriously enough sensitive issues women faced as they sought redress. **JUSTINE M.** shares their concern. *Women's social perspective on issues such as reparation and truth telling seems to differ from that of men. Our transitional justice mechanisms have primarily been conceived by the government* [led mostly by men] *and not by victims.*

Inevitably, the process was slow. Justine continues, *With legal and judicial reform, you don't tell a society to drop what they've known for so many years. You have to slowly by slowly marry the two systems and obviously also apply international norms.* That's a rational consideration. But deeper is her sense of urgency, an internal beckoning to do more.

AGNES, an attorney, is haunted by memories of women she couldn't help. Their despair clouds the eventual legislative victory. *You know, since rape had been used as a crime of genocide, many women were contaminated with AIDS, so even those who made it through the genocide alive are now dead. Some came to me as a lawyer to talk about this, but most died before we had resolution.*

· · ·

Many of the suspects accused of plotting the most atrocious crimes during the genocide were tried at the International Criminal Tribunal for Rwanda, set up in nearby Arusha, Tanzania.

The court's first trial began in 1997—the case of Jean-Paul Akayesu. The former mayor of Godelieve's hometown of Taba, where many Tutsi perished, was an evil icon. And the survivors preparing to testify against him were about to shape history.

In testimony delivered in court, witnesses told of Akayesu overseeing squads of men raping women who had come to his office in desperate hope of safety. One, identified in court documents as PP, described the rape and killing of Alexia, who was pregnant, as policemen and local militiamen acted on orders from the mayor.

PP said Alexia held up her Bible to a man called Pierre, as he was about to rape her. "Take this Bible," she said, "because you don't know what you're doing." Alexia was then gang-raped until she miscarried. After the rape, Alexia was beaten to death.[3] PP, a Tutsi able to pass herself off as Hutu, was one of the helpless onlookers.

Astonishingly, even with such heinous crimes, sexual assault wasn't included on the list of charges brought against Akayesu or any of the many cases pending before the international court in Tanzania. The UN tribunal's statute explicitly included rape and other forms of sexual violence as criminal offenses, but up to this point, not a single suspect had been indicted on those charges.

But additional indictments were added several months later in the proceedings, thanks to enormous pressure from women's groups, according to UN Special Rapporteur Radhika Coomaraswamy, whose portfolio focused on violence against women.[4]

Lawyer and professor **ALICE** was among those leading that activism. *One of my most important work experiences was advocating for those who had survived sexual violence. I was working with Pro-Femmes and other groups to bring to light the particular experience of women.*

At the time we weren't discussing much about gender-based crimes. Given my background in criminology, I became a watchdog of the Arusha tribunal. I helped create a coalition with organizations in North America, making sure that the court took those women into account.

Alice linked up Rwandan activists with groups like the Center for Rights and Democracy in Montreal and the Center for Women's Global Leadership at Rutgers University in New Jersey. Together, they worked on a campaign around a friend of the court brief (amicus curiae) pressing the court to prosecute Akayesu for sexual violence in addition to his many other charges. The friend of the court brief also called for the tribunal to investigate why none of the indictments had included charges of rape or other forms of sexual assault, despite reliable reports documenting that such crimes had been widespread.

During a hearing, one of the witnesses mentioned the rape of her six-year-

old daughter. But it just passed. Since we activists were following the trial, we noticed this detail. But the court apparently didn't. Looking back, it was like this offense was new. Alice lets out an incredulous laugh. *We come from a background where incidents of sexual violence have always been a natural occurrence when you have war. So it was like they weren't aware it was something to include. We were asking for the court to apply the law, as the statute stated.*

Crucially, Alice brought the concern home. *I introduced the first Sixteen Days of Activism in Rwanda to put a lot of attention on this case of Akayesu. We had a march in Taba, so, first and foremost, it was about awareness raising about this trial. At that time, there were some discussions and rumors saying, "Well, this is the business of North America, mainly, of Western activists." So it was very important that there is support for that here.*

We crafted a whole strategy that had many tentacles: the friends of the court briefing, public campaigns, the press, interviews, and I helped prepare the fact-finding mission of the UN Special Rapporteur on Violence against Women, Radhika Coomaraswamy. We worked a lot with legislators and the executive branch, many different partners, mostly women, to make sure that the trip to Arusha for the trials was organized in a dignified way.

On September 2, 1998, the three-judge panel handed down three life sentences plus eighty years in prison to Akayesu, finding him guilty of genocide and crimes against humanity.[5] After the verdict, presiding judge Navanethem Pillay delivered her now-famous statement about this case as a message to the world: "From time immemorial, rape has been regarded as spoils of war. Now it will be considered a war crime."[6]

GRACE: My testimony helped set the standard for the world.

The Akayesu trial was indeed a decisive moment for international law—for which there has been no shortage of affirming suits, from Yugoslavia to Darfur. But in addition to the advocacy of national and international women's groups and a clear-thinking judge, these historic Rwandan cases hinged on the willingness of victims to tell the court about the unending harm they'd survived.

IMMACULEE was a journalist for a prominent Kinyarwanda newspaper. She first traveled to Akayesu's Taba to report on the hardships of those who suffered rape. *I knew that in conflict there are rapes, but the systematic, massive rapes—that was my first occasion to understand, and it was really terrible. At that time I was thinking it was only Taba, but later I knew that there were other places—in Southern Province, Western Province, Eastern Province. In each place we had at least one group of women, but it took about three years to find them and encourage them to join. I'm very sure there are victims who didn't speak out.*

From that point on, Immaculee claimed an unshakable calling. *I said to myself, "Stop everything else. I'm focusing on this. Everyone has to recognize that rape has been a weapon of genocide, and the international community must take action."*

In the late 1990s, teams from the UN tribunal staff traveled throughout Rwanda to identify witnesses and victims willing to travel to Arusha, Tanzania, and give testimony about the alleged orchestrators of genocide. For those who had been raped, that prospect was truly daunting.

After the genocide, the thoughts in my head weren't good. **"GRACE"** was living down the hill from Mayor Akayesu's office. Still today, her land looks out over layers of quilted hills planted with banana trees, cassava, and beans, a pristine sight that belies the terror that took place in these fields. *I was worried about how it would be to speak about these experiences when I was still dealing with the trauma.*

In addition to the risk survivors faced as they sought shelter and food, those sexually attacked faced extra layers of adversity from the stigma associated with public assaults, rejection by family and friends, health crises, and unwanted pregnancies.

Grace was hesitant about going to Arusha, having never been outside her country, and feeling already overwhelmed by challenges she was facing. *I refused at first, because I didn't see what I could contribute, just me alone. But the people from the tribunal and from different groups said I should go. They explained that I'd seen things that would help the justice process, and it was important for me to give that testimony. I just needed to say what I saw—not add anything, not take away. It would be like a contribution to my country, because it would help bring out the truth. It would be important for the other victims and also maybe for people accused of things they didn't do.*

I asked what they could do to protect me in Arusha, because I didn't know that place. They said I would be secure. Eventually, I accepted.

When the time came for Grace to travel to Tanzania, she had just given birth. *The other four witnesses traveled on a Friday, and I had to wait until Monday.* This would be her first time ever to leave her community. *I traveled alone. We were waiting for the passport for my baby, who was one week old. The baby didn't have a name right away, and we had to have a name so that we could register him with immigration.*

When I got to Arusha, the prosecutor had already explained to the other ladies about the process and what we needed to do. I was nervous because I didn't feel prepared. So the prosecutor helped me, but then I realized how I had come to tell my story, and I decided to go first, because I was ready.

I was scared when I entered the courtroom, because when I walked in, everything was already in place. Even the suspect was sitting there. And when you walk in they ask you, "Do you know the person here who you are testifying against?" You have to say yes or no. It felt stressful to say yes, but that was the truth. My nervousness was less as I started to speak about my experience.

Grace expected that answering the lawyers' questions would be

Judges and chief prosecutor of the International Criminal Tribunal for Rwanda.
BY JACQUES LENGEVIN / SYGMA (CORBIS IMAGES)

Public gallery, reflected in the window of a courtroom at the International
Criminal Tribunal for Rwanda. BY TONY KARUMBA (AFP / GETTY IMAGES)

straightforward. But as she sat in the huge room—a gallery of onlookers with earphones on their heads, peering through a window—she felt unnerved. She sensed she had so little in common with the people she encountered while on the stand. *To be in a foreign country, where I didn't share the language or the skin color of the people asking questions—that was hard. The lawyers and judges were a whole mix of races. The courtroom was very big, and there were people from all over the world who came to hear my testimony. Lots of people were writing down what I said, and there were many, many spectators, who came just to watch. It was hard to believe.*

I spent three full days in a row giving testimony, and I was suffering because I had just given birth. I couldn't believe some of the questions they wanted us to answer. They wanted a lot of detail. It was very intense as I went back and remembered. But I didn't feel afraid. I decided that I could take my time if the answer was difficult. I could think about what to say and respond when I was ready.

Grace may have mustered a dignified response to the taxing environment, but for activists in the audience, the unfolding scene was intolerable. They had worked closely with the tribunal team to encourage women to testify, and they objected to what they saw as insensitivity toward the survivors.

The cadence of **IMMACULEE**'s voice quickens as she recalls the scenes at trial. The journalist accompanied several groups of women to Arusha to provide moral support. *Those defense lawyers. They were trying to intimidate, to humiliate, as if the women hadn't been humiliated enough. Questions like, "Are you sure that you didn't enjoy it?"*

We wrote a petition to the United Nations. I even traveled to New York to request that the UN Security Council not renew the mandate of Carla Del Ponte. The tribunal prosecutor was not defending those women. They went there to testify, so they were under the prosecutor's protection. Yes, they had physical security. But defending them in court? Never.

Immaculee says that Del Ponte made the point during their meeting in New York that the defense had a right to press the witnesses about the validity of their testimony. But for Immaculee and other activists, the questioning crossed a line. The Security Council replaced Del Ponte with Prosecutor Hassan Bubacar Jallow in 2003. Activists claim the dismissal as a victory and say the treatment of female witnesses improved under Jallow.[1]

However, the procedure for engaging witnesses and survivors to testify about sexual violence remained fraught with dissonance. While human rights organizations and local women's groups documented sexual crimes in ghastly detail and provided counseling support to victims in their ongoing trauma, a myth persisted at the Arusha court that women were reticent to speak out. "African women don't want to talk about rape," the deputy prosecutor, Judge Honoré Rakotomanana, told Human Rights Watch for its seminal report, *Shattered Lives*.[2] "We haven't received any real complaints. It's rare in investigations that women refer to rape," he said, seeming not to notice that most of his investigators and translators were male.

As of 2005, despite the extremely high prevalence of sexual violence during the genocide, a stunning 90 percent of the court's judgments contained no rape convictions. Stunning but logical: 70 percent of cases before the tribunal didn't even include rape charges.[3]

• • •

In contrast, in safe environments with female activists, women were openly, if quietly, describing what had happened to them. Those who would testify in the Akayesu case gathered frequently at Godelieve Mukasarasi's two-room adobe house on the main road in Taba. A social worker by training, Godelieve founded SEVOTA in December 1994 to assist, in particular, women who had children as a consequence of rape.[4]

IMMACULEE emphasizes the importance of SEVOTA's reaching out to help women, in juxtaposition with the initial approach of the UN tribunal. *To collect women's stories, we started with those ladies from Taba because Godelieve had done a wonderful job of bringing them together.* Godelieve and Immaculee knew each other through the larger advocacy network Réseau des Femmes. At one of their meetings, Godelieve described the support group she founded, and activists like Immaculee were moved to lift up the stories they were hearing. Immaculee continues, *As we talked to the women, they understood that they weren't alone. They trusted those who came to them through Godelieve, so then it was easier.*

Despite their willingness to open up to trusted visitors, survivors in rural areas knew their lives were in peril, singled out as people with powerful information. They lived with daily distrust of their neighbors and debilitating uncertainty about what had become of their aggressors. Women drawing attention to a socially taboo subject like sexual violence were particularly vulnerable, and even more so if speaking out about their own suffering.

Over time, the tribunal set up a unit for gender crimes and made some other structural changes aimed at protecting and supporting victims. Still, anyone associated with the judicial process, whether witness or advocate, was putting herself at risk—a fearful reality that **GODELIEVE** has lived with for twenty years now.

Even though the women's names weren't given, in the community they were known. People notice who is absent, and people recognize those women's voices on the radio. It was easy to figure out who was giving testimony. And even before the women went to Arusha, the court investigators were visiting them.

Rwandese are curious. They see the fancy car driving up and parking in front of someone's house, and they start asking questions: What's this person doing here?

Even before they went to Arusha, they faced aggression in their village. I remember one kept finding notes slipped under her door from someone threatening to kill her if she spoke out. So certainly when they returned home they faced stigma and taunting. Some people were implicated by the information the women had shared. I was with them in their community, and I saw the risks they faced.

It's only after her descriptions of others' peril that Godelieve explains, with a kind of numbness, just how well she knew the hazard. The story may be overwhelming, yet Godelieve is anything but overwhelmed. In a flat, quiet voice she describes how her Tutsi husband had taken their five children into hiding during the 1994 genocide. Emmanuel survived the war, but not the peace. Less than a month before he was slated to testify in Arusha, suspected militia members burst into their family store and gunned him down, along with their eleven-year-old daughter Angelique.

· · ·

Trauma is not an independent experience. It exists along with grief, bravery, terror, strength, wisdom, guilt, appreciation—each maintaining its own color but in a marbled swirl. Part of the gut-wrenching confusion of those who are attacked is that one internal response isn't neatly isolated from another.

"GRACE," all but destroyed by the physical assaults she endured, brings up the psychological challenges she encountered when, after three weeks in Tanzania, she returned to her hillside plot, her simple house with a corrugated metal roof, and a neighborhood riddled with gossip. *Although this testimony was supposed to be confidential, and even the fact that I went to Arusha was supposed to be secret, when I got back everyone seemed to know. People were constantly asking me questions about what I'd said, what the suspect had said, what was going to happen. I chose not to respond; I just kept to myself.* Then her understatement: *But it was a really rough situation.*

When the verdict was delivered and a life sentence handed down to Akayesu, Grace was listening to the national radio. *I heard it from the evening news when I was just sitting at home, coming from my work. I felt that my truth had done something that is right. Going from this horrible experience, then traveling to the tribunal and telling my story. . . . Women could be heroes. We could be strong. We could contribute to elevating our rights. For that, I feel proud.*

She continues, fervently, *Just like in the national Rwandese courts, the international tribunal found that rape in war is one of the worst crimes there is. I found the strength to stand up against a crime that is committed against so many. My voice contributed to a triumph for the women of Taba, first of all. For the women of Rwanda. For Africa. For the world.* After all the agony and the degradation, she says it again, and then again. *For the world.*

I also want to add that for the people who chose not to testify, it was difficult for them. They didn't have the chance to explain what happened to them. These terrible stories swell inside of you if you don't talk about them. There were some who testified but didn't say that they had been raped. They guarded that secret because it was too much to say.

The crime of rape affects the heart, the mind, the body. . . . People who didn't want to talk about their experience couldn't share their suffering with others like we could. These experiences continue to traumatize if you don't talk about them. It's hard on you to hide from what you've lived through, and that makes it hard to move beyond.

Moving beyond may be too far to hope, but moving forward isn't. And

Grace is right; bringing the darkest suffering into shadow, if not full light, is excruciating but vital. Activists emphasize that the Akayesu case's historic dimension establishing rape as a weapon of genocide wouldn't have been possible without the courageous testimony of women.

Still, that's a theoretical point. Like Grace, at a more intimate level, **GODELIEVE** ponders not only the harm, but also the value of the UN tribunal. Her own family paid the ultimate price for the ideal of a successful court. Even so, her appreciation is inspiring. *Women were traumatized by attending the tribunal, by having to answer all of those questions. But at the end they were proud, because their involvement changed something. Sexual violence was, and still is, a taboo subject. This was the first time women had testified about their own attacks, perpetrated in such an intimate way. It's one thing to give testimony about violence you've witnessed being committed against another person. But to say what happened to you. . . . It had a transformative effect socially for these communities, but also globally.*

And then Godelieve's tribute: *Most of these women are illiterate—these women who bravely came forward and told the truth, who dared be open about what they had endured, who dared to go not just to Kigali but to an international court to speak in front of strangers. Really, this was an exceptional example of courage. They honor Rwanda.*

DOMITILLA: In every square meter there were crimes committed.

Seven years after the genocide, Rwandans had grown frustrated by the very slow accountability process, one that seemed severed from the hillside villages and neighborhoods where the crimes were committed. The country had to come to grips with having a national judicial system crushed by the scale of the bedlam: in a nation of about eight million, lists of suspects eventually (over the course of a decade) included 800,000 names.[1]

Attorney **DOMITILLA** was one of those set on navigating through seemingly endless obstacles that were hindering justice. *During the first six years, the courts tried only 6,000 genocide cases—out of 120,000 people who were at that time in detention. Can you imagine how long it would take to try just those people? More than a century! No one would be there! And justice delayed is justice denied.*

But there were other practical considerations. The perpetrators had targeted the country's elite, which meant the most educated. Those who weren't killed had fled. *You couldn't find enough prosecutors to try all of these crimes. You couldn't find enough trained judges. And suppose we had a miracle: enough prosecutors, enough university-graduated judges. Still, the ordinary system says, "You lose. You win." There was no reconciliation.*

People were afraid of everything. That's normal. That's a genocide. To break this fear, this sense of collective responsibility of one group against another, it was important to set up a system that could let people say, "This is how it happened." "In this family we have these people who destroyed this house, who looted the property." "It was the father," for instance, "not the son, not the daughter, not the mother." For the sake of stability, we needed to bring people together to find the truth about what had happened. *How could our families coexist in the future, if there were unsolvable problems between us now?*

Drawing on a tradition for mediating local disputes, the procedure known as *gacaca* (pronounced ga-CHA-cha) was established to hold accountable the masses implicated in violence. The word "gacaca" means "grassy place" in Kinyarwanda, a fitting name since the trials typically took place outdoors, often under the shade of a tree. In the past, gacaca had been used for land and family problems, with three main goals: to reveal the truth, to punish, and to reconcile.

Using a traditional form was easier for citizens to accept, since it was familiar. But to take on such heinous crimes, the time-honored system had to be expanded and revamped. Confession remained essential, given the emphasis on establishing a true rendering of the wrong. However, the range of crimes the process needed to address was startling: A precious cow—a villager's most valuable possession—was stolen. A home was looted or burned down. Even torture made the list.

Frenzied bands of simple farmers, carpenters, motorbike drivers, trusted teachers, and even revered pastors had carried out the crimes gacaca would handle. (Orchestrators of massacres and militia leaders were typically tried in Rwanda's standard courtrooms or at the international tribunal.) The setting and tone of the trials varied because, crucially, members of the community played all the roles: defendant, witness, and judge. Eventually, more than 12,000 community courts would be set up in villages and towns across the country. Despite the variety of settings, there was commonality in the colossal sense of betrayal, piercing pain of the victims, and near-impenetrable distrust and anger on both sides.

INYUMBA, by this stage the head of the audacious new National Unity and Reconciliation Commission, says the government's approach to justice was designed to reinforce the work her team was already doing to promote dialogue among deeply divided communities. *Part of our reconciliation process was stopping the culture of impunity. There had to be remorse. We had to help even the perpetrators understand that genocide is wrong, that killing is wrong. But we wanted to take them a step further. That's why we opted for a grassroots process. If you could come up and confess, and genuinely acknowledge the harm you'd done, there would be pardon. Your* *punishment would be reduced, because the whole spirit was justice that promotes reconciliation.* She couldn't help but add, *And women were going to be very instrumental in the process.*

Although few have described the new system of justice in gender terms, in fact, Inyumba's prediction of the integral role of women would come to fruition—and make a dramatic difference.

. . .

There are almost no relatable experiences that evoke the same fear and powerlessness a woman feels who has watched her home burn to the ground, has been gang-raped, or has seen her children hacked into pieces. Some of the terror was suppressed as many attackers were locked away, but it couldn't be forever. Those horrors were reawakened as women wondered how and if gacaca would work. The environment was further charged by the sight of prisoners in their unmistakable bubble-gum pink and orange suits being transported in groups to worksites or trials.

From the start, the system proved to have a devastating blind spot. Justice efforts focused primarily on killings, a daunting task in itself. But untold tens—perhaps hundreds—of thousands of women had been raped and were being ignored. One survivor told Human Rights Watch that she went to the authorities near her home and tried to report her rape to the police inspector. She even offered to provide names of the men. The official told her "that rape was not a reason to accuse a person and that there are no arguments to bring those sorts of cases before the courts." She didn't try to report the crime elsewhere, because she didn't have enough money to travel.[2]

Against this backdrop, local judge **"MARIE CLAIRE"** observed the impact of seeing female neighbors and friends come forward to participate in gacaca. As Inyumba had predicted, they not only helped design the system but also implemented the process. But, Marie Claire notes, it's not as if the women were primed to participate. They were already overwhelmed trying to rebuild their homes, to rebuild their families, to rebuild their country. Could gacaca help them rebuild their lives?

Women are naturally shy. They don't want to talk in public. They don't want to speak about problems they've gone through. But under these extraordinary circumstances, particularly with the stress they were under

A panel of seven people of integrity weighs the testimonies of victims and witnesses to judge alleged perpetrators in grassroots courts. BY BOBBY SAGER

as new heads of their families, and with sacrifices they were making every day just to get by, counterintuitively, many felt compelled to take a more assertive role. Their presence proved assuring: *Once women saw others there, it gave them the comfort to be able to say what they'd seen. There was someone like them, so they had more confidence in the gacaca.*

The multiple roles women played were interlocking, reinforcing each other, as **ALOYSIE** explains. *A commission was put in place—the National Service of Gacaca Jurisdictions—which included women. Then women's organizations worked in collaboration with the gacaca offices, knowing that without women testifying it would be very hard for the courts to succeed. After all, they were most of the victims who survived, and they were bearing the brunt of the problems.*

The women were victims, often raped. It was very important to have women judges, because victims of rape had sexual trauma. Having their fellow women as judges was an encouragement for them to come out and talk about what happened to them.

"ROBERT," another judge, agrees. Even though the new law provided for portions of trials to take place in closed chambers, it would still be difficult for a woman to testify before a panel of judges composed only of men. *Once she finds women there, she's more comfortable and has more* *confidence, because at least she knows that people will be able to understand. That encourages her to speak out. So there will be justice for women too.*

Women did not occupy public positions such as gacaca mediator prior to this new iteration of the system. Elderly, respected men—known as "people of integrity" (*inyangamugayo* in Kinyarwanda)—took on that role. The shift to include women was both novel and valuable, says **JOY M.** *Traditionally women did not serve in roles where they would be in the spotlight. During the postgenocide gacaca grassroots justice process, however, communities elected judges based on their virtue. A lot of women were chosen because they were regarded as the most honest, tenacious, and resilient.*

ISABELLE was one of four female magistrates (out of eight) appointed to the Department of Gacaca Jurisdiction, a position she held for several years. Women's newfound influence, driven by necessity as well as an increased awareness of equal rights, made it natural for others like her to take on leadership. But there were still challenges. *We had to encourage the women—to tell them that they had as great a capacity to be judges as their fellow men.*

The encouragement worked. In the first election of judges (in 2001), 35 percent of the seats went to women. Beyond handing down decisions on innocence or guilt, the gacaca law gave judges the vitally important task of determining punishments to match the crimes.[3] This was a dramatic reversal of the gendered power structure, as thousands of women judges were deciding the fate of tens of thousands of prisoners.

There were other striking dynamics going on behind the scenes. Confession usually led to a lighter sentence. Activist **SAMVURA** explains the crucial responsibility the wives assumed. *They played a very big role in getting their husbands to accept what they did, telling those men, "Look here, what you've done is so embarrassing and bad." That's how she talked sense into him. Most were able to convince their husbands, so they were among the first released. When these men are asked about their wives, they say, "She convinced me to accept that I committed these atrocities."*

In the same way, outspoken women in civil society helped steer other women, knowing the invaluable perspectives their sisters brought. They knew to take them by the arm, then stay by their sides, helping them stand up in their communities and bear witness.

SUZANNE says women were hesitant at first; they had an especially hard time finding their voices when it came to sexual violence. But the rationale was compelling. *When the government started the gacaca process, our group Pro-Femmes said, "This is an opportunity for us to get involved— and to get women, in general, involved." They could no longer be on the side-lines. Some had lost husbands or children. Now they had to give witness to what they saw. And they had to play the role of reconciler.*

So we started a project where we trained organizers and community lead-ers across the country, the majority of whom were women. Their role was to inform the general public and the local authorities about the process. But they also encouraged women to be witnesses, explaining that if they refused, no one would know the truth.

The web was dense: women helping women, women helping men, men hurting women, women judging men. And **INYUMBA** adds another strand: *It's true, women can be misused like other populations can be mis-used. It's not that women are bad. But if they're fed the wrong information, if they are not properly directed, if they have no opportunities, they can do it—they can kill. Women in my country killed.*

As the minister for women, I would always feel so bad when I went to visit the prisons, and I'd just see women, seated, testifying, "It is true. My name is Maria. I killed so-and-so, I killed so-and-so." Every time I would leave the prison just shedding tears, you know. But that's a reality.

In the complexity of the time, there were many reasons to shed tears: deaths of dearest ones, years of detention before acquittal, and profound physical pain and mutilation that would last a lifetime. But in addition, this was an inner torture unlike anything we outsiders, with all our so-phisticated turns of phrase, data gathering, and public policies, could ever comprehend.

Lawyer Isabelle Kalihangabo.

IMMACULEE: When I listened to those women, it was like . . . no, I couldn't even imagine.

In the quiet of the SEVOTA compound in Taba, and with the understated yet emboldening presence of activist Godelieve Mukasarasi, in whom they had confided over many years, three women sat outdoors in a circle of plastic chairs, reflecting on their motivations for testifying and whether they would make the same decision again.

For me, I was raped very many times, by many men. **MAMA DIANE**'s voice becomes more sure as the conversation unfolds. The other two women lower their eyes in a reverent moment as she speaks; the attack on Mama Diane was distinctly notorious in this town. *I didn't really have a choice about whether to testify, because my attack was in public, so everyone already knew.*

Mama Diane points down the road toward the village square, where the mob of men assailed her one afternoon, a short walk from where she lives today. *I was sixteen years old, still a child. I looked like a madwoman—in the street, naked. Everyone saw me. After, I had to tell my story to try to regain my honor. This crime was inhuman. In public. How could I deny it when everyone knew already? My testimony about my attack was even on the radio.* She repeats yet again: *So everyone knew.*

Everyone knows a mad person.

I have my mother still. My mother knows I was raped, just like everyone on the hill knows I was raped. My mother knew that I was going to gacaca, but she and I have never discussed my attack.

Even today, Mama Diane can't find a husband, because everyone remembers what happened to her. She participated in just one gacaca case.

Survivor Mama Diane.

Her other attackers were never found or not known. Mama Diane says she isn't sure she would recognize them all; there were so many.

A theme begins to appear: the forever effect—scars seen but also unseen. And not just rejection by men, but also of men. After her assault, **MAMA MADINA**'s relationship with her husband was always strained. They continued to live in the same house, but Mama Madina could never again be sexually intimate with him after the night when militiamen barged into their home, pulled her out of bed and into the yard, and raped her until she lost consciousness. *They returned my body to my husband and said, "Here, take your wife."* She was in a coma for three days following the attack.

Now there was a process for those who felt soiled and silenced to perform the impossible: to speak the truth, in front of an audience. *When gacaca began, the authorities issued summons to those people who would be held accountable and who would be giving testimony,* Mama Madina says. *That was difficult for me, because you would see the prisoners coming out in a big truck. When we saw them moving around, I wanted to hide. But after the summons, I understood the process better, and others like me helped me feel strong about saying what I knew. People would say to me, "But it wasn't you who did these bad things; you didn't commit genocide, so why are you hiding? It should be those people who want to hide themselves."*

Little by little I felt more comfortable, but I still didn't want to participate in gacaca. My neighbors and friends urged me to be strong. Eventually, I realized I could face my aggressors. I would have to talk to find justice. And anyway, I couldn't hide what had happened, so it didn't matter.

When I went to gacaca, I never talked about it with my husband. He knew there was a process, because the authorities brought the summons to our house. But he never spoke about it. He never asked me about my testimony.

If it wasn't seen as properly feminine to speak publicly, it was unthinkable that a woman would stand in front of an audience and incriminate a man. But what did she have to lose? *With my attack, too, everyone knew, even though it took place near my house during the night. All the neighbors could hear the commotion and imagine what was going on, so it was public in a way.*

Mama Madina's neighbors weren't just imagining her suffering; they were the perpetrators—a group of husbands and a son from a few doors

Survivor Vestine and her Taba sisters.

down, joining with men from across the street. *No one had come from outside to do this.*

One of her attackers died as the RPF fought their way across the country, routing the extremists. She says another was freed because he was a juvenile—*he was still not mature*—and the four others are in prison.

Eighteen years old and unmarried when she gave birth nine months after the genocide, **VESTINE** had a different reason for testifying. *I had a child because of my rape, and to have a place to say what had happened to me was an opportunity I had to take. I didn't hesitate or feel scared. I thought eventually this would help me explain the past to my daughter. Gacaca gave an identity to my child.*

The child looks like her father's family, and they live next door. Everyone can see it. Now that the crime has been made known, even my child knows her identity. Thankfully I had the support of organizations like SEVOTA. And after the process, the family of my aggressor gave my daughter land for her inheritance, because after a court process the family recognized that she was part of them.

The man who impregnated Vestine was the ringleader of a militia who regularly came to her house and raped her, drunkenly, frenzied. By the end of this purgatory, they had killed her sisters, brothers, and mother. At gacaca, Vestine would call out that band of men for all the ways they had gruesomely robbed her, the sole surviving member of her family. But she never faced her baby's father in court. A notorious fighter, he evaded capture until 1996, when he died in a shoot-out with police who were trying to arrest him.

GODELIEVE: The suspect would be brought from the prison, and people would watch. Then they could see the witnesses going in.

With gacaca, judges carried great sway in the proceedings. The participants in the community also played a significant role in how each trial unfolded. On one hand, this was an important check on the lay judges; however, a verdict might swing in one direction or another because of local dynamics and grudges, or by the simple chance of who attended on a given day.

Judge **"ROBERT"** sees that intimacy and interest as an overall positive. *The judges were not everything; they opened the door to everybody in the community to participate in the judgment. That's very important, since people had lost hope and trust in the judiciary. Gacaca was for people who knew each other, who'd been together for a long time, and that was an incentive. When you talked to people you knew, you weren't afraid to say, "So-and-so did this."* The closeness promoted truth telling.

That may be. But long-standing relationships between local judges and the friends and families of the accusers and the accused also created unpredictable ties or rifts that undermined objectivity. To combat the likelihood of a case being skewed by personal allegiances, the accuser or the defendant could appeal for a judge to be replaced if they believed he or she was biased.

VESTINE raised that alarm during the trial of one of the inciters of the gang that raped her. *I lost eleven people from my family, so I was constantly at gacaca to give testimony and observe. The judges came to know me, and eventually when it was my turn to testify in my own case, they said, "Oh, it's you again. You're always here. Are you really telling us the truth?"*

If you think about it, the majority of people who participated in the process weren't genocide survivors. They were family members, friends, or had other connections to the aggressors. It's simply a fact of the numbers; the people who survived were few. I refused several judges because they were neighbors or friends of my attacker.

The dynamics that unfolded in the local trials could be volatile, making some observers understandably concerned that the event was retraumatizing the victims. Critics also noted how the local proceedings could stir tensions that might again put people in harm's way.

When gacaca judges began prosecuting sexual violence, testimony was given in closed sessions, with just the judge, defendant, and accuser present. But from her experience providing moral support to women before and after their time in court, **GODELIEVE** paints a much more troubling scene. *If you saw the district offices in a place like Taba, you'd understand: it's a house in the center of the village.*

When the judicial process was taking place, there were windows, and often there was no one guarding. So people could hear what was being said inside—even testimony about sexual violence. We can say the process took place in private, but it wasn't really confidential.

The environment within the makeshift courtroom was also daunting because the woman was face-to-face with her assailant, likely for the first time since he violated her. While she had been coping with the trauma of the attack and trying to piece together some semblance of a normal life, the perpetrator was likely to have spent his prison time preparing his defense and conferring with other accused about the legal process. *The setting was very intimidating. Some suspects would verbally harass the woman to stress her. Often she left her deposition in tears,* Godelieve says.

JOY M. felt a civic duty to attend some of the gacaca proceedings. Even though she had been living outside of the country during the gruesome one hundred days and the volatile years leading up, as a postgenocide ambassador, she had the responsibility of raising awareness about the system in the international community and among Rwandans in the diaspora.

Gacaca was a very grueling and complex process, so we really should give credit to the people who carried out the trials. It's very difficult to keep your balance, not to succumb to emotions but to try to get to the truth. These peo-

ple in the village were often not trained in legal matters; some were not even educated in any field. But they had a lot of courage.

Judge **"MARIE CLAIRE"** spells it out. *We could have used law enforcement around when the gacaca courts were taking place. We might preside over a judgment and the next day be killed.*

The threat to witnesses was, of course, even greater. **JOY M.** continues, *I remember this one woman who was testifying saying that even in that moment she was still under threat. She pointed out two young men she said were harassing her for testifying. Her entire family had been killed and she was the only one who survived. It took a lot of courage to stand there and face her attackers.*

The two men were at the roadblocks where her family members were murdered. They stood up and were denying it and being very, very insulting—even aggressive—toward her, right there in front of the judges and Inyangamugayo. Those young men could go after her at any time. And there she was, alone in that community. I don't know how it ended, but it touched me because I felt so helpless as there was nothing I could do to guarantee her security.

As Joy points out, remote parts of the country posed greater security risks. Witnesses and survivors were targeted to prevent them from speaking out or in retaliation after they gave testimony. Some community residents quietly evaded taking part in proceedings, to avoid being drawn into potential stirred-up tensions. Judges and other local officials coped with the risk that their involvement could make them vulnerable to suspects or convicts who might lash out because they felt they had nothing left to lose.

Women who participated in gacaca in any of these roles were particularly at risk because of their weaker social position. Some calculated that their long-term interests were better served by keeping quiet, because relations with neighbors and even their aggressors were best managed by not trying to hold them accountable. But at the other end of the spectrum, that "nothing to lose" attitude motivated some women. No disastrous consequence could deter them after all they had endured; in fact, through gacaca they could be agents of stability as the country was remade.

While acknowledging the risks, advocates of gacaca argued that a more detached judicial proceeding wouldn't get to the heart of the need: to help people reestablish trust with their neighbors so they could go on

The community turns out en masse in gacaca courts countrywide.
BY BOBBY SAGER

living side by side. Those involved with gacaca often describe their work as a public duty, albeit one with inescapable perils and imperfections.

Judge **"MARIE CLAIRE"** reflects on the exposure she accepted for what she felt was a purpose beyond herself. *When you look back at the genocide and what happened to the country, and you know you survived, not because you are mighty or there's anything unique that made you survive, then you feel indebted and have to lay the ground for your country's future. That's why we had to contribute everything we could.*

The proceedings also brought into sharp focus the trauma on both sides of the conflict. At times, accounts of how an atrocity unfolded in 1994 revealed the complicated calculation on the part of the person who eventually did the deed. Not all killers were hardened murderers. Solomonic choices had been made. Poverty and illiteracy played a role. Propaganda exploited ignorance. Violent threats overwhelmed the truth. It was necessary to air and understand this deadly confluence.

My experience studying and working with people on gacaca was less about discovering extremism—that was a given. Activist and lawyer **ALICE** studied the gacaca model as a tool of reconciliation. *The situation was extreme, driven by ideologues pushing toward a "final solution." More puzzling were the links between extremism and life's hardships. The more I looked at gacaca and heard people speaking about their experiences, the more the judicial process made sense to me, because of the connections between people. They were not only sharing geography and social space; they were sharing lives.*

Alice witnessed the trial of a seventy-eight-year-old man who pled guilty to killing his wife. When the judicial team brought the man to the community to give his confession, it was clear he was in poor physical and mental health—*he was a finished man.* He said that he tried to resist the men who told him to kill, but they gouged out one of his eyes and threatened to do worse if he did not obey their order. *His young brothers had forced him, threatening to murder him if he didn't kill his Tutsi wife and then find a younger woman to marry. As he confessed, he broke down in tears.*

Alice remembers another case, this time where the defendant was swept up in the emotion of facing his victim's family. *He was on his knees, imploring, begging forgiveness. He said, "I can see Mr. So-and-So. You know, your mom . . . it was me. It was me who killed her. I'm not saying anybody forced me. I believed it was the right thing to do. I apologize. I'm not apologizing to have my sentence reduced, but I apologize."*

The level of intimacy in this outdoor courtroom was different, because these were people who had taken extreme actions toward each other. Gacaca was designed to deal with that: First, because it put the issue on the table, not from a distance but in the community. But second, because gacaca used the simple words of everyday life, describing the everyday means used to commit extreme acts.

Alice is certain a more formalized judicial system alone wouldn't have worked for Rwanda. *The usual way of dealing with extremism is to go to a very important building, use elaborate jargon barely understood even by the most educated person, and make decisions in unintelligible legalistic terms. How does that transform?*

This was a popularly perpetrated genocide: extreme killings by people who had never killed before, of people they knew. Gacaca domesticated the extremes.

·   ·   ·

Lawyer, professor, and activist Alice Karekezi.

After shepherding the grassroots experiment for nearly a decade, **DOMIT-ILLA** was at the helm of the National Service of Gacaca Courts when the proceedings ended in 2012. *People from the outside sometimes try to compare gacaca to an ordinary court, but our situation is different, and the solution is unique. In the beginning, I was thinking maybe gacaca wouldn't work because I thought that perpetrators wouldn't be honest and that their families and neighbors—I can call it a negative solidarity—would protect them. But with the participation and goodwill of our people, gacaca is a successful story. People have seen it as their solution, and as really the only solution that we have.*

By 2012, nearly two million cases had been tried. And while the system came under fire from some for not meting out punishments commensurate with the horrible crimes committed or for convicting people on incomplete evidence, the model has been commended by most for its ability to confront a legal challenge of unprecedented magnitude, for the cost of between $23 and $33 per case. By stark contrast, the UN-backed International Criminal Tribunal for Rwanda completed seventy-five cases from 1997 to 2013, for which donor countries spent around $2.6 million per case.[1] However imperfect, the local courts helped the country stabilize socially, allowing millions to confront debilitating uncertainties and look ahead.

It's a grim closure that **ANNONCIATA** knows well, as she came to grips with her husband Innocent's disappearance. Fifteen years after soldiers had beaten him in their home in Kigali, a gacaca case opened in southern Rwanda that suddenly brought to light his fate.[2]

As soon as the genocide ended, Annonciata had searched for her husband. Despite seeing him dragged away by his fellow soldiers, she reasoned that if he had managed to escape he might have defected from the Rwandan national army and enlisted in the rebel Rwandan Patriotic Front, which he had always admired. In the following months, she sought out people who might have news of her husband or know his fate.

Maybe he had survived. I'd never seen his body or met anyone who'd seen him die. I talked to soldiers who'd known him and those who'd been at the RPF training area where he might have gone. No one knew anything. Eventually, I was exhausted and gave up.

More than a dozen years later, the gacaca proceeding opened for a former county official, a *sous-préfet. During the trial I heard that my husband had come to this area to see his family. I never learned how he managed to escape those men who'd taken him from our house in Kigali. When he got here, he learned that his whole family had fled to Burundi. But the neighbors in that area knew him, and they called the authorities. People were apparently scared because he was wearing his uniform and had his gun. We don't know if it was the police who were taking him to the sous-préfet who killed him, or if it was the sous-préfet himself. The sous-préfet said that he took my husband to a military base near Butare. You know, it was all soldiers there. . . . He testified that he had no authority to deal with military people. He said maybe it was the soldiers at that military school who killed Innocent, but no one knows.*

Annonciata accepts that those questions will probably never be settled. But the closure has enabled her to move forward with her life, because she's no longer holding out hope. She's left it in a grassy place.

PART IV
Signposts

M oving past one milestone after another, it's time to pause.
Put most simply, the theme of our book is that the rise of
Rwanda's women and the extraordinary gains of that country
postgenocide are not coincidental. After seventeen years connected to
Rwanda as well as a score of other violent conflicts, I'm comfortable
claiming that hunch.

And my second assertion is equally intrepid: it's worth trying to understand how they came to have so much influence, because our planet
would be more livable if women had that much influence worldwide.

But who can prove it's made a real difference having so many women
in top positions? The question intrigues social scientists, who study the
novelties in Rwanda's experience to tease out causation, or show where
it can't be proven. Such a study is seductive, but it's not the purpose of
this book.

Another reminder: this is no coffee-table collection of fascinating and
world-class women. As tempting as that tribute would be to write, I'm
leaving the privilege to others. Instead, here's an inside look at how they
came to have the positions of influence that they do, what they've done
with that influence, and how they're thinking about securing their sway.

At a more in-depth level, I've spent time with friends at various stages
of the rebuilding: putting together and then rolling out an innovative
program to stop rape; puzzling over how a political campaign back in
villages might take hold or backfire; recognizing that easing the pressure
of overcrowded prisons requires riveting attention, even if the approach
still eludes.

For each of the women's accomplishments I'll lay out in the next pages, a host of elements were at play. I won't try to quantify the extent to which one woman or a collective impacted the final results; that's part of the complexity obvious in this book from the beginning. But intersections and influences are becoming more intricate as pages and stories go by. Essentially, this book is becoming more true to life, with all its mess. Not only are developments on the ground in Rwanda moving at different speeds. They're stepping all over each other—and they're trampling on the outline of my book.

For example, this section begins with a new inheritance law allowing women in the family to receive property from men. That law was a precursor to mass weddings, as women realized that they needed to be married to be eligible for the inheritance. With those marriages, women would eventually gain other protections and rights, including joint titles to land currently owned by their husbands alone. But those titles didn't just follow marriage. The land reform built directly on the inheritance law, with the very idea of women owning land. So the first reform— inheritance—was both a direct and indirect precursor to others.

Looking more linearly, as women became landowners, people (including the women themselves) were more able to imagine women beyond homemaking roles. Land was also collateral, and thus a step toward bank loans and business ownership. With a stronger self-image and greater capability of supporting themselves, women were more able to bring themselves to report men who were beating them, as the new gender-based violence bill said they had a right to do. And of course, with the higher income, they could take better care of their own health and afford their kids' school uniforms and supplies.

Inheritance, marriage, titles, loans, self-image, safety, health, education, mothering—each has required shifts in public policies (a special interest of mine), as well as changes in widespread attitudes. Yet these rights seem so basic, almost pedantic. So what makes this story worth your time?

It's a different list: The harrowing history. The high-priced peace. The colorful context. The fabulous personalities. The inconceivable struggle. The unlikely joy.

FATUMA: We also had resistance, especially from old women, who were saying, "Why don't we stick to tradition?"

With women taking on pronounced roles in rebuilding, they were well situated to help usher in more permanent protection of rights. They set about changing discriminatory laws and establishing ones designed to dismantle the huge obstacles women and girls were facing.

An early project launched by the Ministry of Gender brought together lawyers, gender experts, and others to review existing laws and pinpoint discriminatory provisions or gaps in protections. The commission found that while some reforms a few years before the genocide gave women greater rights, key laws would leave women and girls acutely disadvantaged under the extraordinary circumstances after the genocide. Foremost, the system for handing down property to family members in the event of a death needed an overhaul.

FATUMA was working with the gender ministry during those pivotal years. *The existing law didn't allow wives to inherit property from their husbands or for daughters to inherit from their parents. Immediately after the genocide this was terribly problematic, because so many households were headed by women, including widows and orphans. Property of a widow could be taken by her brother-in-law, especially if she never had sons. Or you'd find a distant uncle taking property from an orphan girl heading her household.*

The women parliamentarians had created an advocacy forum, and the ministry worked closely with that caucus and with Parliament as a whole to revise the discriminatory laws. And, of course, intensive sensitization had to

Some 85 percent of women work as farmers, but until 1999 they weren't allowed to inherit so rarely owned land.

happen because we were dealing with not only laws, but also the mind-sets of both men and women who didn't see the need to change the laws.

Because it is an agrarian society, Rwanda's reform of the inheritance and succession law had implications beyond the promotion of equal rights. Women and girls would be able to inherit land, the most valued commodity in the densely populated country, for the first time in their history. That one fact would impact their families' access to food, where they would live, and what vocations they could pursue.

Fatuma remembers how many, if not most, questioned whether change would usher in trouble. *"But how do I inherit property? I inherit from my husband and also from my father. How will my brother manage?"*

It wasn't just people in rural areas who needed to be convinced. **PATRICIA** became an MP in 1994 and served through most of the transition period, right after the genocide, that led up to the 2003 constitution.

We had a long, long sensitization campaign. . . . This was a very big debate where we asked, "Okay, fine. You think only men can inherit, not girls and women. But as a man, you have a mother who might lose the property from your father because your uncles will take everything away from her. Would you like that?"

Then we said, "You're a man. . . . You have children. You have a daughter who owns property with her husband. Would you like to see that daughter of yours, if her husband dies, have everything taken away?" When you personalize things, they tend to understand.

SUZANNE saw how legal reforms could make all the difference in the world for women saddled with hardships after the genocide. Coordinating Pro-Femmes' countrywide Action Campaign for Peace placed her at the heart of discussions about women's most urgent needs. *When the bill was introduced in Parliament, we mobilized women from everywhere: the activists, women selling goods in the market. . . . The assembly hall was full.*

JEANNE D'ARC K. was one of those women in the packed gallery, looking down the sloping room to the podium where the representatives debated the bill. It must have been a spectacular sight—the bright red, blue, and green bold-print head wraps turned toward each other, bobbing up and down, or tilted forward toward a sea of gray suits. *It was unusual to have so many people from the public come to watch the session, so the MPs kept turning around: "What are all those women doing?" When one of the speakers said something good, we would all clap and cheer. It was a different mood there compared to most days!*

SUZANNE chuckles. *The president of Parliament was asking, "What's going on?" We said we want this law to move forward as quickly as possible, because we have widows who can't inherit, young orphans who can't get the property their parents left behind, women with husbands in prison who are kept from managing their families' affairs.*

The inheritance law passed that day in 1999, and it's consistently cited as a crucial early step in the advancement of women's rights. This was the first of several reforms that would explicitly protect a woman's ability to open a bank account, control her own assets during marriage or jointly manage them with her husband, file for divorce, and pass on citizenship to her child.

The women were on a roll. A 2001 law defined and criminalized child rape, which marked the first time the courts took a stance against sexual violence. That legislation paved the way for more sweeping prohibition in subsequent years.

The changes weren't all at the legislative level. **ISABELLE**, from her position as permanent secretary (second in command) at the Ministry of Justice, wanted to be sure that the importance of having women in the judiciary was fully appreciated. *Okay, this is very important: the Parliament needs women to make sure laws are in conformity with women's rights, not discriminatory. In the judiciary system it's the same. We have many cases about matrimony, divorce, even succession. We have to have women involved in this court and even in the executive branch, because they'll be more sensitive about these problems than the men.* She adds a critical point beyond the words on paper: *Plus they'll have a different role to play, to make men understand women's issues.*

It's hard to overestimate the importance of these initial legal protections. They were a triumph of progressive ideals and a testament to the synchronizing prowess of women leaders across government and civil society. But Isabelle is right. The focus needed to shift toward making the new policies actually work.

During her first two years as mayor, **FLORENCE** noticed the discrepancy between the encouraging new protections that the inheritance law afforded and women's real ability to claim them. Couples were often married only informally. They might live together for years and have a family but not have a marriage certificate registered with the government.

About 80 percent of people in my district weren't legally married. If anything happened between them, the woman would be told to get out. The inheritance law gave us room to break this practice. To solve that problem, I—of course not I alone—we, as the team from the district, campaigned for these people to be officially married.

Culturally, the informal practices were deeply engrained. And they were advantageous for men.

After the genocide, you can imagine how young girls wanted protection. Even a place to live. So if a young man said, "Come to my home and we can stay together," then they would be married in the community's view.

Women were the weaker group. Men were economically capable, so they

Mayor Florence Kamili Kayiraba.

could have one wife today and another later. Since they were switching be-tween women, they didn't want to tie themselves to one. You understand? Staying with a woman in an informal marriage was dependent on the man. The man was, you could say, profiting from this arrangement.

When we started working on this, polygamy was acceptable. Some men had two or three women, and they had to choose one. Some would be left out. The men would usually choose the young one and leave the old. There were some tough feelings. So we'd say, "Okay, we'll register with the district that these are your children with Harriet, but you're no longer the husband of Harriet because you're choosing a different one." We'd tell the man that he still needs to give a portion of his land or his cows to the children he had with Harriet, and Harriet would be trained to manage the family on her own.

We were telling the men, "Your lives will be simpler if you stay with just one wife, rather than having so many women." Some men were convinced. We could show them the economic advantages and the support the district would give. We were teaching them about social norms, but it was a free thing. No one was forced into it.

As the campaign made progress, Florence and her team confronted a new obstacle. *People were telling us, "But to get married requires a lot of money. You have to produce a ceremony, have a nice dress, and book a hall for a party." So we said, "Okay, you don't have to book halls. The district is going to handle this and do the ceremony for you."*

We brought the ceremony to them, because even transportation was an ex-pense. The day for the wedding, we came with tents, drinks, food. The couples made their vows and we celebrated. It wasn't just a family wedding party. It was a district party.

At the first mass wedding in Florence's Kicukiro district, 312 couples married.

FELIX: People saw that keeping a secret would support the rapist.

Moving from laws into action always seems slow on the uptake. Still, those legal requirements were a crucial starting place. Women leaders took up a new cause, with the country relatively stabilized and the political environment working in their favor. Like inheritance and formal marriage, this issue was beset by not only traditional underpinnings but also mortifying stigma. Sexual violence had been a particularly abominable manifestation of the genocide coupled with a lawless environment. But women leaders were blunt: male-on-female violence wasn't just a recent phenomenon.

Having distinguished herself as a strong and vocal advocate for women's rights on the constitution drafting commission, **JUDITH** had been elected to Parliament in 2003. There, she took up the presidency of the women's caucus with a similarly ambitious flair. Their goals were far-reaching. *We'll target domestic violence, but also the parts of our culture that make women very weak and allow men to beat them. We'll be very clear about the consequences of being violent, but we also want to change behavior. We'll use media, we'll use research, and we'll do advocacy with leaders across the grassroots level. We'll also empower women not to be victims of this violence. Those are different strategies. The law is only one.*

Parliamentarians, activists, and brave witnesses who testified about rapes had dramatically raised awareness of this abuse during the genocide. Now the brutalization couldn't be chalked up to a sideshow of war. Studies by the government and other organizations drew attention to the staggering scope of the peacetime problem. A Ministry of Gender report ten years after the genocide drew open the curtain: in a one-year period before the ministry released its 2004 study, half of the country's women had experienced domestic violence.[1] The same year, Human Rights Watch found that in every province, complaints of sexual violence against girls far exceeded the number of complaints filed for adult women.[2]

Judith knew well that the public advocacy she wanted to do would rattle people. She approached **IMMACULEE** to join a small group of informal advisors strategizing about how to approach legislation and cultivate allies. *Women activists, at that time especially, thought it was very important to denounce gender-based violence wherever it was happening. Judith was really a wonderful woman—very passionate about this issue. She was so dedicated to women's empowerment, and you know, when you are a victim of gender-based violence you can't be empowered.*

This was a new language in the culture. But Judith knew you can't have big change without shocking people.

Immaculee points to the activists' successful campaign at the Arusha tribunal: *We convinced the UN that rape had been used as a weapon of genocide, so when we were lobbying to end sexual violence, it would be a pity to see that the international community has accepted our message about rape, and now in our own country, our husbands, friends, and the authorities don't want to understand us. That's helped change the minds of the men here.*

The Rwandan government hosted a conference in the capital in 2005 to develop recommendations for a new law that would prevent and punish these attacks. With Judith as president, the women's parliamentary forum launched a mass media campaign over television and radio to begin alerting communities far and wide. The violence was damaging to the entire society, and this obscured issue was being pulled out of the shadows. Citizens could call in to live-debate radio programs, using free telephone lines, and weigh in on what could be done.

With this surge of exposure to pave their way, parliamentarians returned to their home districts to engage their constituents in the first stage of a lengthy and fruitful public consultation on the gender-based violence law. Seventy-six parliamentarians (out of 106) participated in these historic community meetings. Nearly half were men. The women's parliamentary forum also coordinated with the National Women Coun-

Member of Parliament Judith Kanakuze.

cil to convene large, female-only groups. They invited smaller groups of local women activists to visit Parliament and share their perspectives in committee sessions.[3]

These conversations with constituents infused the work of parliamentarians with an invaluable dose of realism. For many lawmakers, years had passed since they had lived in their villages. And even if they'd spent time with these communities, their level of education and financial security set them apart from some of the dynamics underpinning violence against women and girls.

Former parliamentarian **AIMABLE** described a conversation about men's rights. Aimable, who passed away in 2011, asked one man whether he ever physically abused his wife. *The man answered, "I don't beat my wife, but I could beat her because I paid a dowry."* Aimable also understood that the dowry price was particularly high in the town of Ruhengeri, narrowing the pool of eligible men. As a result, polygamy appealed to families of women looking for a husband who could meet the bride price, even if he was already married.[4]

Attorney **JUSTINE M.** was hired to conduct interviews and draft legal language for the gender violence law. She too described the value of going to a range of settings to hear directly from citizens about the underlying drivers of assaults and possible solutions.

How would you know how to prevent someone from being raped if they're in really remote places? How do you know the best protective measures? You don't know where they live; you need to ask how they find the police if there's no road to get there.

Citizens proposed creating watch groups of neighbors who would keep an eye out for and report suspicious behavior or crimes, especially targeting women. Some called for a legal obligation to speak up about abuse.

The women's caucus assembled a committee composed of female and male parliamentarians and representatives from the ministry of gender, ministry of justice, and Rwandan National Police, plus the legal and women's rights advocacy communities. The committee met monthly to write the legislation. When they unveiled the draft bill in 2006, the influence of the citizen consultations was apparent. Sections mirrored specific language and recommendations from the community meetings, reflecting perspectives about why the practice persisted. The draft also included suggestions for spreading the word, and recommendations for punishment. This direct link proved compelling in parliamentary debates when lawmakers questioned the rationale behind proposals. The awareness raising was so pervasive that, across the country, many Rwandans thought that men beating women was illegal long before it was.

Public debate spanned nearly two years, and **IMMACULEE** explains why: *The delay was the hesitancy to talk about some cultural topics. How can a man rape his wife? It was seen as a normal thing. Women didn't know they could say yes or no.*

Some sayings in Kinyarwanda directly reinforce this supposed right to violence and a woman's vulnerability. Immaculee mentions a proverb about how two (revered) cows in the same space inevitably push each other ("Nta zibana zitakomana amahembe"). But that doesn't mean they don't love each other, so the saying goes. Immaculee clarifies that the justification applies only to men; the notion of a woman physically taking out her frustration on her husband isn't in the realm of possibility. *The woman is in his house, so it was difficult to convince people that these practices should be prosecuted.*

While in the midst of planning the legislative drive, **JUDITH** comments on the benefits of the process: *Even during the preparation of the law, some attitudes can change. We want prevention and protection. We want penalties to be the exception.*

The public engagement had a powerful effect in connecting lawmakers to the needs of their communities and bettering the chance of buy-in from citizens. But the sensitivity of the topic warranted careful navigation among MPs themselves. Judith mentions one lawmaker who told her he was "living the contradiction" and approached her to ask that she not request his support as a cosponsor. He would be the first in prison if the bill passed, he'd said. Other male parliamentarians refused to cosponsor, asserting that it wasn't consistent with Rwandan culture.

Not surprisingly, women leaders were deliberate about how they spoke to male colleagues. They avoided discussing violence as a conflict between husband and wife, which could touch a nerve. *For all you knew,* says **JUSTINE,** *you could be talking to last night's perpetrator.* Instead, by framing the issue as a matter that could affect someone's mother, daughter, or sister, the conversation became about guarding a vulnerable loved one.

The women among themselves had the numbers to pass the law. Still, they wisely recruited four male MPs as cosponsors to introduce the legislation alongside the four female MPs. Gender-based violence was thus a broad policy matter rather than a women's issue. The draft bill highlighted abuses that could befall males as well as females, such as crimes against young boys. To use **JUDITH**'s words, the law wasn't *coming to beat men.*

The gender-based violence bill became law in 2008. In the years since, gendered violence prevention has become one of the most prominent campaigns in the country, with flashing billboards urging Rwandans to stand together to prevent sexual harassment and violence. Activist **SUZANNE** sums up the trend: *Before, it was taboo to talk about sexual violence, so the prevalence and the cause of the problem was much less known. Now when there's a rape, everyone understands it's wrong. It's a crime, and victims don't have to be afraid or ashamed.*

Because there's more discussion about sexual violence, it may seem like it's happening more. For one thing, it's not just the activists who are speaking about this now—many more people are involved, from national leaders to local officials, police, psychologists. And so people who are attacked feel they can speak up because the perpetrators will be punished.

We don't have numbers to actually compare to the time before all this work began. But even our current reports show that people are aware, neighbors are aware, and the police have programs in place. Violence against girls and women can be given air and begin to heal.

> JANET: People talk about women who are MPs, who went to school. But there are these other self-made professionals—weavers who can interpret an intricate design yet can't read and write.

Newly promoted to the presidency in 2000, Paul Kagame delivered a momentous speech in Parliament that articulated the rationale for the new government's proactive approach to women's advancement: "My understanding of gender is that it is an issue of good governance, good economic management, and respect of human rights."[1] The president's focus on the strategic importance of equality was particularly significant in a deeply patriarchal country. Resistance could, and would, come from quarters where human rights, much less women's rights, were not at the top of the list. Whether women would be valued contributors to the post-war economy was on the cutting edge of economic development debates.

Public arguments about women's legal rights had made it crystal clear that male-only ownership of land perpetuated inequality, and remedying that imbalance would boost women's standing. But as the neatly laid out bands of finely terraced hills dominating the countryside attested, land in Rwanda was already spoken for.

After serving in the transitional parliament, **PATRICIA** held several leadership positions at the government ministry in charge of land and environment. She'd seen the practical hindrances women faced as they tried to manage their family affairs and finances, and she was struck by how they were fighting the same battles after laws had been changed. Her 2002 interview makes it plain and simple. *Land and resettlement have always been a male domain.* Her ministry's study the same year found that

In a rural country, owning property is central to economic empowerment.

nearly all of the country's land was owned by men, with women's names on titles in only the rarest of cases.

Here's her 2002 assessment: *It's difficult to transfer land men already have. However, we're undergoing rural land reform and showing how women, too, can get access to land. Of course it's still minimal because of our culture. We're an illiterate society. People don't know their rights. Even if they have property rights, they don't know how to access them. I've tried to count annually how many women have actually applied for land title; it's an insignificant number. Even among the very few who have a right to ownership, most don't apply.*

The ministry made two key recommendations to boost female land ownership. First, since much of the country was claimed by developers or farmers without title, all land had to be registered. Second, a legally married couple had to register the land already in their possession as co-owned, a provision that went hand in glove with the mass weddings Florence was organizing.

A new land law in 2005, with amendments since, adopted the recommendations made by Patricia's team: unless a person requested otherwise, marriage meant sharing a plot as well as a bed. An important new avenue for women's economic opportunities had officially opened.

Longtime land reform expert **DIDIER** explains how the changes work on the ground. Sipping a beer, without hesitation he rattles off article numbers and language from the laws. (He helped write much of the regulation.) *With the earlier provisions, when registering a property for a land title the registrar wasn't required to ask someone if he or she is married or if there's a female, or a male for that matter, co-owner. The reform states that every co-owner should be on the title. And another thing: I can't transfer that land without the consent of the other person on the title. So now before I sell my land, we need to decide to sell, I together with my wife.*

The mind-set, the assumption, of male ownership changed dramatically over the next years. Instead of being a rare exception, the most recent figures from Didier's office, the Rwanda Natural Resources Authority, show that women actually own significantly more registered plots than men.

· · ·

Then came another economic policy change benefiting women. To encourage people to merge their resources, a campaign incentivized working together in local cooperatives.

The success record for these local groups is mixed. Their members seem to share a commendable ambition to pool their knowledge and create a thriving business. That said, illiteracy, lack of basic management and accounting skill, little start-up cash, and difficulty getting a first loan hamper many cooperatives. But cooperative members told **JANE U.**, a university researcher, that even with meager and irregular earnings their lives had improved since they started working together.[2]

At first the women weren't so keen, because they had those different backgrounds, with confounding variations of ethnicity, wartime pain, peace-

Government leader Patricia Hajabakiga.

Coffee is a main export, and women dominate the industry, as farmers, pickers, sorters—and company owners.

time trials, *and they would dwell on them. But they were forced by circumstances—like being very poor or living next to one another—to look beyond their differences and find ways to earn a basic living. So they decided to start working together.*

The cooperative I studied started as an association supported by a church. Many of the members were street women, and the church tried to bring them together to find other ways of earning a decent living, or at least enough money to survive. The women learned how to make jewelry out of recycled material, and their specialty is newspaper and magazine beads. They cut magazine pages into strips and then roll them tightly to create layered, lacquered beads popular at tourist markets throughout the region. *Eventually there was a problem with the church's support, but since the members were by then*

Evangelical congregations swelled after the genocide.

used to being together, they created Plan B and kept working. Issues like ethnicity still caused them problems, but since they had a common need to earn money, they continued trying to keep focused on that. This is when their cooperative was born.

As time went on, their cooperative started to thrive. This isn't to say that the women were fully satisfied with what they had achieved. *I still visit them from time to time, and I can say that they struggle but are hopeful.* They work out of a shipping container partitioned into an office, a storeroom for the finished products, and a workshop where women making beads sit side by side on the floor, their sleeping babies next to them on mats. *Their place is metal on all sides, and though they've cut out some windows, it gets very hot in there when the sun is out, and when it rains there's a hail of noise.*

The women don't make lots of money. Some of the leaders go for trainings once in a while, so the cooperative members are encouraged. The leaders come back with some skills that they share, like how to manage finances or how to make different jewelry designs. Some of the members have found small jobs outside of the cooperative, as janitors or housekeepers or vegetable sellers. But there isn't enough opportunity for everyone. It's not every day that you find a job, and sometimes it's by sheer luck.

The group members have been disappointed about the lack of support from the Rwandan Cooperatives Agency, but they are understanding. *All cooperatives are registered under the RCA, and the agency has a fund. But the group I worked with has never received tangible support.*

Still they say, "However far down we are on the waiting list, our turn will eventually come." They are women of faith, too, telling me, "God somehow always sends us help, and that's why we're still surviving."

ALPHONSINE N.: Women tend to stay small. They think that big projects are for men, that they can't afford it. But I know women can do it.

It's a sign of her success over the past decade that **BERTHILDE** is beginning to fret over her legacy and the handover of her company. *I think this place will not only benefit my children but also the people who work in the mushroom business. I want them to put in mind that this is going to be their own, and I want them to share my vision.*

A few years ago Berthilde added a training center to her mushroom company. She's speaking from a chair with a pop-up desk, in a freshly painted classroom where hundreds of adult students have learned the meticulous science of mushroom cultivation. They've become extensions of Berthilde, launching their own small farms on their property.

An idea piqued her interest at an unexpected moment, as with most entrepreneurs. It was a decade earlier, in Zambia. *I went to visit my relative, who said, "You know, we have so many farmers around here. Take a look if you're interested." I was thinking, "Yeah, what are the benefits from this trip?"*

The first visit we did was to the mushroom site, to speak to the farmer who grew them. A small market in mushrooms already existed in Rwanda, but unlike the crop Berthilde found in Zambia, the Rwandan variety was wild and found only during the rainy seasons. Plus, the spores were difficult to harvest.

With some Zambian spores in a water bottle, Berthilde returned home and began experimenting. She had to modify the growing conditions.

Rwanda had little cotton, which was plentiful in Zambia and worked well as a habitat in which the mushrooms could sprout. Instead, she repurposed bean plants after harvesting the pods and grew the mushrooms in heaps of the dry leaves.

Berthilde was also running a moderately successful brewing company that specialized in banana wine and was connected to her commercial vegetable farm. But her entrée into mushrooms drew attention and, soon, accolades. *I'd been going to the agriculture show, but just exhibiting alcohol, like liquor or beer. So I got the idea that if I'm taking my brews to the show, why not take my mushrooms too? It wasn't mainly for selling; it was to introduce mushrooms to people and give them a taste, and we showed people how to cook them.*

We won first prize. I was given a trophy and a cow by MINAGRI, *the Ministry of Agriculture. Two weeks later, I got a phone call, and suddenly I was going for training in China.*

Berthilde spent two months on a study tour of mushroom farms in China, supported by the Rwandan Ministry of Agriculture. She saw the potential to scale up her production. *I saw how mushroom growers had a good life from their businesses. So when I got back, this was the first structure we built.* She points to an open-air shed with a tall sisal roof. Above the front door is a wooden sign carved with the words Mushroom Village. It's now one of a dozen small buildings, including a pristine, white-tiled laboratory, in the company compound built on several levels down the side of a steep hill.

A mentor par excellence, with loans from the Ministry of Agriculture and investment by her husband (who owns a contracting company) Berthilde has trained three thousand people. They grow mushrooms in their yards and then sell them in their communities. The farmers can also sell the mushrooms back to Berthilde's company, BN Producers, which processes them into a variety of products, like soup, flour, and meatballs.

This visionary entrepreneur has built slowly; she's skeptical about bank loans. Her painstaking approach she relates to a Rwandan proverb: *The bird picks out of its little claw a small piece of mud, and it builds a wall gradually, until the whole nest is done. The bird can't do it in a day. It takes time, but the nest becomes strong.*

Entrepreneur Berthilde Niyibaho.

Workers at Berthilde's mushroom company cultivate spores to distribute to small-scale farmers across the country.

Her nest has been expanding with each year as she forges promising corporate partnerships. She even travels across East and Central Africa to scope out prospective markets, although the work in Rwanda is clearly her first love. As her eyes scan her compound and the fields farther down the hill, her gestures and her voice quicken. She speaks breathlessly about the vision that keeps her up at night.

Whether I'm asleep or just imagining, I start seeing trucks coming from the field with mushrooms and vegetables and they enter here and then go into the processing site and the mushrooms go on this side and the vegetables go on the other side and we have a big production making soup and packaging it.

• • •

While there are encouraging stories of business owners who persevered and now direct flourishing companies, the private sector remains riddled with added challenges for women. Education is certainly one impediment, but so is the obstinate perception among lenders that women aren't cut out to manage businesses, even as the women increasingly prove the assumption wrong.

With these hurdles in mind, the Ministry of Gender teamed up with the central bank to create a special fund that would serve as a guarantor for women and young people without collateral. In 2011 management of that pot of money shifted to the newly formed Business Development Fund (BDF), with its spangled blue glass façade on a street downtown in the modernizing capital city.

INNOCENT, head of the BDF, wears a smart suit. He looks and talks like he's straight out of business school, with statistics at the ready as he speaks primly about the potential development these new business owners could drive.

It's demographics. Women and youth make up 72 percent of our population. Females are 52 percent, so the government realized that these numbers could help bring about economic growth.

By the time women come to BDF, many have a history of entrepreneurship that has signaled to the bank that their new venture will also succeed, but it's not a criterion. *We support start-ups, and a woman does not need a track record in business to be supported. All she needs is a strong idea.*

So you walk into your bank; they appraise your business; they evaluate you. If they think it's a good concept, but you don't have sufficient collateral and wouldn't be eligible for normal credit underwriting, the bank comes to us and we provide supplementary collateral.

The purpose of the BDF is to promote small and medium-sized enterprises. It serves as a guarantor and also offers women grants worth 15 percent of the loan, just as an extra incentive.

Economic empowerment of women, that's a quite recent thing. The government started with political empowerment and policies to advance women, like the quota in Parliament and appointments to the president's cabinet. It's only recently that there's been a recognition that women aren't borrowing or that there aren't as many women-led businesses, so the government has put

Stringing beads to make a living while remaking a tradition.

in place some institutions like this one dedicated to encouraging more women to start businesses.

Even with these government incentives, women are still taking out fewer loans, evidence of enduring obstacles. Of the 2,900 loans backed since 2011, four hundred borrowers are women. But those who do seek financing are paying back their loans more reliably than their male counterparts, almost two to one.

ALPHONSINE N. has theories on why females are proving a more reliable investment. She draws from her own experience not only as a business owner and property investor, but also from her extensive work on the board of a prominent bank and her leadership role in the Private Sector Federation. *Most women entrepreneurs are very hardworking and serious about developing their enterprises.*

Part of that determination comes from having to multitask, as women care for their families while also sustaining a tight rein on their business. It also comes from having something to prove as women.

The small details really matter. They matter because you need to be orga-

Layers of fabric, ceiling high, for sale at Kigali's Kimironko market.

nized. *If you're in these positions and not organized, you can't make it. You need a plan every day. They're going to ask you questions, and if you're not prepared, you're lost. Then they're going to say, "Oh, women. They're really not strong. She shouldn't be in that position."*

Alphonsine appreciates government-led initiatives to foster female business ownership. She singles out the inheritance law as distinctly significant. But she emphasizes that the real impetus for women's rise in the private sector has to be the ambition of entrepreneurs themselves. *Yes, the government promotes women in its leadership. But the private sector is different, because to be elected to a leadership position, first you have to be a businesswoman. They can't just say, "Oh, 30 percent are going to be this. . . ."*

Suits and stilettos.

It's a domain where traditional views about gender roles still tend to rule. Even women with drive limit themselves.

It's like when you give a public speech, you feel somehow scared. Women think, "I'm not going to do this as well as a man would do it." You see? Lack of confidence comes from lack of exposure. If you come to one, or two, three, four public events, you start to feel free to express yourself. But your first time, you're scared! You feel like everyone is looking at you; everyone is wondering, "Who is that woman, and what's she saying? Is she making sense?"

It's up to us women to change it, to show that we're as capable as men.

One Sunday afternoon at a trade fair in the northern town of Musanze, vendors from across Rwanda and a few from neighboring countries hosted stalls selling handmade baskets, seeds, solar lights, and farming equipment. When the governor arrived, Alphonsine joined him to survey the grounds before the opening ceremony for the fair. Representing the Private Sector Federation, she gave her remarks about the value of regional trade and introduced the governor, commanding esteem with her assured voice and radiating confidence in her finely tailored pale green batik dress and patent leather stilettos.

Then she coolly took her place again in the front row among the other dozen dignitaries—all men in dark suits.

GODELIEVE: Especially the woman who was raped, she realizes, "You too? That is what happened to you? It's the same as what happened to me." And then someone else shares, and other connections are made. Soon, the women feel they aren't alone in their suffering.

A Rwandan proverb says, "The tears of a man flow on the inside."[1] Being stoic in the face of adversity and keeping an even keel when confronting grief are proud traditions taught to children—boys especially and girls to a lesser extent—from a young age. But when adversity means living next door to one's rapist, and sorrow means coping with the slaughter of an entire family, the ideals could be suffocating.

The impression that everyone was suffering in the aftermath—correct as it was—compounded the cultural urge to shutter emotions. What good would it do to start talking about deep personal sadness when friends and neighbors were also beset with grief?

GODELIEVE had studied psychology and was a social worker focused on trauma counseling. Before the genocide, her patients were typically coping with domestic violence, AIDS, and their children's malnutrition. After the genocide, they were being pummeled with nightmares, flash-backs, anger, self-blame, and unrelenting depression.

Right from the beginning we focused on counseling, and the clients were almost all women. I started something we called Advice Saturdays, where they could come together and share their experiences. It was through these sessions where I first connected with the genocide survivors like Mama Madina, Mama Diane, Francine, and Vestine. That's how SEVOTA *was born, just*

Social worker Godelieve Mukasarasi.

months after the fighting ended. (This was the local group that would help these women and others find the courage to speak up at gacaca and the UN tribunal.)

When a person is alone with the counselor she trusts, she can talk about things that maybe she hasn't voiced before, that she isn't comfortable talking about. But once she has opened up, it's important for her to speak about the experience among her colleagues—her acquaintances and friends. *Maybe they hadn't been subjected to exactly the same traumas, but they were having similar experiences after. So I grouped them together based on their needs.* Godelieve draws circles with her finger on the white plastic tabletop as she describes how she organized the women into clusters. She's sitting in one of the sparse meeting rooms of the cinderblock house-turned-office for SEVOTA. *We had a gathering for women who'd been raped, for those who were widows . . . with this kind or that kind of challenge.*

The joint counseling sessions proved helpful, as women began to more actively process what had happened to them. But talking about trauma wasn't sufficient. *We needed to liberate all the negative energy that people were still holding, so we decided to introduce traditional dance, singing, some games and skits that would make people laugh. When you're dancing, you get some exercise, you feel more joyous, and so you let go naturally of some of the injuries to your heart, to your spirit. It happens automatically. And that's how these women, little by little, began to restart their lives.*

Godelieve's stories (and her calendar) reveal the sheer passion she brings to her work. She has counseled many different types of patients, but she shows a special fondness for women who survived rape, especially those who came to those early gatherings as young mothers nursing new babies intimately attached to their trauma.

With the women who were raped, there were, of course, children who'd been born because of those attacks. So we used similar techniques with the children alone and along with their mothers. There's one called therapeutic dyad, which strengthens relationships between children and their parents. Globally, the therapy is often used with adopted or foster children and their new families, to help build trust and bond. This was how women like Mama Diane and Vestine managed to let go of the negative energy, the intense feelings of anger, sadness, guilt. When you're plagued by these feelings, you feel like no one loves you. You can't find energy or do any work. You just exist.

Godelieve's name doesn't generate instant recognition, the way the names of some government officials and longtime activists do in Rwanda. Watching her bustle between meetings, overloaded backpack slung over one shoulder and reading glasses haphazardly perched on her head, it's clear she has no interest in playing the role of perfectly coiffed public figurine. She's ebullient, but also serious and down to earth. And she has a special talent partly based on her personality, partly on her profile, for bridging divides: She stays attuned to the distinct ordeals facing people in the countryside by still living in her hometown of Taba, though her work often takes her to Kigali. Also, she's a Hutu who was married to a Tutsi—her husband, Emmanuel, who was killed in 1996 for daring to testify at the UN tribunal. He was brave like his wife, and like the women with whom Godelieve works.

Eleven communities across the country now host SEVOTA's activities. *Sometimes we work in places where the women live, but typically we have them come from different regions to meet here in Kigali. The journey from the countryside is a positive experience. It gives them a sense of purpose and a chance to leave their home areas. And it gives them a new outlook when they go home.*

The memories of horrors they lived through may fade. But daily reminders crop up in empty places around the dinner table, the quiet in the yard where small voices once squealed in play, the extra weight of work in the fields.

All of our activities are focused on finding ways for people to live positively with their trauma. If all of your children were killed, you're not going to forget that you're alone. You have to find another way to live. If you were raped, that memory is with you for life. Mama Diane was raped when she was sixteen years old, and everyone saw. If she hadn't focused on living positively, she would have had to leave the region. In her village there were constant reminders of her attack, but as a teenager so emotionally fragile and without money or skills, how would she have fared elsewhere? *With the support of this counseling, she has started her own business. When there were village elections, she was chosen by the community. She even was a gacaca judge.*

Mama Diane found another way of living. You know, these techniques don't always work—that is for sure. But we try. We organized some short trips to beautiful places for the women who had been raped. Do you know Kibuye?

The serene lakeside town is a favorite spot for a weekend getaway, where steep hills bursting with the bright hues of blossoming trees seem to plunge into the deep green water.

Another time we took these mamas and their children to Peace Island, a precious spot near Kibuye. We want them to spend time in nature and have time to share with their children. Away from routines and the daily judgments of those who know their histories, the women start building positive, new memories. *The children form friendships, and the mothers continue to deepen their relationships with one another and with their children. It's very important for those children also not to feel alone. Many of them have grown up hearing these terrible stories about their mothers, and their relationships are very complex.*

In addition to her work with SEVOTA, Godelieve has for many years coached other counselors. Few in the country had psychological training, so the skills of those who did sorely needed to be shared. Eventually thousands of community social workers received three months of instruction through programs set up by women's groups or the government, often backed by international specialists. Then they went home to begin outreach. The needs were immense, and so were the hurdles, remembers **JANE A.**, head of the Rwandan Association of Trauma Counselors.

It's very expensive to train counselors, so we have worked with other people in the community who do basic counseling. When we started, the first group was women. We thought: Men wouldn't be able to listen. They aren't patient. They aren't concerned with other people's problems.

After some time we tried to start training male counselors, but about 85 or 95 percent of their clients are female. Women are more open or easily . . . I don't know . . . they seek counseling more than men. And we did some research. The major problem was our culture, which encourages women to cry and talk out their problems, whereas men are taught not to cry. Their tears should flow inside. "You are a man or a boy. Don't cry." But normally women are more free to talk of their problems.

When women talk about their inner feelings and emotions, they end up stronger. They come out with determination, with new plans and a new way of looking at things. Sometimes when you are full of sorrows and problems in your soul, you can't see properly. You can't think properly. You can't plan, you can't—you know? You're confused. Your heart is grieving.

We receive people from different backgrounds. We even have some soldiers. But they say, "No, a soldier can't behave like that. That's a weakness. How can a soldier go for counseling?"

The broader society had a major stake in this progression, beyond individual healing. Jane's organization trained counselors to work for gacaca, the National Unity and Reconciliation Commission, and various public and private institutions.

We work with an individual to come to terms with what has happened and to understand sorrow and other reactions that may prevent reconciliation. If somebody has feelings of hatred, guilt, or despair—those are some signs of trauma—it's not easy for them to reconcile with another person. They don't feel secure. They still have suspicion. They are still grieving. Some are guilty. In Rwanda, people killed each other, and you have to live with it. So it's normal that they fear each other. And they can't reconcile when they haven't talked together.

The government has pushed to place mental health nurses in centers across the country. They are trained specifically to support patients who are HIV/AIDS positive, in line with the nation's goal of not only reducing the spread of the disease but also caring well for those already infected. (They're outperforming the United States on that front: some 92 percent of Rwandans in need of treatment remain in care, compared to 51 percent in the United States.)[2] **ANITA**, a physician and former Ministry of Health official, points out how, as with many of the government's programs, the impact reaches beyond the intended purpose. *We have now close to five hundred centers, and each one will eventually have a mental health nurse. We want to reach people where they are.*

INYUMBA: Women decided to take up *productive* roles, not just the reproductive role we've played traditionally.

The Polyclinic of Hope started as a project of Rwandan Women's Network in 1997. Living in Switzerland, **MARY** had been active in the global antiapartheid movement. She moved back to Rwanda with a mind to put her social justice activism to work at home. *We realized that so many women had been raped, and so we wanted to create a space for them where they could freely open up, feeling supported as they register for assistance. That led to so many other programs in the space. Sometimes our centers are like a shelter. Women come and stay when they're in crisis.*

In 2002, Mary spoke about the pressing needs she and her team aimed to address.

We use the word "hope" in our name, because this new confidence is a healing process. When we talk about "polyclinic," we're thinking holistically: physical health, but also trauma counseling, economic empowerment, human rights, the inheritance law. We offer legal aid, through which we assist women to come forward and speak out about how their rights are violated and assist them through the court process. But we also integrate women prisoners once out of jail. This helps them gain back their lives in their communities.

We're putting all these together in a puzzle. Mary's goal is for the clients to have a sense of ownership over the polyclinic, shaping it, but also letting it shape them into a cohesive force for change. *We make referrals when necessary to hospitals and legal services. Our counselors also accompany them when they need services elsewhere. But the women always return to these safe spaces we've created, like a home base.*

The Polyclinic of Hope now has locations in twenty-four of the country's thirty districts, and Mary is eager to expand further. A large health center near the capital is outfitted to handle patients with more serious medical issues, especially those related to gender-based violence. Their staff members also regularly venture farther into areas where they're based to provide trainings and encourage women to create safe spaces in their own homes where other women can come for information, comfort, or refuge. At the end of the day, it's about solidarity and connection to each other. Mary is unabashed in her pride for the group's women-helping-women approach.

With her candid delivery of her opinions and at times booming voice, it's no wonder Mary is on the cutting edge of current debates about how to move beyond women-friendly policies to protective actions. After years of organizing among national leaders and local beneficiaries, activists like Mary are focused on how to make the gender-based violence legislation, for example, meaningful in practice.

So what we've been doing is mapping who are positive men, bring them on board in our spaces and train them to be community mobilizers. Our women from our spaces are out in the communities speaking about all these issues, the ways laws are changing and maybe creating new relations between men and women. We've seen that the inheritance law especially has attracted the men. They are keen to understand the impact the law has and how it affects them as men and heads of their families. The women meet these men, and really we're very selective about who we invite to join us—we want to be sure they won't bring in their manly attitudes. But we think they have a big role to play with the gender-based violence work. We tell them, "This is also your business. It can't be women's business alone." Then we let them take the lead in training people in that message.

Other issues, like abortion and birth control, are newer frontiers.

Mary is a vocal supporter of a burgeoning pro-choice contingent of activists. *What we're missing is a focused, smart awareness about abortion and how we come to this. It starts with our hesitancy to talk about sexuality. Before we even get to the discussion of choice, we have to fix this stigma towards women's health that leaves young people uninformed. This new abortion law is being much talked about now, and activists are asking, "Is the current law really working for women?" We're pushing to give freedom to abort when they*

Activist Mary Balikungeri.

feel they need to. But this is a very Christian country, and they're saying, "Why are we promoting abortion when we should be promoting morality?" The fact is that people should be making choices about their health before they even get to the question of abortion. But it will take us ages because of this taboo. So let's start with accepting we must talk openly about sex and the right to make healthy, informed choices.

The Polyclinic of Hope has also started hosting sessions in more private settings, for women to meet with nurses and discuss family planning, in its many dimensions. For instance, women start new birth control regimes and then discuss how it's working. Mary says these exchanges are insightful for her and her team as well, as they strategize about how best to reach out to the women they aim to support. *We're learning a lot about empowerment of women and how they make decisions about their sexual rights, making sure that a woman determines when she has a baby, that the family has access to contraceptives. It's really opening up a new conversation, with lots of learning for women. It's amazing to hear what they say about sexuality, being forced in bed when you're not even willing. To some women, this is normal, to others, no! So it's really showing how important it is to be sure women across the country take leadership with rights issues.*

Finally! says **ODETTE**. When she finished her tenure as the head of the Ministry of Social Affairs and took a seat in the Senate in 2003, she came with a mission: to spearhead the country's first-ever bill on health and reproductive rights. She teamed up with fellow physician and former minister of health Ezechiel Rwabuhihi, who had also just joined the Parliament. They surveyed Rwandans' views on increasing their families. Their team spoke to older students at secondary schools in every district and met with community and religious leaders, soldiers, police, and women's associations. *We would first make a presentation on the health status of Rwanda, the poverty situation, and what can be done. Then we would ask, "How many children do you think one should have?"*

Their presentations described how other countries have developed not only by building industries, but also by choosing to have fewer children. They highlighted the time a family spends devoted to raising many kids, compared to developing their farm or pursuing a career outside the home.

If a woman gives birth to ten children, that's at least twenty years of not

Taking charge of their own health means women planning at what age to have children.

working full time and mainly taking care of the children. Especially consider that people were only living until their late forties! So it's very easy to explain what is poverty and what creates poverty.

We asked the students what they thought. On average, it was two children they wanted. And women wanted no more than four children. And men wanted five. So we put in the average: three. It was a recommendation.

We wanted to put it in the bill. But it was very difficult to do, because you cannot punish someone who has four children, or it gives the impression that the child is unwanted. So instead the bill was proposing incentives: If you have only three children, after ten years of marriage, you will be given free health insurance. Taxes will be waived at this rate. We also put in some articles on

Mother and child fountain, a Kigali landmark, features as a backdrop for many a photo shoot, especially wedding parties on Saturday afternoons.

abortion, because I thought it should be a right for women, especially in the case of rape. Finally, we wanted to oblige the government to make available birth control options, centers for reproductive health, youth counselors. . . . It was a very nice bill.

The draft received immediate pushback. *First of all, the Americans were against it.* Odette says that a delegation from the U.S. embassy came to her office to urge her to not even introduce the bill. Rules under President George W. Bush restricted recipients of U.S. foreign aid from receiving funding if they provide abortion counseling or advocate for reversal of laws banning abortion.

By the time Odette left Parliament in 2008 to join the East African parliament, the lower chamber had approved the legislation. *But when* it reached the Senate, they said, "No, this is mostly a policy," and they took it back to the lower chamber. I was not in the Senate then, and I don't think there was somebody to lobby for it anymore. The lower chamber redid it, and it was taken back to the Senate. In 2009 the Senate rejected the bill once and for all.

Many parliamentarians wanted it. I can't say that it collapsed just because the Americans didn't want it. Yes, we can be influenced by foreign opinions, but I think in the end, even the government didn't like the bill. They said that they should put those details into a policy and a mechanism to sensitize people, instead of putting in place a law.

Odette, who soldiered on to get her medical degree in the 1980s and disproved her father's claim that she would never become a member of the president's cabinet, is used to defying expectations. Her composed, affable demeanor belies her dogged determination and crusader bent. For women's health rights, Odette may have been too far ahead of her time.

As a woman, as a medical doctor, I know what it is to be pregnant. I know how difficult it is, and how women suffer when they have more than four pregnancies. In medicine, we call all pregnancies above the fifth high risk. Your body, your uterus, everything is tired. And some women continue, continue.

It's unhealthy for women and also for children. When you have so many children, how can you care for them? And I always wished to see people develop, and to have developed people around me. Not beggars. And so I would wish that in our country people develop. But you can't with this situation—it's not possible. I'm very passionate about this. I want women to be free.

Odette says that even when she was a little girl she wanted to have three children. She always knew her career would be central, though even she was surprised to find herself holding such prominent political posts. Balancing family and work was difficult enough with two sons, a daughter, and a husband who was similarly devoted to his medical practice. With her children grown, Odette now shuttles between home in Kigali and capital cities in the region to fulfill her duties as a member of the East African parliament. She's content in this new phase of her life.

Now all my children are gone, and I am only with my husband at home. And I feel well! That's because I had only three. If I had ten, I think I would *still have some children at home. I have some colleagues, even older than me, who still have babies! And I find that it's inappropriate. It's bad for those babies. They'll never see their parents when they are old. When they marry, their parents may not be there anymore. So I think that as humans, we have to regulate our beings, to make sure that our lives are better than they used to be. We're no longer in the jungle!* Odette laughs out loud at her joke.

PATRICIA: Ah, there are so many priorities, there are so many priorities.

Even years before the genocide, Rwandans on the whole were dying younger than almost any other nationality in the world. In 1990, the life expectancy was thirty-three years. It fell to twenty-eight by 1994.

But twenty years later, people can expect to live at least into their early sixties, longer than in any other country in the region. Part of that impressive rise can be attributed to the peace. It also has a lot to do with the focus on basic well-being and the strategy of bringing care to the far-flung valleys and homesteads where people live.

In 2000, the government created its Vision 2020, which mapped out a host of development goals and strategies for meeting them. National policies have since built upon that ambitious plan, and in many of them, people's physical condition is central. Most citizens live outside of cities, so ramping up services has meant fanning out through a huge network of clinics with newly skilled community health workers. *All this hinges on one principle*, explains **ANITA**, the medical doctor now heading clinical services at Rwanda University Teaching Hospitals. *How do we make sure that we offer services that are good quality, timely, and closest to the people?*

Many centers have been built, but, most importantly, many have increased in size. Those that existed were like a one-room, very basic thing. It was called a health center, but it was not offering services defined to be a health center. Even before 1994 we had some of these, but if you look at what they were offering, it was not anywhere close to what one would say are quality services.

Anita credits President Kagame for setting the tone. *Strongly behind this work is people-centered leadership that says, "All are equal." I must say that we're learning from a very tragic history that separated the people. Let's face it: where we ended up in '94 was because the leaders were teaching that some are favored, some are not. So we want our little ones to grow up knowing that we're all equal. We should not create a moment where some feel superior or inferior to others.*

Currently leading that charge in the health sector is Minister Agnes Binagwaho, a pediatrician who made a name for herself through various high-level posts focused on HIV/AIDS prevention and treatment. She served as the technical lead (permanent secretary) in the Ministry of Health starting in 2008, a position she held until 2011 when she was appointed minister. Friends say she is principled and driven, an excellent manager who gives clear guidance and attracts talent.

ANITA has worked alongside Minister Binagwaho for many years. *She stands her ground. If she thinks something is best for the people, then it doesn't matter what you think—not in a negative sense but in a very positive sense for the sake of the people. The health sector has many partners. When you have many people coming in to work with you, if you are not strong and focused on where you want to go, you can easily be disoriented. But she has always helped this sector stay focused. "What is our national plan?" she always says. "Where do we want to get to? If you are coming in to work with us, please stick to our plan."*

Minister Binagwaho seems personally ruffled by the suggestion that her being a woman has been a factor in her professional success, as if that would take away from her star-studded reputation. Similarly, she is loath to attribute to women traits that make them more helpful as health care professionals.

ANITA concurs that pinpointing gender as the deciding factor is fraught. *Is it because they are women, or is it because they are holding particular positions? That is always hard to tease out.*

But the reality is that women have played an outsized role in developing these plans to improve citizens' physical condition, to stunning effect. *An army of community health care workers,* as Anita calls them, has swelled to 45,000, all volunteer. Two-thirds of them are women. Each village chooses between three and five neighbors to receive training from the Ministry of Health. *They are elected because people trust them. The*

Doctor Anita Asiimwe.

community health workers are people with integrity, who the community feels they can be comfortable with to advise them. Among their many duties, they learn how to give immunizations, teach their neighbors how to use bed nets to ward off malaria, coach new mothers to breast-feed, and monitor cases of illness so they can refer patients to clinics.

If I look just five years back, for example. . . . Or even worse, if I go ten years back, malaria was claiming most of our children. That's because prevention was not as good as it is today. Now mosquito nets are available. People know to sleep under them every night, and they understand the need not to have stagnant water around their homestead. They also have learned to seek treatment with the first signs of the disease. The result? Death from malaria has dropped nearly 90 percent.

Being female doesn't necessarily predict how effective a representative of the community is in teaching about malaria transmission and treatment. But, as in politics, those who elected her may have more trust in her advice because she's in a caretaking position, as their mothers were.

For other programs, Anita highlights an advantage.

One area where I think being a woman has contributed is in fighting malnutrition. A lot of work has been done there, but it's a complex area. The patience that comes hand in hand with being a woman can help you to continue working on it, because it's not an area where it's easy to see immediate results. If today a child is stunted, and they are already two years old, there's no way you're going to reverse that. You have to come to terms with it. "I can help this child carry on, but it's already happened. I can help all the others who are not yet two."

Still, malnutrition among children remains high. The rate is declining, but there's much to be done. As Anita notes, it's a complicated public health issue because malnutrition may be about scarcity of food, but more often it's a lack of adequate information about nutritious food. *That's obviously to the detriment of the nutrition of our people, who are unfortunately not yet knowledgeable enough.* Doctors and nurses can advise a mother whose child is already suffering from stunted growth, but the best hope lies with the community-based workers to head off the problem.

We have very many examples of parents who have chickens, not like a poultry farm, but a few chickens. They lay eggs, but then the family sells off the eggs to buy the baby a Fanta [soda] because they think . . . I'd like to say, Coke has done a great job of advertising, and everyone thinks that Fanta is the best thing you should drink—even in the deepest part of our villages.

So a poor lady will sell off her eggs to buy a Fanta, thinking she's doing something good for her baby. I'm talking about people who are not rich, but who still have access to basic food. When these mothers sit and talk about it with their community health worker, they help each other—learn how to cook nutritious food, what to give their children, or how to take care of a pregnant lady.

After finishing her nearly four-year stint at the Ministry of Health, Anita took up her post at the teaching hospital in Kigali. She's passionate about making policy and educating future health care providers, seeing both as contributions with the potential to have far-reaching results, beyond the individual patients she used to see when she practiced. But her exposure to the real-life conundrums facing families clearly influences her current role, even as she sits behind her orderly desk on campus, with students rushing by. As she recounts numerous stories of former patients and conditions in rural clinics she has visited, her ambivalence about the differences women bring to their leadership in her sector becomes more nuanced. Finally she says: *I know I'm biased because I am a woman. But I tend to think—I tell this to my husband and he'll just laugh me off—there are details I pick up that he doesn't pick up when we look at people. Like when they tell me that a child in village X has died, I have a feeling that I get much more interested in why and how could we have avoided it. Not that a man in my shoes wouldn't do the same thing, but I always have a feeling that the instincts of my being a mother—and now here I am emphasizing how I'm not only a woman but a mother!—always puts me in a state of, "That can be my child. That can be my sister." It's not that guys don't take care of children, but the way we do it is quite different. We are kind of more focused on the person than just what they'll eat, what they'll wear, which school they'll go to. Those details come in, but there is something bigger too.*

And of course sometimes as women, many times, we have flaws. We get too emotional sometimes, and we stay focused on a small thing and use much more energy, yet we should leave it to another group of people and concentrate on something much bigger. I think that's how at some point—and again, I don't think this is true of all ladies and all men—but I guess somewhere the men help us, kind of wake us up: "Hey, it's important to concentrate on that one baby, but you want to move faster. There's more to do." If I use myself as an example, there's a good chance that when I go visit a clinic, I'll see this one child on a bed who is not well, and that stays in my head. I pick up my phone and I call: "I left this child on this date. How is he doing?"

Of course I haven't talked to my colleagues and asked how often they do that. Maybe among my colleagues there are ladies who don't or men who do, but I feel that I do it because of the mother in me. So I think there is something to it. I can't measure it, and I can be biased, but I know that in me, I do certain things because I am a mother and a woman. I have accompanied a sister of mine who I love dearly through labor. I have stood with women while their husbands were standing outside—not because their husbands don't love them, but because society hasn't prepared them to be involved in that way.

•   •   •

Deeply set hurdles remain, but the concerted focus on physical well-being has generated spectacular results, for which Rwanda deserves and has received hard-won accolades. True to the ideal of avoiding complacency even when life is looking up, **ANITA** cites these impressive milestones, even as she explains what she sees as one of the biggest challenges.

We've seen mortality rates going down; we've seen under-five mortality rates going down; we've seen malaria no longer be the number one killer; we've brought down the rates of death from HIV by more than 80 percent. . . . But all these successes are fragile. We must make sure we maintain them.

Her optimism lies in the collective contributions that she feels the progress now epitomizes. *One point I'd really underline and put in bold is that the achievements we're seeing in health came because of the many other ways our country is developing.* The availability of clean water, the electrification of places that never before had power—that gives a big boost to the services that rural health centers can provide. *Just imagine if we were not safe enough, if those responsible for security weren't doing what they're doing. Do you think people would elect volunteers to come into their homes to take care of them? No. A neighbor would be fearing the other. I can go on and on. . . .*

So we cannot relax. Not even a little bit. People have to understand that. If I used a mosquito net the last two years, and in my house there was no case of malaria, that's the reason I must continue to use it. Just a little moving away

A carefree childhood rests on great care from adults.

can easily shoot malaria figures up high again. At the end of the day, the bottom line is behavior change.

Shoring up and continuing the gains depends on policy makers like Odette to understand the needs of citizens, and on activists like Godelieve and Mary to engage with those at the heart of these public health puzzles.

ANITA has it right. All of the bustling and organizing will be for naught if Rwandans don't see the value. *Most of these health initiatives hinge on the will of citizens, and we know this is something that takes long. So we have to make sure we don't get tired, and we carry on, and carry on, and carry on. The change—like the mosquito nets—has to have a positive impact so people feel this is the right thing to do. They don't have to wait for someone to say so. It becomes automatic in the way they live.*

31 LITTLE ONES

> KIRABO: We've come to a point where we need to justify our presence in leadership by creating change for the especially vulnerable: the woman and the child. That means projects targeted toward them. That is the main message that will change the world.

Children anywhere in the world require special attention from their community—and influential adults to advocate on their behalf—to make sure they receive proper nutrition and clean water, don't lose their lives to childhood illness, have a safe place to live, and go to school. In Rwanda, where poverty already complicated access to these necessities, the genocide and war leading up to it dramatically intensified the adversity children faced. Schoolchildren had been killed in their classrooms. They survived because of pure chance or their own ingenuity: taking cover under dead bodies or escaping into hiding places like latrines. Other children had seen their father or brother wield a machete, or had themselves been forced to kill.

Just a year after the genocide, a team from UNICEF, the UN agency focused on children, interviewed more than 3,000 Rwandans between the ages of eight and nineteen. Some 80 percent had experienced a family death during the genocide and 70 percent witnessed a killing or an injury. Their fear of being killed was acute: 61 percent had been threatened with death, and 90 percent believed they would die during the slaughter.

UNICEF estimated that 90,000 children were orphaned when their parents died in massacres, and more than 300,000 were separated from their families in the bedlam and subsequent imprisonment. AIDS has orphaned many more since the genocide. Traditional social networks that

Chores of daily life, like collecting water from the village tap, often fall to children while parents are farming.

would typically have helped absorb abandoned children were undone by the violence, compounded by new depths of poverty and the HIV/AIDS epidemic.[1]

While several international organizations reunited children with their families and supported orphanages, the Ministry of Gender took the lead in trying to find more permanent homes, with distant relatives or in adoptive families. **FATUMA** saw the scope of the challenge when she worked in the town of Byumba even before the genocide ended. *There were so many children just living on the street. They had literally nowhere to go.*

Fatuma says that as the Ministry of Gender began its work, encourag-

With 42 percent of the population under age fifteen, children are some of the most vulnerable.

ing adoption and fostering was an immediate responsibility. *In our tradition, every child has a right to have a family and to be treated with dignity. These were driving forces as the ministry took a leading role in sensitization to adopt children. It worked. But it also didn't just stop there. There was also monitoring of the fostering system, to ensure that the new families were caring well for the children, taking them to school, not forcing them to work.*

We were being inspired mainly by our family values, our culture. But we also were a nation that wanted to care for its children as the future of this country. Orphanages weren't the solution.

We worked on this issue through women's empowerment initiatives, like one called Shelter for Women. It became a popular program, especially for widows, returnees. If a woman has a home, a child will have a home. Plus,

The government encourages adoption and fostering, with no child growing up without family. Little ones rest together on woven mats at a Kigali orphanage.

most of the people adopting children were women; a very poor woman, maybe with several children of her own, would take in three more.

Having so many children without families took its toll. Many—especially those poorest or severely traumatized—lived on the streets. Everyone knew someone with a young relative, neighbor, or even stranger under her wing. Sometimes these blended families worked smoothly; other times, the chaos was so crushing that relationships shattered.

The country faced a new flood of orphans and imperiled children in the late 1990s. **INYUMBA** was heading the Ministry of Gender. *The influx was predominantly Hutu children coming back from Congo. So we'd just mix them in with the Tutsi in our orphanage centers. We women said we have to look at the basic need of the child. Most of them didn't even know a parent. They didn't know whether they were Hutu or Tutsi. This was a perfect opportunity for assimilation.*

ANNE MARIE M., charged with working on orphan programs at the Ministry of Gender, was acutely aware of the distress at her doorstep. As a mother of four, her job assignment quickly became personal.

I was working to try and get street children into centers where they could receive care. Sometimes the mamas who took in children would have problems with the orphans they adopted. So I—or our family, really—had the idea to adopt. We thought we could be a good family for children who needed a home. And we thought we could be an example for other families.

Since her military husband defected from the rebel group in Congo and walked with her back to Rwanda, their family's lot has shifted for the better. Anne Marie tells her stories very deliberately, as if reminding herself that the twists that reunited them and enabled her family to grow cannot be taken for granted.

There was a call to Christian families from our church, through the Radio Adventist. They said that there was a center that was hosting twenty-eight children during their school break, because they didn't have families to return to when they weren't at boarding school. We wanted to help, and we put together donations like clothes, and even some money. Then we decided we wanted to follow one child from there. Even if we didn't adopt, I thought I could be like a godmother.

Piece of papers were piled up, like this. Anne Marie builds an imaginary stack with her hands. *On the papers were children's names,* she says slowly, savoring the memory of that momentous day. *We chose a piece of paper, and on it was written the name Ntabanganyimana Noël—our son. At the time we didn't know him. We had never met, but that's how we came to adopt him.*

Noël, who was eighteen at the time, didn't come and live with them right away, because he had responsibilities at the center as the leader of a group of children. But he participated in family events, and Anne Marie and her husband supported him financially. They've been planning for his future too—for graduate school, for a wedding someday—a detail important to say, since it was a way of overcoming differences that could divide their family.

One year later, while Noël was home from boarding school for the holidays, he found out that his two younger sisters who had been living with a foster family had been sent away. He came to us, very distressed. We told him, "Bring the girls here." So his sisters started living here with us. Soon, Noël started university and began living close to campus. His two sisters stayed with us, and we adopted them too.

The parents of Noël, Yvonne, and Katherine died during the genocide. In the years after, the trio had mostly lived apart, spending much of the year at boarding school, paid for by the national survivors' fund, and with various foster families. At last, they were settled and together.

Asked about how the children have coped with and have come to understand their history from a time when they were all very young, Anne Marie says her approach has always been to talk honestly. *At first when the children came to this new family they didn't feel free (the Rwandan phrase for "at ease"). But we've had many, many family discussions, to help them reclaim their lives. We've gone to counseling. The younger ones settled in more easily, but all three children have slowly become like our other children. They do well in school. They're healthy and content.*

When we first started talking about wanting another child, we didn't have our youngest son yet, so we thought, we could have a fifth child. Rather than giving birth, we thought we could adopt so that we could provide for a child that was already in need, someone who could really use the support of a family. Then, of course, we had this little one too! She gestures toward her boisterous son Dan, who frequently peeks around the side of the couch to listen to his mother's stories, or turns up the television so that *Tom and Jerry* is playing at top volume to get her attention.

Anne Marie wrote a thick report for the Ministry of Gender about the country's orphan challenge. It's now tucked on the bookshelf next to her other magnum opus, a master's thesis on the role of women in helping to disarm or apprehend Rwandan rebel fighters in Congo. *I look for ways to improve the situation our community is dealing with. Working on things that I'm living.*

SPECIOSE: When one of my children is sick, I am suffering too.
So when we are fighting for women's rights, we are fighting also
indirectly for children's rights. When we are fighting for equality,
it is not for us, but we are doing it for that little girl.

In Parliament, female members dedicated their attention to children immediately upon taking office. Their advocacy for the inheritance law highlighted in particular the need for legal reform so that daughters could inherit property from fathers.

Two years later, in 2001, women MPs helped ensure a bill focused on children's rights, articulating first-time protections for youngest citizens. Beyond murder, it included rape, the use of children for "dehumanizing acts" and prostitution, exploitation, neglect and abandonment, and forced or early marriage, and it set more severe penalties if someone in a position of power over the child perpetrates the abuse.[1] The bill also notes that a child under eighteen cannot give consent and therefore establishes that sexual relations with a minor inherently constitutes statutory rape. The children's rights law represented a victory for the government and civil society as part of a joint campaign against sexual violence, a clear priority amid debilitating traumas faced by young and old as a legacy of the genocide.

The recognition of child rape was a major step forward, at a time when the country didn't yet have a legal definition of adult rape. The children's rights law protected both boys and girls, progress lauded domestically and internationally. The law's turnaround time was also momentous: months, not years, from drafting to passage, due to close cooperation es-

Eager to learn, children attend primary school in higher proportions than anywhere else in Africa.

pecially between women leaders in the executive branch, the legislature, and civil society.

It wasn't difficult to get consensus. Children's rights has been the common thread throughout **ZAINA**'s career as a social worker, stretching back to 1976 when she returned from college in Belgium to start her first job, in the Habyarimana government. *I think we are very sensitive to rights because we had our rights violated in the most extreme ways. Children especially can be victims of abuse—that is, sadly, universal. They're meant to be protected, not to protect themselves.*

The children and women's legal aid group Zaina founded in 1991, called Haguruka (Stand up for your rights), continues to be one of the preeminent voices in civil society. *I designed it with UNICEF in my head, so that when* UNICEF *leaves there will always be some group fighting for women's and children's rights—and it will be Rwandan.*

Bolstered by the new laws on inheritance and children's rights, Haguruka and other groups (like the National Commission for Children Zaina would later head) focused on a basic right: birth certificates. Zaina explains why the deceptively straightforward concept had proved complicated. *Women who aren't married are often ashamed to go and register alone, because they may be looked at like they're prostitutes. So we have to raise awareness that a child can be brought up by a woman alone, that it's her right to register her own child, and that she should do it—it's in the interest of the child, and so on. It doesn't prohibit you from continuing to pursue the father who does not recognize the child.*

The idea traditionally was that the child belongs to the husband. You— you're just giving birth. Your husband's identity card, not yours, included your children. So if you're a single mother, you feel ashamed, because people may think that you aren't a serious woman. The mother would have to register the child under her own father—so the child's grandfather. There was this impression then that these children shouldn't be seen as equal to other children, because they weren't recognized by their mother's family or their father's.

The issue of girls' education was especially on **ODETTE**'s mind in 2004, when, as a senator, she laid out a conundrum. For poor families, having girls at home was a great help. *How do we oblige parents to put children in school? I tried to persuade those introducing laws to make education compulsory. That would affect girls disproportionately.*

In 2009, the government finally mandated basic education for all young Rwandans, girls as well as boys. It's become cheaper to attend school, though students say related expenses, like uniforms, books, and even direct contributions to teachers, are still too expensive for some families and prompt students to temporarily drop out while they save up money. But the impact of the focus on education is vast, spurring the construction of more schools and mentorship of thousands of teachers. UNICEF reports that Rwanda now has the highest primary school enrollment in Africa at 96 percent. In fact, girls now attend school in slightly higher proportion than boys.[2]

But more than a decade before this sweeping government policy, a small group of women saw the value of giving female students a boost,

Ambassador Zaina Nyiramatama.

a move that challenged the long-standing cultural premise that sending daughters to school was much less valuable than educating sons.

At first people would often say, "Well, you know, girls normally stay at home. So this is a bit complicated. Girls don't do math!" **THERESE** was a refugee who grew up and went to school in eastern Congo but moved to Kinshasa to study molecular biology. She moved back to Rwanda after the genocide and was soon tapped to direct the newly created Kigali Health Institute. Therese and a dozen other female university graduates decided to start a Rwanda chapter of the Forum for African Women Educationalists (FAWE).

It was part of the effort to ensure that the country would not replicate previous policies of discrimination. Even the children of parents who had committed atrocities. . . . We wanted to be certain that those girls would also become the [educated] *elites of this country.* The FAWE women trained young women and men from rural areas to go back to their communities and urge parents to let their children be educated.

When FAWE opened a school in 1999, they chose to focus on sciences. *We wanted to prove that girls can study technical fields, whether biology or economics or physics, and not only the social studies.*

It was compelling to work with prominent women, who could stand as an example of the value of educating girls. My colleagues and I could say, "You see, I went to school, and now I have this important position." Seeing us in office sends the message, "You must give opportunities to your daughter as well, because one day she could become a minister, a director—just like her brothers." Today, Therese is a senator.

Currently FAWE has three campuses and its graduates are engineers, doctors, and students pursuing advanced degrees abroad. It's part of a growing, impressive corps of all-girls schools cultivating inquisitive young minds and promoting holistic education in the country.

Maranyundo Girls School was the dream—and too early, the legacy—of Aloisea Inyumba. Buildings of warm red brick, with gentle archways and wide windows, encircle a central gathering space dotted with saplings. Pathways of loose white stones accentuate the sound of steps as students cross the schoolyard from the library to the science lab to map-adorned classrooms. Opened in 2008 with a convocation by First Lady Jeannette Kagame, the school now welcomes 265 early teens from across

Senator Therese Bishagara.

the country. True to Inyumba's vision of offering an outstanding education to talented students from disadvantaged backgrounds, half of the students come to Maranyundo from the local community on scholarship.

The town of Nyamata, now a thirty-minute drive from Kigali, was particularly brutalized in 1994. Poor soil and malaria-carrying mosquitoes made it an undesirable place to live, so previous governments had seen the region as ideal for the resettlement and banishment of Tutsi. The region therefore became a prime target during the genocide. Its parish, and now the rows of mass graves behind it, freeze in time the details of one of the largest mass murders: ten thousand people killed on the church grounds, most of whom had sealed themselves inside the building in hopes of miraculous salvation. Their rumpled felt hats, calico dresses, and treasured rosaries now lie in dusty mounds. Today, sunlight sprinkles the scene through holes punched in the metal roof by shrapnel from the army's grenades, when soldiers and militia chipped away at the once-sacred, then futile, fortress.

That history isn't lost on the adults involved in the school's creation; Nyamata's mayor said in his remarks at the dedication ceremony that while issuing the land title his team learned that the new school was built on the grounds of what had been a Tutsi concentration camp in the 1970s. But it's a past blessedly far away from the campus scene today, where eleven-year-olds adorn bunks with carefully clipped magazine photos or a special blanket from home, in dormitories tidy enough but strewn with teenage-girl paraphernalia. Or fourteen-year-olds head off to the dining hall in crisp white and blue uniforms, showing off their polished Mary Janes or All-Star sneakers.

Headmistress **SISTER JUVENAL** is from the Catholic order Benebikira, whose nuns teach and run the middle school. She says that the selection process has a separate track aimed at recruiting students from families who wouldn't be able to afford to pay private school fees. Nearly 50 percent of girls come to Maranyundo on some kind of financial aid.

At the time the Maranyundo project got under way, Aloisea was governor of Kigali-Ngali Province. Maybe she was affected by seeing how girls here couldn't get to school.

What I remember so much is that she was very engaged in fighting poverty and supporting poor people, especially women in rural areas. She wanted them to be economically independent so that they wouldn't have to wait for things from men. She wanted to show them that they're capable to do everything. And that's what she did as gender minister, as governor, as senator—she always worked for women to become confident.

Benebikira nuns were Inyumba's obvious partner when it came to educating girls. They'd been in the field of education longer than anyone else in Rwanda. Sister Juvenal's own passion for teaching goes back to her girlhood and the awe she felt as she watched the instructors she deemed all-knowing lead a class. *I always knew I wanted to be a teacher too.* The Benebikira order was founded with education as its first mission. Sister Juvenal recounts the history in her measured tempo, her eyes engaging through pronounced spectacles. It's a teaching moment. She pins the link to the early 1900s with missionaries from Germany.

When the White Fathers arrived in Rwanda they began to teach catechisms, reading, writing, and other skills for developing the people. Since they were men, it was difficult at that time to approach women, so they came with White Sisters too, who were missionaries from Europe. But they found that they had difficulties with the language. When they were teaching people, they saw that some women were interested and open to learning more and sharing what they learned. So the founder created a native order, a Rwandan order, that could teach women and girls.

This was no simple task, given the cultural norms and male privilege that they were up against. *At that time, women worked alone and men worked alone. They weren't used to working together.*

The order began to recruit some girls to become sisters in 1913, and the first Rwandan nuns took their vows in 1919. *They began to teach around the country, first, in community places, such as a parish. But then they began schools.* The Benebikira sisters now run fifteen schools in Rwanda, some of which teach girls and boys side by side. Other Rwandan Catholic orders also specialize in teaching, but Benebikira was the first.

Maranyundo is well known because of our national exam scores. When you have a good record, parents talk among themselves. People hear about it, and they want their children to come. The school's success mirrors a countrywide trend. The Ministry of Education reports that girls complete high school at rates slightly higher than boys, and the percentage of women at universities is steadily on the rise.

Sister Juvenal.

The town of Nyamata also holds a lesson, Sister Juvenal points out. As in many farming communities, people there weren't very well educated, so sending girls to school wasn't prioritized. *The few schools that were there mostly served boys, and girls often stayed home to work.* Sister Juvenal's theory about the impact of a mission like Maranyundo's is a common refrain. It speaks to the drive that has inspired many in the global women's movement to turn to girls' education, as they look at the sustainability of their work.

The girls will be the mothers. If we make sure they're educated, they will make sure their children are well taught. Educated girls will use those skills for the whole family, for the whole country . . . the whole world—why not?

PART V
Building the Road
They're Walking

As headmistress of the prestigious Maranyundo middle school, **SISTER JUVENAL** is mother of the brood for her impressionable boarders. *For Rwandan culture, seeing women leaders is new, but the idea is not new. In our language we say, "The woman is the heart of the family." So if she is the heart, it is she who leads the whole body.*

In traditional life, women were responsible for all things in their families. Not going out and giving orders, giving speeches, but all organization in the family was made by women. And there is another expression in our language that says, "If you have a good wife, you will have a good family." So if all things are led by the woman, why not the district? Why not the province?

She pauses for emphasis but also to let out a little chuckle; the newness of the trend still amuses. *Why not the country?*

Sister Juvenal's look is unwavering, even if softened by the gentle crinkles around her eyes. She's not kidding.

· · ·

A common story line in the country about the origin of women's subjugation pinpoints the Belgian colonial period, with its policies favoring boys' education and limiting women's rights. While this narrative may not entirely reflect the complexity of gender dynamics throughout history, the framing of today's female-focused policies as a return to a bygone precolonial era of gender harmony has proved powerful.

When charting new ground, trailblazers encounter a range of characters: Good neighbors who point them in the right direction and maybe even offer to give them a lift. Or people who misunderstand their mission and unintentionally relay the wrong information. Or others still, who, motivated by competition or spite, purposefully mislead. Ultimately, it comes down to instinct, street smarts, and wisdom to stay the course.

Fortunately for a Rwandan woman on the cutting edge of her society's evolution, she's had plenty of company—countrywomen also energized by the progress of the past and the possibilities ahead. As the title of part V recognizes, they didn't have the luxury of mapping out plans for the rebuilding before getting to work.

Previous parts of this book have emphasized the merging of factors that have enabled advances. Without question, Rwandan women have ample agency in this still-unfolding story, but they're also up against influences upon which they have limited say: broader political dynamics, international interest, time. The meaning of those first two factors is self-explanatory. About the third, I'll say this: just twenty years. The time an infant daughter grows into a free-thinking adult, often bearing her own children. But in the midst of these twenty years, we usually notice changes only gradually. It isn't until looking back across the full two decades that we take in the stunning scope of what has transpired.

Rwandans often point out the positive changes first. While gains may be uneven (and some would contend, ill-gotten), it's hard to argue that the country's lot hasn't improved when comparing circumstances today to the proverbial "before"—before the genocide. Even the absence of mass violence approaches the miraculous.

How lasting are the advances women have ushered in and the unprecedented influence they've secured for themselves and their protégés? What's left to be done? They hold a large majority in Parliament and weighty seats in the president's cabinet, but in other avenues—such as business and local leadership—they're still limited in number and audibility. Furthermore, the Rwanda experience with female leadership inevitably raises the question: Yes, but what difference does it make?

INYUMBA: If you look in my province, I am the governor. My deputy is a woman, and the head of gacaca is a woman. So at meetings I tell the men, "You're in safe hands!"

It's no minor detail to see a woman as mayor presiding over a city council meeting, or a businesswoman featured in the newspaper for her new big idea, or more female than male faces among MPs being sworn in. To those of us watching this trend from the outside, it's remarkable. To Rwandans, it's the new norm. Yet this norm is an almost unbelievable feat, as any development specialist will attest.

As one of the constitution drafters, **MARIE THERESE** profoundly appreciates the achievement of creating laws to protect women, but she's also candid about the potential gap between those regulations and real life. *It's one thing to have those rights, but you have to know your rights and demand them. That's the role of the women in Parliament and civil society.*

My target is to always have women striving to do their best work. We have to, or people will say that the only reason you're in that position is because you're a woman. You have to prove you're able, as able as a man.

You're there because of your value, because you deserve it! It's not a gift. Of course, some people will still say that. Every day is a continuous fight—but it's a good one.

The supportive political climate has meant that Rwandan women typically don't face the blatant hostility that female torchbearers endure in many other settings across the world. But even in Rwanda, genuine openness hasn't set in immediately, in large part because it's in stark contrast to the limits imposed on women for generations that are now ingrained.

Peace, positive leadership, and women's public participation are a reality for a new generation.

It comes down to women having confidence in themselves. **JANE U.** witnessed this dynamic time and again in her interviews with rural women who had created cooperatives to share risks and revenues as they sold baskets, jewelry, and tailored clothes. She wanted to understand why the members had focused their women-only venture on jewelry making rather than more directly lucrative options, like farming. *In a patriarchal society—okay, in the world over—this lack of self-confidence is so deep rooted. You may feel like you can't do something, yet you can.*

There are some areas women look at and say, "That's not for me." For example, before 1994, farming mainly included men, so even though women had started doing other jobs they hadn't done before, somehow they feared they couldn't do a farming cooperative just with women. But they are capable. That's the thing about empowerment: It's saying, "My brother can do this, and so can I." It's venturing into something big and making it work.

The question of confidence affects whether or not women like Esther—whom we'll soon meet—are deterred from becoming a pilot by a poor math score or Alphonsine, who regularly addresses seas of business-men, looks beyond her modest first enterprise. Others point out how self-assured women can have a moderating impact on the whole society, regardless of their professional ambitions.

JOSEPHINE is sitting in her modest living room, with bright blue walls showcasing the many awards that recognize her hero status. In 1994, this house on a steep hill above the banks of Lake Kivu had just two rooms. She points out the cupboard and the space under the bed where she managed to hide people during the genocide until she could pilfer boats and devise their escapes. Her actions—despite her hus-band's protests and her own mortal danger—give heft to her comments on what might have changed the calculation of those without her nerve or her vision.

I compare now to how it was when I was a bride, when I "became a woman," as we say. Before, we accepted to just "obey your husband." Women didn't think they could do big things compared to men. They felt that men would make decisions and shouldn't be challenged. They feared men.

What has changed? Josephine doesn't have grand pronouncements about the impact of high-level women. In fact, she's blunt. *Having women in leadership in Kigali hasn't made much difference for the women in the vil-lage.* Instead, she insists that opportunities they now have to go to school or meet outside their homes gives them a chance to pick up new ideas and social skills that breed confidence.

Women who are married today have a lot of luck. Now, even if women think that they should still obey their husbands, they aren't fearful like before. They have higher self-esteem. They have the right to meet each other, get together and talk, to congregate with other people, even other men. Before, that wasn't true at all. Now women are able to learn about things beyond their house and family.

And then her shrewd link to the time of terror: *If the women had had a chance to be with other people, maybe they would have reacted differently when the genocide started. They might have been able to share information and stop the killers. But back then, even if one had information about her own husband, she couldn't share it and didn't know what to do, because women didn't take initiative like that. If the genocide was being planned today, when women are more educated, when they aren't so ignorant, I think that kind of killing wouldn't have happened.*

· · ·

Solidarity and sisterhood have been prevailing forces throughout the evolution of the Rwandan women's movement. It nurtured healing, as Chantal found among other widows and Annonciata discovered amid diverse women at her church. It inspired common causes, in the way that Veneranda and Judith appealed to their fellow activists. It galvanized work for others, as Godelieve felt when she met survivors in her own town and Zaina when she realized the raw vulnerability of children and their mothers in the eyes of the law.

Solidarity is strongest when it binds people in the face of threat, where there's a palpable sense that, without a unified front, progress could be wiped out or ardent ambitions could come crashing down. Each day in postgenocide Rwanda was lived on tenterhooks. Would the future bring irrevocable divisions? Or could there be rejuvenation, given how everything, but everything, needed rebuilding?

Back when parliamentary sessions took place in a huge, bombed-out building that was in line for attention behind burials and cleanup, male MPs would scuttle off to nearby bars at the end of the day. While unwinding from work, they would inevitably rehash and resolve lingering scrapes from the day. These man-to-man exchanges created cohesion for the group and the institution.

For women, bars were off-limits, and anyway they had families to go home and feed. But in the women's caucus, female MPs found not only a forum with which to build their common agenda, but also a network through which to build woman-to-woman bonds. Hutu and Tutsi members joined together over their new, shared tribulations. Eight women, then twelve, then eighteen, and eventually more than fifty, they were united and undaunted trailblazers.

As years have flown and their representation has soared, the intimacy inevitably has been left behind. The legislators have proven their mettle and reversed some of the most discriminatory laws, but the struggle to advance has dissipated, and camaraderie no longer feels so essential. **AGNES**'s tenure in Parliament spanned the early years before the female majority until late 2012. She has watched with dismay how *nowadays some of this solidarity focusing on common challenges, like balancing family and work, has changed. Women are so stressed, pursuing degrees, chairing committees. We used to talk about recipes, or "Who is your tailor?" These things seem small, but they were important for promoting partnerships.*

To Agnes's point, professional culture is skewed against women in deep-set ways, as **JUSTINE U.** found in her doctoral research.[1] She conducted confidential, in-depth interviews with twenty-nine prominent Rwandan female leaders to understand how their work affects myriad aspects of their lives, from self-worth, to sex life, to motherhood.

Justine's inspiration was personal. After finishing her master's degree, she came back to Rwanda while her Rwandan boyfriend stayed in Great Britain. She was seven months pregnant when she arrived in Kigali, so she had just started work when she gave birth to their son. *Sometimes I would be on the way home, having finished my work, even though it was later than the prescribed working time. Around 7 PM the minister would call me to come back to the office.*

I was living like a single mother, because my boyfriend was in the U.K. I was living off a very low salary, with a nanny who wasn't very well educated, so I had to be there for my son. But my minister, a woman, would call me back to the office to do something someone else could have done. And that was the Ministry of Gender!

So it was clear from my experience, being close to these women politicians, looking at the kind of lives they have, looking at the kind of issues they face, and from my background as an activist during university . . . it was important to me to look at how we can bring up our numbers while also changing the way of life, changing relationships between women and men.

If women were, in fact, able to nurse a drink at a bar instead of nursing a child at home, they would almost certainly console each other about what **PATRICIA** calls juggling triple roles. *We often think of two sets of responsibilities, in her home and at her office. But in reality, the reproductive role women bear is a very big element. So when we talk about the balancing act, we should keep in mind the extra challenges for the woman who is pregnant, or breast-feeding, or with small children at home.*

Even as women assume more powerful posts, they have scarce influence in how tasks are divided up at home, **JUSTINE U.** found during her research. Most work a double day—coming home from the office to oversee the homework, dinner, and other chores, with little help from their husbands. Support from house staff is viewed as support to the mother. If the father stays with the children while she stays late with her colleagues, it's a favor to her, rather than his responsibility.

Women are not unaware of the social injustice. They are making a calculation about how hard they can push. There's a strong belief *that men fear stigmatization based on losing their boss status if they get involved in female traditional roles in the home*, as Justine says. More insidiously, some she interviewed explained that a man who does family work is considered "bewitched" (*baramuroze*) by his wife.

The women I spoke to mentioned that some men had started to do some chores around the house while their wives were away for work. But they said there was the perception of those men being helpers to their wives rather than equal partners with a shared to-do list.

Justine reads the testimony of one of the female leaders with whom she spoke: "*He thinks that he is just helping, like a replacement, a rescuer when the wife is not there, just when the woman has gone for an official duty . . . and he comes in to help, but not as his responsibility. So the day a husband will understand that he can do domestic work even when the wife is around; then that's when we can talk about change.*"

MARY: The message is out there. The conversation is on. It's public knowledge: gender-based violence is wrong. Now we have to engage the men. They must feel part and parcel.

The symbolic value of so many women in prominent posts doesn't ensure future successes, but neither should it be dismissed. Like any major social change, gradually watching a trend look less trendy and more ordinary defuses many opponents. Once in powerful positions, female leaders have proven they're capable, undermining the view that women aren't suited for public leadership. But behind the scenes, women have pushed along this evolution by proactively recruiting allies and wisely considering who will make the best messengers.

MUTAMBA is one. He returned in late 1994 from Kenya, where he'd been teaching high school economics. Having fled Rwanda as a seven-year-old, he was eager to contribute to the rebuilding however needed, so he submitted an application at the Ministry for Public Service and waited for placement.

Slender and starting to gray, Mutamba seems professorial as he cites one example after another, recounting stories in intricate detail. *When we were sitting in the waiting room before the interview, they told us that the Ministry of Gender was recruiting that day. One of the questions I was asked was, "What measures would you propose to promote the role of women in Rwanda's reconstruction and development efforts?" I had no idea what that meant!*

You have to remember that having a Ministry of Gender was new. This whole idea was new. So I was thinking about this question as an economist,

Women are now represented in professional settings, sometimes in even greater numbers than men.

and it clicked in my mind—*development and the big role women play. I answered with an excited tone, "We cannot reconstruct this country without engaging women."*

Mutamba admits he wasn't angling for a job promoting women's advancement. *Little did I know this was going to be my life career.* But it suited him from both a social justice and an economic standpoint.

As a young boy, I noticed how women lived. How, if a husband decided he didn't like his wife's character or if they had a disagreement, she was forced to go and leave the children behind. In a patriarchal society, children belonged to the father. They would often suffer being separated from their mom. Luckily, it never happened to mine, but I saw mothers of some of my friends in our neighborhood going through this ordeal, and I used to feel it was unfair.

When I was studying economics, I also noticed how we generally think that whatever is produced that is not sold on the market is not considered work done. I used to say, "No, a mother produces many things that are not sold, and they're very useful to making society function. So why don't we attach value to that kind of work?"

He astutely shapes the rationale behind gender equality to suit his audience. He has spent the past twenty years leading trainings for numerous government officials, including the prime minister and members of the cabinet, and he now consults for UN Women. Mutamba has created a niche for himself.

CHRISTOPHE, a big man, quick to smile, trained as an agriculture specialist and now represents Rwanda in the East African Legislative Assembly, the region's parliament. For a long time, in the years before 1994, he shunned politics. He loved working in rural areas and advising farmers, and he didn't want to get caught up in the volatile political scene under the pregenocide government of President Habyarimana. But the president's party (MRND) wanted him. *When you're in a leading position, you're supposed to be part of what the party plans. If you don't agree, it's as though you are opposing the process.* Christophe's attempt to stay neutral as the murderous fervor rose proved devastating.

Charismatic and warm, Christophe has a somber tone as he offers up this story: In April 1994, he was in Kigali for a workshop. His wife, a Tutsi, was at their home in the lakeside town of Gisenyi with their two children. *When the genocide started, the Interahamwe came to my house the first day.* The initial round of murders by soldiers and militias targeted Tutsi and also Hutu known to oppose the extermination, and extremists had put him on their list to eliminate. *That day, they killed my children and my wife. They also killed my sister-in-law and our housekeeper. But they had come looking for me.*

Christophe, now a high-level Rwandan Patriotic Front figure and strong advocate for women, and Mutamba, now a high-level consultant focused on women's issues, were easy converts to the women's movement. But as men who grew up with Rwandan proverbs and warrior role models teaching them about masculinity, they understand the social pulls that drive skepticism or downright opposition. Helpfully, they're also vocal about what they see as not just the adequacies women bring to their work, but also their exceptional attributes.

Christophe finds that women's central role managing the affairs of their homes, tending to children and husbands as well as extended families, and balancing their careers makes them adept at thinking several steps ahead. *Normally the decisions of women are more analytical than those of men. A man can make a decision without thinking about it as much as might be necessary. But a woman takes enough time to think about her impact.*

• • •

A crowd of police officers and nurses converges in a room painted brightly with alphabet letters at a hospital in a central neighborhood of Kigali. A plush frog and a couple of dolls with Afros lie on the table, props that might be used by a child to entertain herself while her mother seeks care, or to act out to a counselor a haunting scene of abuse.

The Isange One Stop Center is just the first in a growing, countrywide network of clinics where survivors of sexual violence can seek medical treatment and counseling services. They can also file a legal claim against their attackers. The design is intended to ensure the patient has to tell her story only once.

Rwanda's top police commander, Inspector General **GASANA**, comes across the street from his headquarters to make introductions at the center. A wide-chested, muscular man, he peppers his comments with phrases like "prevention mechanisms" and "gender budgeting."

When we first started this gender-based violence work, we started to see the numbers going up. I was asking all the time, "What's happening?" But because of the campaign, it moved things. Women began to see attacks as crimes and, very gradually, as traumas they've endured for which they shouldn't feel ashamed, Gasana explains. His gentle words seem incongruous with his gold-festooned epaulettes and the pants of his navy police uniform tucked into polished boots. But he speaks with obvious pride.

Community policing committees are also on the case—90,000 civilians across the country, Gasana reports—charged with helping maintain security in villages and towns across the country. He spends an hour talking through the program. With his booming voice and the detailed operational plan, he could have been describing a military strategy rather than a remarkable system to protect women from predatory men they might face in their communities, including in their homes. He explains that the leaders of these citizen committees are given cell phones so that they can call in reinforcements. *Center stage among messages we give them is domestic violence prevention, because this is their department.*

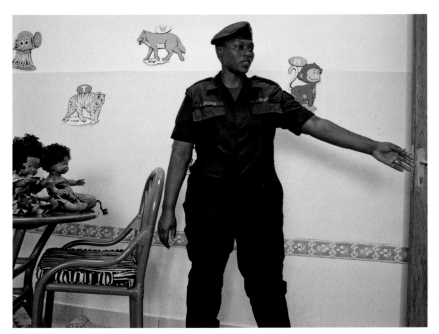

Afro-coiffed dolls and plush toys soften the mood in the children's area at a
One Stop Center, where survivors of sexual violence can seek counseling as well
as medical and legal services.

Over at police headquarters, the atmosphere is strikingly different,
with lots of saluting and flags—a command center humming along.
Tackling gender violence is one of their most publicized campaigns, and
Gasana is pleased to show it off. *I'm lucky: every morning when I'm here
at my desk, you can ask me the situation in the country and I can tell you,
because of those community committees.*

The One Stop Center and the inspector general's emphatic descriptions demonstrate the determination of the government's zero tolerance
for sexual violence. It's the push first set in motion by the late-night strategizing and organizing prowess of many, including activist Immaculee,
lawyer Justine M., and parliamentarian **JUDITH K.**

We don't want to just make a law. Judith laid down the marker in 2005
when the work was still under way. She wanted to change behavior—stop
men from beating their partners and stop women from tolerating the

beating. The law would be one element in a larger strategy to change accepted expectations that made life dangerous for women.

Deciding who should deliver those messages was key. **JUSTINE M.** recounts how the feminist agenda at the 1995 Beijing Conference sparked the interest among Rwandan women to write their own antirape legislation. But framing the issue for the majority of citizens required a different approach. *The way you start is very important. Don't mention activists like me—"Oh, you mean those women who have no respect for men?" Then it becomes like a men-women thing. And it takes away from the gender-based violence thing.*

Pragmatically, **JUDITH** points out that the beliefs that make women most vulnerable to sexual violence are the same ones that make them less effective as advocates, because the males they most need to reach won't listen to a female. *Women are the victims of traditional practices that regard them as weak and vulnerable, unable to lead. But even if our society is patriarchal, it must change. And how? Some men are gender sensitive, and they can explain more quickly how to make equality between women and men.*

Agreeing, **MUTAMBA** says that some of the most promising new work comes from other male advocates who are trying to bring along the stragglers, now that there's a general acceptance of women's leadership in society. *To complete the equation, we need really to work on men, to empower men—though we don't usually use that term, "men's empowerment"—to be partners for gender equality. Some elements of our cultural values can be used as the basis. It's not strange to see women engaged—before, more behind-the-scenes and now, more publicly.*

One other component is important: We have this generation of leaders, like those of my age, who grew up seeing our mothers effectively cope with refugee life. They were able to find ways to be leaders—I call that leadership. Managing in a crisis, being resourceful, keeping the children well, giving children our values, and maintaining our dignity. And we have male leaders who appreciate that. We have to remember that and capture it; otherwise, we have a new generation with no experience seeing women deal with crisis.

JANET: All our weavers are wearing shoes. Their children are wearing shoes.

Acceptance and even appreciation of women's leadership is creating enduring space for new players. *Their gains are no longer about legal structures.* Minister of Foreign Affairs **LOUISE**, one of the president's cabinet members most often in the spotlight, is unequivocal. *Women and men see their capabilities and vote for them. This is a permanent cultural shift.*

While women and men talk of a movement, the word "feminism" almost never arises. Nor is Rwanda's brand of women's revolution modeled on emulating men. Instead, they've earned their credibility as leaders through their experience as mothers—a sentiment that would vex many Western feminists. In a society where it's very uncommon not to have children, either biological or adopted, and where motherhood is particularly revered, justifying women's ability to lead by venerating their talent in managing family and home is an authentic point of view raised by both women and men.

Like many others who spoke to this theme, **FELIX** draws a direct link between women's honesty in the public sphere and the society's long-held maternal ideal. *Our culture teaches that as a mother she's the heart of the family. The wife sets the tone and coordinates everything, even if the husband retains his ultimate authority over big decisions.*

Women are more trustworthy. That's why in most situations you find them in charge of finance. They oversee the treasury in associations, and in extended families, women handle management and support. Once women have a job, they want to keep it to make their kids' lives secure. So she can imagine that if she goes to jail her kids will be alone, without anyone to take care of them. I see it as the combination of cultural roles and their big hearts wanting to always protect their kids that makes them less corrupt than men.

From stints in high-level posts in Parliament, such as vice president of the Senate and president of the women's caucus, **MARIE** says she recognized a conscientious attitude in her female colleagues. *Women manage public assets better than men. They're more dedicated to the progress of the country and thus less corrupt. Why? Women come into positions with a purpose: developing, proving they can do things better than what used to be done.*

•   •   •

JANET didn't set foot in her own country until she was in her early thirties, when she and her older sister Joy moved from Uganda in 1994. Janet had a background in art; her sister had a restaurant in Kampala, the Ugandan capital. In Kigali, they started out running a hotel, but soon the duo launched Gahaya Links (named for their family) to market high-end handicrafts.

Though raised in a refugee camp herself, Janet was dismayed by the utter poverty she discovered in her country. *Most women were wearing soiled rags. Their children had nothing to wear, no shoes. You may think I'm exaggerating, but they had no food, nothing in their homes, which were the most basic grass-thatched huts with dirt floors and no doors.*

In one village we visited, it was very, very challenging to see women with dirty hands, who didn't have enough soap to wash well and who had to make a very clean basket. You'd find somebody in unwashed clothes but with this beautiful basket she'd made. That's what made me realize that this dirtiness wasn't their lifestyle, not part of their values. It was because of poverty. The key reason they weren't clean or didn't have food was because they had no means of earning an income.

It's not in the Rwandan tradition to beg. The women we met felt embarrassed, saying, "How can we go back to ask for food again?" So they walked into the hotel I managed, with baskets in exchange for the food we gave them.

Janet recognized the shapes and designs as cultural emblems of her homeland. *As a little girl I always saw my mother and the other ladies in our camp weaving together.* Like American quilters, they socialized in each

Entrepreneurs and sisters Janet Nkubana and Joy Ndungutse.

other's homes or backyards making crafts. *I thought, "Everybody knows how to make baskets."*

And so the sisters started their company, with groups of vulnerable women. *As time went on, we taught them how, with their earnings, they could buy a piece of soap and wash their clothes.* But deep issues arose as women from both sides of the genocide shared the space. At first they segregated themselves—Tutsi with Tutsi, Hutu with Hutu. Over time, and often with guidance from Janet and Joy, they began to open up about their prejudices and insecurities, as well as the difficulties they faced at home. *With common cause, they came together. Sitting beside one another to work, they had time to talk, to understand each other.*

A pool of artisans has grown up. Their expertise in basket weaving is an extension of the tradition of limiting female ambitions to family roles and not mingling in public. In a pleasant irony, a cultural restriction has spawned a marketable skill.

Janet has taken the distinctly Rwandan forms and patterns of yore and given them a modern touch. The high contrast of the traditional black-and-white painted *magongo* (cow dung) decorations plays out in beadwork. Delicate woven designs that adorned practical containers now embellish—in miniature—buttons, cufflinks, and earrings.

Once we had created an export strategy at Gahaya Links and got into the international market, women started making money. Today, married women are more respected by their husbands because of their contribution to their families and the community, and because of the change of attitude toward women as the government has emphasized a new equality.

So, as we work with the women, we also pass on the message that you shouldn't be subjects of men. You're contributing equally, so you have equal rights. That means if a man beats you, you have to report it. But also, for the men it's more difficult to get up in the morning and beat the person who is working so that you can eat.

Another thing that inspired women to have confidence is that the government instilled a kind of mind-set that we're all able-bodied. Women used to think they could not go on a construction site or drive trucks. "Don't underestimate yourself!" That was the message.

But what I'm really very proud of is that when you meet our weavers, you won't understand that these are rural women, from the villages. They're well groomed. Some have fixed up their hair. I asked one woman, "What do you think is the impact of our business?" She said, "Look at me! I dress like a model! Better than the schoolteachers!"

This whole chain is a transformation being created by women. If mothers had not passed on the skill to the daughters, it would have died, and whatever we're achieving today wouldn't happen. But today, even a child of a weaver tells you, "Oh, my mother sells baskets." And if your child is proud to talk about what you do, that child will even be willing to take it over when you're not there.

Janet is proud, and rightfully so, when she talks about how the women involved with the company have seen their standing in their families and communities rise, even though their work producing handmade Rwandan crafts is decidedly feminine. The weavers we work with are now contributing at home because men don't have jobs. Some are widows but supporting their families with their own hands, through a tradition inherited from their parents.

Stacks of just-assembled boxes stamped with the Gahaya Links logo fill all the floor space around banquet tables completely covered with baskets. The designs are slender or squat, mostly natural beige, but with red, black, and other colors in geometric patterns, and tiny enough to hang on a Christmas tree or as tall as a child. One model with five pieces comes nested together like a Russian doll. These are the shipments heading overseas. I send baskets to Uganda, to Kenya, or abroad to an international market like we have now. It's something that can change lives. What we're giving women is not so much a market to buy and sell baskets, but a life of opportunity.

Gahaya Links has become a powerhouse conglomerate of women-run groups whose members have mastered their crafts. The success of their model may come as a surprise to some, but less so to this hardworking duo. For a long time, people said, "Women can't do business." Because of our cultural bias, they never believed a woman could make it as an entrepreneur. But now we compete with men; we're doing the same jobs. We're into export, and the most in retail are women. When you go to the villages, women are the majority of those growing the crops.

Janet's sister **JOY N.** puts a fine point on it. The men keep asking, "How do you do it? How?" I tell them, "You know what? You men all go borrow

Recapturing the artistry of basket weaving, with a modern twist.
BY TESS SAGER

money from the bank and then use it for something else instead of the project you've borrowed it for!" Women don't take risks, and we make things happen. Those who started borrowing twenty thousand francs are now borrowing two million, because they're growing. Growing! Women say, "I have goats, but I want a cow."

While outspoken activists deplore men's rebuffing of household chores—and many more women quietly do—activities seen as feminine become prized once they're marketable. Although they may shun the task at home, men are often more open when it brings in money, and that twist raises the perception of value. **JANET** explains, *We've exposed the weavers to what it means to do business. And because these women have now changed in nutrition, in appearance, their homes have changed. It's being passed not just from generation to generation, from mothers to daughters. Men are coming into weaving.*

Behind Janet's voice is an example: the whir of more than fifty Juki industrial sewing machines fills an otherwise quiet workshop. Tailoring is the newest addition to their company's specialties. Scraps of cloth pile up under each machine, destined to become headbands or earrings or quilts. Mingled in with the women, all eyes peering down, intently following the needles and thread, are two men. *For women it was a hobby. For men, a skill.*

· · ·

Joy and Janet's exquisite beaded jewelry, intricate baskets, and handbags stitched from vibrant African fabrics are sold in the American department store Macy's, the fashion and home decor store Anthropologie, and the designer boutiques of Kate Spade. Their enterprise may be one of just a handful known outside the country, but in Rwanda it's among a throng of other businesses owned and managed by women. Many of these entrepreneurs see the economic development potential of their operations to include the development of the talent and skills of others — often younger — in the community. As these businesswomen offer personal encouragement to some, they help shape the mind-set of more.

Yet despite the many strides, there are also controversies and obstacles tied to the notion of a cultural shift that has led to expanded opportunities for women and girls. **ROSE M.**'s own trajectory from practicing law to becoming the first female president of the lower house of Parliament is stunning. But while a remarkable number of women have outstanding careers like hers, she points out that many, many more still watch from the sidelines, unable or unsure about how to step up into leadership or stand up against abuses.

A lot has been done in our country about women's rights, women's promotion, but there is a lot to do because of history and tradition. I worked in the Association of the Defense of Women and Children's Rights—Haguruka—where the main activity is training in laws protecting women. Each year, we'd see about six thousand cases of domestic violence, and we'd provide legal assistance to the victims.

As a result of the gender-based violence law, many sexual abuse cases, including domestic violence, now pass through the police. Researchers say that the number of reports annually has risen, likely because of the increased awareness that such violence is a crime.[1]

Rose continues. *Another problem is that these laws protect only legally married couples, and we have a lot of "illegal marriage," as we say. It's not polygamy, but unions between couples that aren't registered and, therefore, are unrecognized by the government. Polygamy is illegal in our country, so sometimes a married man takes a younger woman. He has his legal wife on this side and on the other side a couple of girls, and he has children through those illegal relationships.*

The law doesn't protect that kind of union. There's a long procedure for those children to get their rights as legitimate. The problem is, most women don't know these procedures. They don't know they can ask for justice for their children and there's legal assistance to do so.

Rose's point about how protections exclude women (and men) in informal relationships leads back to the mass marriages organized by Mayor **FLORENCE**. Surprisingly, despite the legal advantages formal marriage affords, the institution as recognized by the state still adheres to a traditional view on gender. The Family Code states that "the man is the head of the family and his opinions must prevail."

The original Kinyarwanda version uses the word *umutware*, which translates to master or boss.[2] There's an intriguing divide even among women's rights activists about how that clearly discriminatory language makes them feel. Florence seems to choose her words carefully, knowing that her stance is unexpected. *The constitution makes us equal, but in the marriage vows we say men are the head of the family. It's for the proper management of the basic unit of society, which for us is the family.*

Yes, there are some who say, "If you say we are equal, but in the family unit that the man takes the lead, then we are not equal." It's still being debated. But I for one would leave the management to men, because even in the army, school, any group or gathering, you must have one in command, with the final say. And if it's not well stipulated in the law, we'll have chaos in the family.

Florence doesn't feel that this arrangement strongly disadvantages women, who she says are astute at negotiating to get what they want. *You have to outsmart him and convince him! You know, I can force him to take up my position, but not by telling him, "This is my position." You lob it from the other side, and then he may think it was his idea.*

However clever, women need allies. Priest **EMMANUEL**'s gentle demeanor made him a confidant for his rural parishioners who needed to speak about delicate burdens. He lets conversation breathe and doesn't interrupt, leaving space for difficult details to seep out. With a tilted nod for emphasis and eyes peering up as he recalls (but doesn't betray) stories and faces, he says, *Where women are not educated, they still have to put up with a lot from their husbands. They still suffer.*

While new laws guard against abusive behaviors, Father Emmanuel says that in tiny villages especially—where everyone knows everyone else's business—the calculations playing into a decision to draw on those safeguards are complex. *For many women it doesn't feel like an option to expect better treatment. And even if they know how they can fight back using the law, they feel like too much is at stake in their family and small community. To take your husband to the police is hard.*

DOMITILLA: When we are in these posts, we really feel like we need to work with our hearts, with our competencies. And if need be, we have to add our feminine aspect. Meaning we are not only public workers—we are mothers to our children, and we are mothers to this country.

Perhaps the most pronounced impact of women in leadership is on the homemakers, teachers, farmers, and lawyers who themselves decided to jump in on the trend. Whether they followed the organic early trajectory of realizing their survival would depend on embracing new roles, or they watched the first waves of women get involved and felt inspired, women describe their sense of purpose as a deep motivation. Often their work has required a rebellious streak as far as their families were concerned, even if the politics of the country overall were encouraging. Having so many women pushing against barriers has undeniably broadened their expectations of themselves.

With new examples of what success looks like for Rwandan women, learning foreign languages, studying math, or pursuing advanced degrees are less easily dismissed as frivolous. The gas station on the corner; the freight company near the airport; the complex with the grocery store, furniture showroom, and gym? Female owned. Expanding the range of roles women can play means less need to define identity by domestic duties.

First of all, I say to my peers: "Your aim has to be success, no matter how you do it." DOMITILLA knows that helping draft the constitution and then heading the commission running the gacaca trials—challenging

Lawyer Domitilla Mukantaganzwa.

and groundbreaking as the jobs would be for anyone—were particularly momentous because she's a woman. She embraces that chance for boldness but suggests not dwelling on it.

Asked for a piece of advice based on her experience, she says, *We're a model for our daughters, for our sisters. But also for our sons and husband too!* She laughs, but she's serious. *Girls and women need to get the message: We're capable and shouldn't put so much attention on being women. You have your own characteristics as a woman, just like a man does. But when it comes to the business of public or private business, you'll succeed depending on your inputs. If you have a business, your outputs will be the same level as your inputs.*

Personally, I don't think I've had any problems in my career because I'm a woman. We've been with men since school. I'm not here to compare myself to men. If I deliver, that's good. And if I don't deliver, we now have our Parliament, our ministers, our president, who will watch our work and see that it is correctly done. If I'm not getting the work done, I'm not going to be excused just because I'm a woman. No! For a public program like gacaca, justice that promoted reconciliation, you have to be competent. We're working with the people who are effective.

Our current political leadership has made all of this possible. We don't have to pretend that we aren't mothers. Or that we aren't wives to our husbands. You know I'm a lawyer and I'm a peace builder, but I am also a mother and a wife. I can't stay in the office of gacaca for twenty-four hours forgetting that I have some obligations waiting for me. So we have three roles to play. We have to combine them all—and we're doing it.

While political appointments and government policies jump-started women's involvement, many say that seeing others thrive in leadership or in typically male-dominated careers has been their most powerful motivation. **ESTHER** became a veritable celebrity as the first female Rwandan pilot when she was just twenty-four years old. CNN and the national television station have interviewed her on camera, and she regularly speaks to schoolchildren around the country about her exhilarating job, which started as a passion even before she'd ever been on a plane.

Although her family is Rwandan, Esther was born in the small country to the south, Burundi, where her family lived because of violence and fierce discrimination at home. They returned to Rwanda when Esther was a child, so most of her memories of growing up in Burundi's capital are vague. But some are vivid. *When I was four I noticed a plane flying over our house in Bujumbura, and I told my dad, "I want to be a pilot!" I had never seen a pilot before and didn't even know what one looked like.*

A family vacation to Disneyland, while her father was working with a church in the United States, solidified the dream. For seven-year-old Esther, the flight to California was the highlight. *At that age you don't really care about the technicality of anything. It was this whole flashy experience. I knew right away I wanted to do this someday.*

Esther's father traveled extensively to England, the United States, and throughout East Africa as a popular Pentecostal pastor. With five children at home, Esther's mother decided to care full time for the family. But she had studied electrical engineering, so even in her handiwork as a homemaker, Esther's mother was a role model who challenged the stereotype of a stay-at-home mom.

If we had a short circuit in the house, my dad wouldn't go out to fix it. My mom knew exactly what to do. So at home, I never saw him fixing the lights or repairing things. It was always my mom. I guess it was surprising for everyone else, but for me it was normal.

When Esther was nine, her father died in a plane crash in eastern Congo while on one of his mission trips. But that didn't deter her from learning to fly. *I don't know why, but I wasn't really scared. People always asked me, "Oh, my God. Do you want to go find out what killed your dad?" Aviation was really a mystery back then.* People were baffled by Esther's career choice, thinking it was prompted by the crash. *But my decision was made way before, and I didn't want to change. That moment when you first take off . . . I didn't let anything take that away from me.*

With the loss of her husband, Esther's mother needed to work, so she sent Esther and her sister to boarding school in Uganda. The school was prestigious, but Esther wasn't impressed. When she didn't score high enough on her entrance exam for the math and science track, the school enrolled her in arts and history. *But I said, No! This isn't what I want to do! I need to do math. This is my dream.*

I packed my bags and changed schools just like that. This was a very good school. If I'd consulted my mom, she never would have agreed. But when she

Pilot Esther Mbabazi.

came to visit, I'd changed schools and she had to deal with it. After that, when I said I wanted to fly, she knew I was serious.

Esther was studying for her pilot's license at a school in northern Uganda when she caught the attention of recruiters for RwandAir. They hired her before she had finished her training and sent her to Florida to get her commercial license and then to Canada to learn to fly the Bombardier CRJ900.

During her training, she met several female pilots who had faced harassment and threats for going against the grain in their societies. *I have a friend who was flying in Saudi Arabia. She had a very tough time, because people didn't think that she should be doing this work. And one of my instructors was Pakistani. She had to leave to fly in the States because in her culture this was frowned upon. But everyone in Rwanda is so encouraging. They come up to me: "Oh, I've heard your story. I like what you're doing."*

I've had no bad experiences about being a young woman in this job. We have a lot of women in the company now who are pilots—from India, Ethiopia, Kenya. So it isn't that surprising anymore. Several other young women are training with RwandAir, and the police force has hired a handful of female helicopter pilots.

Esther counts off on her hand the other Rwandan women in her field, emphasizing how normal it is to see women in the cockpit and seeking to downplay her own achievement. She offers to lift up other pilots by making introductions—to share the attention she receives as the very first. But she evokes obvious admiration: People turn to look when she walks by in her uniform, pulling behind her a rolling bag with a small, glistening insignia that reads "Pilot." The old-guard activists inevitably nod with approval when her name is mentioned.

Women like Esther wouldn't be venturing into new realms if they'd been taught from a young age to feel limited in their aspirations. It's a generational shift to see opportunities within reach. But **MARY**, a longtime activist and mother to two adult daughters, points out that young women still face competing demands. *No doubt, there's a new pressure on the next generation. We have to say to them, "Be yourself. Your time and our time are different."*

For women worldwide, as opportunities open up, priorities have to be shuffled, creative ways dreamed up to save time. But unlike societies that increasingly respect the array of choices that free up space for their careers (such as having children later, foregoing motherhood altogether), Rwanda has a narrower acceptable realm. If legitimacy in leadership comes from homemaking, what becomes of a single or even married career woman without children? Very few have tested the scenario.

The vast majority opt to do it all. They hire a housekeeper, a common arrangement for Rwandans at almost all income levels, where basic tasks like washing clothes (usually by hand) and making dinner (often over a small charcoal stove, in a pot that needs stirring over several hours) are far more time consuming than in the West. Career mothers find child care, often by a younger relative. Still, many are plagued with self-doubt about how they're managing the balancing act.

In Rwanda, of course, there's the added dimension that most women faced great loss. Now they cope with an array of challenges (for example, folding orphaned children into their traumatized families) unlike their peers in other countries. Even for those with families intact and thriving, secondary trauma takes a toll. The pain they see close colleagues and friends confront on a daily basis looms as a reminder.

GAKUBA explains how she and her family made sense of an unexpected period of joy paired with deep tragedy, at a time when she was in the public eye as a promising young city council member in Kigali. *I thought I was finished having children at that time. I had two daughters and two sons. But after five years, I got another one! My littlest boy was already nine years old, and then I had Jonathan in 2005. It was challenging, I will say, but I realize so many people want to have children. He was such a blessing! Especially because we had Jonathan at the time we also lost our daughter. . . .*

Emmanuella was thirteen. One afternoon she was playing with David, who was eleven, and who loved his big sister. They were very close. In between our plot and the neighbors' there was a wall that wasn't finished. They were just kidding around and playing, and she fell in the other plot and got internal bleeding. It was . . . so strange, unbelievable, really. In hours she passed away.

I was home because Jonathan was only two weeks old. The emotions . . . truly, I couldn't be so sad because I had a baby in my arms. After a month I went back to the office.

Gakuba says she never really considered taking more time off or moving into a career that would be less scrutinized. *Being in the public spot-*

light . . . even though people are trying to be helpful, they bring up those hardships to you, and you're always reminded. So that was tough. Sometimes even a simple "How are you doing?" felt like it abruptly jogged her out of her deliberate focus on work.

But on the other hand, I thought so much about people who lost beloved ones during the genocide. And I felt I can't even talk about this loss, because I'm so fortunate to still have my family, to have children, while so many others are just single people living alone now. Like a mother who had eight children, and all perished in the genocide. Or children who lost both their parents. In this country, these experiences were too strange and too hard. My situation was still in control. That gave me some perspective.

37 PLANTING DEEP

ODETTE: From the time you're born, you're told not to speak when men are present. When I go to my village and talk, they know me. They know I was a minister, and I am a senator, so I can speak; I am considered as a man. But if another woman gets up to talk, they say, "What about that one? Who is she to talk?" But slowly, slowly things will change.

LOUISE moved back to Rwanda permanently in 2008 to take up the post of minister of information. She had spent more than two decades abroad, first going to university in Delaware, and then working in Washington, DC, as a lobbyist on Capitol Hill and eventually communications director for the African Development Bank in Tunisia. Her reflections on gender are against this broad background. *When we have balance, our jobs are much easier. Our male colleagues in Rwanda don't mind sharing in the workplace and creating a friendly environment. They're wonderfully encouraging, available to talk and help. It's not easy, the hours we work. Not being always available for our families is a problem, because, of course, family is first.*

We should export Rwanda's tips on the attitude of men about women rising. In a number of countries, ambitious women who are high achievers end up in conflict with their husbands, with their colleagues in the workplace, or with men in society in general. When men share small daily life activities, it gives us more confidence. When you're changing broad attitudes, it's important to be in a supportive environment.

As one of the most prominent female leaders in President Kagame's cabinet, Louise does indeed cut a striking figure when representing Rwanda at international events or taking to her popular Twitter feed

As a whole, members of the potter community in Rwanda are among the most impoverished.

to stalwartly defend her government. She is eloquent and composed, a fierce debater who doesn't shy away from an argument with a critic. They're characteristics that also distinguish her from most other female leaders in the country. Given her years overseas, Louise now brings a prized fusion of cultures to her role as foreign minister.

Like Minister Louise, many women in the top echelons recognize the cluster of factors—not least, their drive and savvy—that have enabled their rise. They vocalize a common refrain about cultivating opportunities for other women to command influence, especially those from disadvantaged backgrounds.

That has actually been one of my preoccupations. **INYUMBA** raised the point even back in 2002, after she'd gotten a sense of the everyday challenges Rwandans faced, through her work as gender minister and head of the National Unity and Reconciliation Commission. *I felt the best way to contribute was to train other women to come and do better work than me. And I think it's a credit for us that if you look at the region, Rwanda has led in giving importance to women's contributions in the construction of our country.*

Inyumba says she would remind herself and the women around her not to forget about the privilege to serve, even if it came through sacrifice and hardship. *"You have to understand that you are not just a leader. You are a woman leader." Very big message. We should not forget.*

We tend to take it for granted that we are there. But how many other women have a chance like me? To perform the kind of assignments that I have done in this country? Just remember, we are talking about four million women in Rwanda. How many other women can have such an opportunity like me? It's because I went to school. So through my position as a woman leader, the first question should always be, "How do I create opportunities for other women?"

That philosophy had a direct impact on **JEANNE D'ARC M.** She comes from what's known today as the potter community, a euphemistic term (and Jeanne's preference) referring to indigenous Rwandans who traditionally made a living creating ceramics out of clay found in the forest. (In the attempt to reunify the country, "Twa" is rarely applied to a particular person.) As a group, her ethnic community is among the poorest Rwandans, and is unfairly stigmatized as uneducated and uncouth.

In school, some people from the potter community are really sensitive. And sometimes when they're being discriminated against or made fun of, they give up. But those who have emerged and have finished school without being too sensitive about their ethnicity, like me, we don't really care what people are saying.

Jeanne d'Arc went to a school run by Catholic nuns near the town where she grew up in western Rwanda. She excelled and became the first person in her family to finish high school. She won a full scholarship to university, thanks to a fund set up by the government to assist talented students from the potter community. Fewer than fifty potters have ever finished college, and Jeanne is one of them.

Finding stable work has been another matter. As in most places, jobs

Activist Jeanne d'Arc Mukasekuru.

are competitive and tend to go to well-connected people. As Jeanne d'Arc puts it, *For people coming from nowhere and knowing nobody, it's so hard.*

Discrimination is illegal, but prejudice persists. *Like my husband. We're not the same ethnicity. His family discouraged him about me before, but he kept calling me, because he doesn't really care about my ethnicity. And I don't care about ethnicity. When I go to meet people I don't see myself as only that. I see myself as someone who can bring my ideas and talk to someone.*

Jeanne is definitely a bright light, and happily the first lady's foundation saw her spark too. Jeanne d'Arc interned with Madame Jeannette Kagame's Imbuto Foundation during university and was then hired by an advocacy group in Kigali that works on issues affecting the potter community. But the organization has struggled financially. *When you are begging, the giving side always decides the timing. So sometimes you run low of funds, because you can't anticipate when the support will come. But that's normal—it's a global crisis. Sometimes money comes, and sometimes it doesn't.*

Jeanne d'Arc makes the introduction to a woman named Emma Marie in a village outside of Kigali. Emma Marie talks about how five of her ten children went to school but gradually dropped out because of costs or when they got married.

Jeanne explains the rationale. *For some in this community, they aren't thinking for the long term because they are preoccupied with their very serious poverty and the daily challenge to find enough food. Sending children to school might not feel like a priority. It doesn't bring livelihoods.* Emma Marie's neighbor Mediatrice speaks up, adding that they feel discrimination even at church, where adults in the congregation make insulting comments like, "No one will ever marry your sons."

Emma Marie explains that they're entrenched in poverty because selling pottery isn't profitable; Rwandans have stopped wanting to buy their time-honored goods as the country becomes more developed and people can afford imported items. But more fundamentally, they don't own property and instead work on other people's farms. Jeanne d'Arc translates: *They don't have land because their grandfathers never had it.*

Behind her house, Emma Marie proudly presents her cow, which she received through a government program to provide livestock to poor families. But the cow stands still in a dilapidated pen just bigger than its body. It's her prized possession, but Emma Marie doesn't have space for it to graze. In a storage shed near the cow pen, metal molds for sculpting small ceramic cooking stoves are stacked up. It's the newest pottery design, which they hope will be more marketable.

Driving away, Jeanne d'Arc launches into advocacy mode. *You have to know that they are Rwandese. Even if Rwanda is developing, there are people who are still living a miserable life, being left behind.* In these moments, she often mentions her meeting with Aloisea Inyumba.

There's a program that brings together youth from America and Canada, and they meet with youth leaders here in Rwanda. It's called Global Youth Connect. Jeanne d'Arc represented the potter advocacy group. *We visited many places together, and we went to the Ministry of Gender. Inyumba was the minister then. I would usually speak up to advocate for the potters. That's when I raised my concern about women, and how the potter women are doubly disadvantaged.* It's a theme that immediately animates Jeanne.

I said that, in general, Rwandan women have been discriminated against for a long time, but when it comes to the potters, it's double. So I asked Minister Inyumba what could be done for our women, so that they can see themselves as valued too. Minister Inyumba said that women are looked at the same—there shouldn't be a difference because of ethnicity. She said she wanted to meet with me again, to talk about this issue deeper. This was in 2012. Inyumba was quietly battling cancer, which would claim her life that year. *But she died before we had our appointment.*

· · ·

Life for the potters, on the whole, is dire. But the hardships apparent in Emma Marie and Mediatrice's village aren't so far removed from conditions under which most Rwandans still live.

The country is moving toward what's known in World Bank–speak as middle-income status, but it's not there yet. **INNOCENT**, the polished executive from the Business Development Fund, mentions some recent statistics that illustrate the disadvantaged status persistent among women—chief among them, that women take out 22 percent of bank loans. (That number is low, but the trend is impressive: in BDF's first year, female borrowers held just 12 percent of volume.) But he sets these numbers in the broader context—removed from the bustle and sheen of the capital, or from meetings with poised, ambitious women leaders speaking eloquently in English and French.

The majority of our population is agrarian. People don't have savings. They use the money they earn, even more so the women. Fewer of them are day laborers, digging all day, carrying loads—the kinds of jobs that earn money rather than just food Even today, in rural areas a woman works more in the home, where she surely contributes to the family but doesn't earn money. She is cultivating, fetching water, looking after kids.

I'm not talking about the 1 or 2 percent who are in town and making money, or those who are educated and can get a job. We're talking about uneducated women in the village with a hoe. That's the majority.

Those divides are not only between rural and urban, but also between classes in the countryside and in the cities. Women in the capital have listened, advocated, and legislated on behalf of their sisters, but they know there are still pronounced divides.

Ask **ZAINA** about the benefits of their labor in the twenty years since she launched her "Rwandan UNICEF," and she's prudent. *Laws are there, and policies and good programs. The issue now is to simplify and disseminate them so they're understandable for people who are less educated, who are in rural areas, for young people. These changes have to get into households, affect relationships between men and women, children and parents, but these legal frameworks aren't always easy to understand.*

From the village level up to the national, we have some structures close to the people. In the justice system we have the mediators down to the village level; they have some simple tools to explain laws so that they make sense. But you know, not all Rwandese can read and write. Now, in 2015, the rate for women is around 65 percent. For men it's just over 70 percent.[1] So you still have around 30 percent who can't.

When Zaina set up the legal aid group Haguruka in the early 1990s, she saw a gap that she felt no other organization was filling and that the Habyarimana government was neglecting: advocating for women and children's rights in policy making and ensuring that their clients had recourse if those rights were violated. Fortunately, the needs have changed, she says. It doesn't mean groups like Haguruka are no longer valuable, just that their focus should shift.

When I was an adult and thinking about starting Haguruka, it came out of my frustration. But the dynamics began to change once the Rwandan Patriotic Front assumed control of the government in 1994. *Now when you look at the work of the RPF, their program was the same as the one Rwandans were fighting for before.*

Zaina became the head of the National Commission for Children in 2011. *When I left civil society to come to the government, I thought, "This is really good. Here I can make more change." I can work for children directly by influencing government institutions that are working on children's rights and yet I have the government backing. I don't have to go and struggle, write proposals, plead for some small dollars. The government policy backs this work. By assisting women—a focus for the RPF—I'm also supporting a child.*

I was telling my former colleagues from Haguruka, my friends from there, "Dears, now you should do the research about these policies, about the implementation. Do communication, advocacy. Use media. You are there in one district, or maybe in a few sectors, but the government is everywhere. We don't need to compete. Create transparency. Don't try to replace the system. Before it was not there, but now it is there—see if it works well." A nongovernmental group can make its own name by being a watchdog. It should grow to suit the context.

The challenge to Zaina's proposition is that there is limited space for criticism of government programs and policies. The preference for consensus politics—an understandable approach to postgenocide healing—leads to the view that opposition is divisive, and division is dangerous. Differentiating between healthy debate and strife is fraught when tensions and traumas still run high. People deliver even the most benign critiques in hushed tones, cautious not to offend.

In this climate, there's ample room for proposals and initiatives in line with the ruling RPF's agenda. Fortunately for most activists, the government's stance on nearly all social issues is among the most progressive on the continent. For example, on universal health care, access to education, social services for marginalized people, the Kagame government is proactive and creative, modeling approaches that activists elsewhere in the region covet. But observers wonder if the advancement of women leaders, like many of the other impressive experiments under way, will prove vulnerable if it's overreliant on support from the government, the ruling party, or the man at the top.

• • •

The high number of women leaders is an undeniable feat. But now comes, arguably, a stiffer challenge, says **JUSTINE M.**: making it count. *Frankly speaking, we realized that, like in any organization in the world, the real activists became politicians, and then there was nobody left behind to be a real activist. The government also wants those people who can bring their messages across. So even though women have risen from the ashes to the top, the spirit of pushing the issues forward has died.*

I remember coming to Rwanda a few years ago, and I was so furious. I spoke to a group of my friends—Judith Kanakuze was still alive—and they all looked at me like I was crazy. And I said, "Seriously, how can you sit in the ministry, in a cabinet meeting, without raising your finger and saying, 'Hey he-he-he-hey!' Yes, not all these projects to embolden women have gone as well as we hoped they would, but maybe we can turn it around. Why aren't you defending our interests? Whatever happened to your activism?"

And I said, "Yes, things change, and I see they change. But you guys, who have spent sleepless nights building this whole . . . and then what you present to the international community are the statistics, but I don't care about the statistics! Make the women in Parliament 98 percent! But give me the action, give me the tangible, give me the woman who will not cower, who will not hesitate to raise her voice."

If there's insecurity somewhere, it will affect women—that's my kind of activism. It's not about pointing fingers. Our country is still building itself. We don't need to point fingers, because any other country will also face these things. . . . When there are problems in America you're not going to frame Obama, but you're going to question him. And when women don't have the voice to question, I wonder: What are they doing in the Parliament?

Justine's plea will sound familiar to feminists the world over, who have watched their hard-won progress lose momentum once they aren't fighting for every inch. Many have cringed seeing their stockpile of successes frittered away by generations who can't fully appreciate (or remember) what was earned and what was sacrificed. In Rwanda, there have even been calls to revoke the gender quota in government. As elsewhere, women in Rwanda are beginning to face the question: Isn't it enough?

DINAH: When I stepped outside of Rwanda I realized all the things we're doing right. Of course, deep social changes take time, especially when dealing with communities where education levels are still low. But it's clear how, pushed along by political leadership, there is a change of attitudes in people toward women in Rwanda that I do not see in almost any other African country.

The most tangible, unequivocal consequence of all this organizing is its effect on young women. This next generation may not know the details: of Immaculee and Judith staying awake until dawn to polish the gender-based violence law; of Alice coordinating the letter to the Arusha tribunal to demand full recognition of the suffering of the women in Taba; or of Inyumba's dusty treks across the country to learn what people needed most from the innovative reconciliation commission. But young adults now have grown up in a culture steeped in this new narrative about the rise of women.

For Foreign Minister **LOUISE**, remembering how she was once barred from going overseas to study because of her ethnicity, the shift toward inclusion within just one generation is remarkable. *It goes all the way down to young women. I've visited a number of schools and see the daring kind of approach young women have, the kind of self-confidence that translates into academic achievement. They feel there's no limit to what they can do. It's quite amazing, especially when you look back at a country that was basically nonexistent in the summer of 1994.*

That summer, **NADINE** was two years old. *As you can see, I can easily remember, because I got burned during the genocide. This, here.* She brushes

Nadine discovered a photo of herself, age two, in a display in the Children's Room at the Kigali Genocide Memorial. She recognized the matching shirts that her mother had sewn for her and her sister Belinda, age five.

her hand over a rippled patch of skin on her forearm. She's wearing a cute sleeveless sundress for her last day of school. Tomorrow she'll graduate from college. *And I, I was with my mother and two siblings. My younger brother was three months old, and I was just two, but I can still remember how we . . . when we were leaving our house, seeking refuge. We were hiding in a church called Holy Family. I even have my picture in the genocide memorial site.*

The snapshot hangs at the Kigali Genocide Memorial in a room dedicated to children who perished in 1994 and those, like Nadine, who made it.

Miraculously, Nadine's whole family survived. Her mother was alone raising Nadine, an older daughter, and two younger sons, and she prioritized their education. But at times they couldn't pay school fees. Nadine remembers with a tone of distress a time toward the end of high school when she had to miss a national exam. *I stopped going to school for two months. I kept dropping off and dropping off, but I was lucky. I completed high school.*

University felt out of the question. Nadine took a job at a supermarket, where she could make money to contribute to her family. Her supervisor, the shop owner's son, thought she had promise. *One day he was asking me, "What do you want to do? What are your dreams?" And I said, "I really wish to go to school, because I don't know what's going to happen to me next, in my future, if I don't have education."*

I think he kept this in his mind, and when he heard about the Akilah Institute for Women, he came and told me. He's like the first person in my life who ever told me I had potential.

The Akilah Institute for Women is Rwanda's first all-female college. Its debut class graduated in 2012, and First Lady Jeannette Kagame gave the convocation.

But in my mind I was like, "No, he's just encouraging me." I couldn't believe him because it's like . . . how could I even get this? I didn't really go to good schools, and I'm only a high school graduate. I came from this less advantaged family, so . . . I even told him, "You can't understand. You went to study abroad, and your father and mother were supporting you." He said, "You have to trust me that it's true. If you really work hard, you're going to achieve something better, and you're going to be someone better."

I started believing what he said when I got to Akilah, but not even right away. You know, as women, we're raised not to speak, or even believe in ourselves. But I remember once, when the teacher encouraged everyone to talk in class and express our ideas. I stood up, and I gave an opinion—it was a leadership class—and my teacher looked at me and was like, "Oh, Nadine, hold on! I think that's brilliant!" She said, "You can keep talking and give your ideas to everyone."

My classmates afterward were like, "Wow, that was amazing." And I was like, "Yeah, maybe . . ." So I started thinking about that. I thought maybe I have this potential, if I really work hard and trust in myself.

Nadine became a standout student and was selected to represent the Akilah Institute at the Women Deliver conference in Malaysia. *It was really, really cool. We were five thousand people together, with a lot of high-profile people, like Melinda Gates, Barbara Bush, and Chelsea Clinton. They*

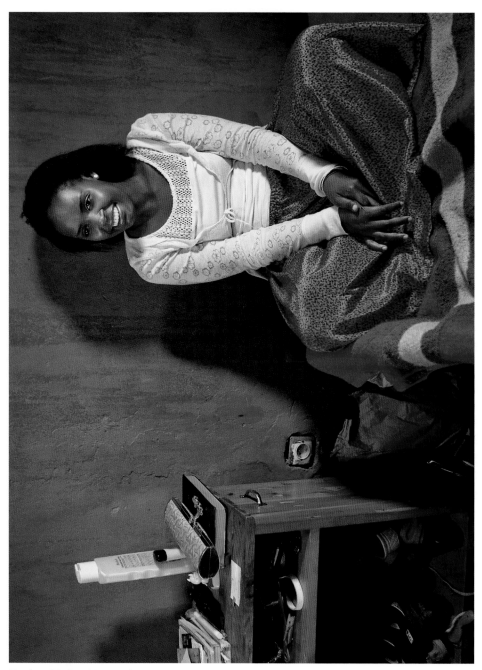

Student Nadine Niyitegeka.

gave speeches, and it was so inspiring. I think that's when I got that spirit of being a leader at Akilah, and I thought, "Okay, there are other women who are doing amazing work in the world so I can be part of that in the future."

The international exposure made Nadine feel that she was part of something bigger, but it also shifted the way she saw her opportunities at home.

While I was growing up, we had some great women leaders, like Jeanne Gakuba, Aloisea Inyumba, who died, and Rose Kabuye. They showed how powerful they were, and the government started believing in women. It was especially Aloisea Inyumba who woke my inspirations. When I grew up I heard about her, and she was really inspiring to me.

Now I think that one day I can become like her, and I can contribute something to my country. I believe that I will become a great leader with the skills and knowledge I get from Akilah. Five years ago my future looked dark, because I couldn't think that I'd be someone with talent, able to speak out and defend herself.

Marriott International was about to hire Nadine and move her to Dubai, but the Akilah Institute made her an offer she didn't want to refuse. With a modest salary, Nadine could pay for her two younger brothers to go to school. She would spend part of her time recruiting students in Rwanda and part recruiting donors abroad.

I said, "Hold on. Akilah helped me so much. I wouldn't have all these opportunities I have now without my school. I'd love to give back and be an inspiration to girls who are coming up." I think they'd be very inspired to come to Akilah if I'm showing them, as someone who went there. "Look at what happened to me now, how I'm helping my family, thinking differently than the way I did before." I'm being a world citizen! Not only an African citizen!

For a while, Nadine's standard answer when asked about her future ambitions has been that she hopes to someday serve as minister of gender. After a recent stint in the United States, she entertains another idea: maybe head of the United Nations.

JEANNETTE: Having 64 percent women in the Chamber of Deputies is not that big of a deal for Rwandans today. It's actually the opposite that raises eyebrows: from the smallest village to cabinet, people are uncomfortable when women are not visibly represented.

One of the lessons those in leadership have wisely gleaned and now pass on to their successors is about how to navigate with men. It's an essential skill in a patriarchal society that operates on a strict hierarchy. The topic generates a fair amount of dismissive gestures. "Double standards," women, and some men, mutter, where an "assertive" man equals an "aggressive" woman.

But women like **ALPHONSINE N.**, who operates primarily in the masculine world of business, is a pro at delicate maneuvering. *We're not in competition—that's what I'm trying to say to other women. We are not in competition with men. But we do need to show that we are capable. Then it's going to be easy. It will be natural when they appoint you to a higher position. You don't have to make much noise. No. Do what you think is better for you, and for your family, and for your country. Know what you need to do, and then go and do it.*

When **KIRABO** took on the powerful role of mayor of Kigali, a city of more than a million, she led a city council and an administration composed mostly of men. *If I have a problem with a man I'm working with, I don't say, "Oh, men." If I say that I'm lumping together the whole constituency of men. I try to identify the specific problem with that particular person and address him as one man, so that the others who maybe don't share that prob-*

Mayor Aisa Kirabo Kacyira.

lem will not be brought on board unnecessarily. Then the rest of the team will actually help us out of it. That builds trust.

I've had situations where I had to choose between my pride and my country. In the case of that man, I need to make him comfortable, to let him realize it's not about his manhood but about an issue. Often when there's a dispute, it's about the person feeling challenged by a woman. Or maybe how we're discussing it. I may need to go a bit lower, so that he has space to come up. Then I must make sure that when he's starting to come up, I don't let others pull him back down. If I make it a specific issue and the rest get on board, we all come up.

I always pray to God that I never, ever think I'm indispensable, because that will be the beginning of my failing. I'm part of a team. Sure, important, but not indispensable. So however tough that man might be, he's actually working to make me better. I see a lot of opportunity in that. On the other hand, there are so many other men around me who are out to help me, whom I may not see if I'm defensive. Ultimately, it's about my attitude.

An approach that has proven compelling is to emphasize the complementary role women play to men, harkening back to Rwandan tradition. Discussing the value of female leadership, people invariably mention the distinctive perspectives women bring to their work. It's part of a narrative reinforced by government officials but not an empty story line; **INYUMBA** and others supply ample anecdotal evidence.

When I was governor in the Kigali-Nigali province, I was in charge of ten very big districts. Visiting people in all these sectors was so educating. I learned how the communities already know their issues, and that they have proposals for how these issues can be addressed. People assumed that as governor I would know the priorities, but the communities would always challenge me.

If you talk to women about health they would understand more because these are their immediate needs. If you talk about food, women deal with food. If you talk about water, we are the ones who use water for domestic use, for washing.

I think that's why we women are more responsive as leaders, because we're there. These are not things we read about or watch on video. It's our daily life. I understand issues of children, of health, even legal reform and access to land—we're the ones tilling the land.

That link between women's fitness for office and their lived experience, or inherent qualities for that matter, is an argument made by not only women but also men. On the other hand, in private conversations or public addresses President Kagame does not make that link when he emphasizes inclusion and participation as fundamental to his long-held goals. Instead, he sounds like many feminists' dream as he expounds on how women have been systematically ignored and need what some would call positive discrimination—extra opportunities for education and training, in addition to the chance to learn on the job in appointed or elected positions.

The new leadership is people centered. Children's activist **ZAINA** uses a common phrase. *They don't want to leave anyone behind—women, children, young people, men. It's inclusive.* She then moves beyond the value of participation as a principle. *Laws or policies are more comprehensive when it comes to everyone's sensitivity and needs, and so they're more relevant. For example, having so many women in the Parliament means there's more concern for women and for children. They are mothers (or they're meant to be—most have children).*

Appreciation of the new inclusivity is personal to Zaina. In 1976, fresh from Belgium with a degree in social work from a prestigious institute, she applied for her first job, as a teacher in a school that trained social workers in southern Rwanda. She was refused because of her Muslim-sounding name and was hired instead as a civil servant in the Habyarimana government.

A few years later, Zaina, whose family's ethnic allegiance wasn't clear, was rejected in that job too. *I was pointed out as somebody who was not the person they wanted. People said, "We aren't sure if you are a Hutu or Tutsi." "We don't want you. . . ." I was called several times to my boss's office to be warned that if I didn't tell the truth, they would think I changed my identity. She was saying, "We aren't sure when you were in Belgium. . . . We heard you were fraternizing with the [Tutsi] refugees."*

Now, to Zaina, the presence of women throughout government structures shifts the atmosphere and priorities. *When women came in, they brought their sensitivities as wives, sisters, grandmothers. They're everything! That improves the quality of our work.* She says she doesn't necessarily believe women are by their essential nature sensitive, but rather that they're attuned to their personal experiences as they design policies.

Zaina draws an analogy: At the National Commission for Children, *we need the policy we're designing to be checked by children, who bring their own sensitivity. Every year we have a summit for children. This is also one of the principles of the new* RPF *leadership—that consultation is important.*

The different perspectives complement each other, Zaina finds. *Women can be too emotional, so having men there too is a check on everyone. We organize regular meetings with our colleagues so that decisions aren't made by just one person. Even if you're a leader, like being an executive secretary as I am, if I tried to take the decision alone, my colleagues would challenge me. And other institutions will check any policy I develop.*

This system of checks and balances really strengthens a law. Then, like one woman after another in this book, she refers to the enabling environment of the RPF as steered by Kagame. *It's not only because women came. Of course, having women makes a difference, but it's mostly about the leadership. Otherwise, women may work hard, demonstrate, but . . . niet!*

Asked whether she sees any differences in the way men and women lead, self-proclaimed feminist **JUSTINE M.** bursts into laughter. *Totally different, totally different!*

I actually envy men in leadership, not because I want to be a man. I'm proud, extremely proud of being a woman. But I like some tactics of men. They know it's never the right time or the wrong time to be in leadership, and I'd love to take that lesson for myself or for other women. You'll never be ready unless you're there. You call men, and they say yes. Women think about it. . . . And what I don't like about women, they're never sure whether it's the right time. And they keep questioning themselves.

Having women in leadership is always beneficial, Justine says, because whether or not they're activists, they add a balance to the male perspective. But Justine cautions against the view that women will inherently work on behalf of women.

The government thought—and I'm not defending government, I'm just telling you the way it is—they thought that a ministry of gender can be led by any woman. Ignorance! Just because you are a woman doesn't mean you have what it takes to make a difference in women's and family life with the ministry portfolio.

Western universities have made that mistake too. They think that automat-

At a polling station, female and male elections staff review voter names.

ically a female university chancellor will defend women's educational rights. But then she messes up, because she has no idea how to go about it. She has many other tasks, yet somehow she's expected to also spend her time advocating for women. By now the poor chancellor is pulled in two directions, and then no one is satisfied. *At the end of the day, she leaves her job, and people say, "Oh, we can't find a woman who is qualified."*

Why? Because we expect women to have these skills to promote women, but we don't help the women build them. Having a woman holding a position doesn't mean the question of women's rights advocacy is settled. The wide gap between numbers and outcomes irks her.

DOMITILLA builds on Justine's thoughts with a salient point, informed by her decade leading the gacaca justice process and hearing of atrocities women too carried out. *Part of the reason there were fewer women involved in committing genocide is that women weren't so involved in public life, in these prominent positions.* She mentions a female radio presenter who, empowered to reach masses through the airwaves, directed killers to target certain people and communities.

Genocide is a political crime. Wherever you see genocide, there's state power behind it. In our history, governance was like a family business. You had the wife of the president, and you had the brothers and uncles. So women played a role in destroying this country. But women have also played a big role in reconstruction, in rebuilding.

Then weighing the two points of view, she commits. *Our history would have been different if we'd had more women in leadership positions before. If someone asks me to commit a bad thing, as a mother, as a woman, I can't. For the women in prison, it's very tough. They feel really bad, because what they did isn't natural. Women aren't supposed to kill. They bring life.*

· · ·

The notion of women and men complementing each other may have a major downside as the Rwandan women's movement evolves, even if gender collaboration is grounded in tradition and therefore feels authentic. The idea of two distinct parts making a whole doesn't push change far enough, according to **JUSTINE U.**, as she refers to her interviews with top-level female leaders.

Many women still believe men are the head. Today they also believe that being a boss doesn't allow him to abuse his wife, but as long as we still put someone in the position of boss, there will be problems.

Even women aware of gender inequalities are reluctant to push for them to radically change. *They think this will jeopardize the peaceful, smooth influence they're making to policy and laws.* They draw on conventional roles to legitimize their place in the public square: managing the home, multitasking, and nurturing. The downside, of course, is that they're boxing themselves in so as to be accepted as politicians.

Despite the value allotted to women's domestic roles, no major moves to update husband-wife expectations have accompanied the social and political shift toward women in the workforce. Only four of the women

Justine interviewed said their husbands were more involved at home. In private, many women also face a strong backlash.

Women mentioned that some men become insecure and sometimes jealous of their wives, thinking that they are involved in adultery if they stayed at work until late. Some associated this with stereotypes relating to men's control over women's sexuality. There's a big double standard. We can sit here in the bar together eating lunch, but if you were a man, since I'm a woman, people would talk: "Oh, what's happening with those two?" Even if we are just working together. These kinds of rumors have ruined people's reputations and careers.

Justine has a PhD and she uses words like "phases" and "sampling," comparing feminism across decades, demographics, and continents. *People in the Third World think of feminism as radical—only promoting sexuality rights, like lesbianism, which is, of course, really sensitive in Rwanda and other African countries.*

Women have new opportunities, but they're expected to succeed in work that people feel, at a gut level, belongs to men. Several in Justine's study raised the stigma of being pregnant while in top posts—even though motherhood is seen as a defining characteristic for proper women and especially for those with the stature to be leaders. One MP told Justine it felt wrong to be pregnant as a politician, because one might "appear like a person who is stupid . . . someone who doesn't know what she wants."

Fortunately I had the authority of being gender sensitive, an activist, and Rwandan. So these women would turn to me and ask, "So Justine, what is feminism? Are you a feminist?" And I'd say, "Oh, yes. I am." If there were a way to teach people what feminism is, what gender equality really means, I think they would quickly adopt it.

Unfortunately, with our economic development approach, we talk about gender equality in numbers—such as how many women are in politics, how many have started financial activities so they can be economically independent. Even if these ideas have some link to feminism, it's not clear that we're coming from the angle of knowing our rights and being able to ensure them. We're coming from an angle that doesn't touch on the relationships between men and women.

With her usual bluntness, **JUSTINE M.** says she's hopeful that the upcoming generation will usher in these more fundamental changes. But they won't take hold without the foresight of the old guard. *We must support women to find their empowered roles at all costs and by all means. Use the rhetoric if it makes sense, but if not, find words to really make women feel like they have a choice of whether or not to get married, to have children, to go back to school. And they have the right to change their careers if they want to.*

Both Justine M. and Justine U. observe that the Rwandan women's movement does not have the zeal of a revolution against either the constraints of convention or the abuse of patriarchal power. But that's no surprise. The first wave of women's advancement came to a screeching halt with the murder of Prime Minister Agathe Uwilingiyimana. And those hundred days in 1994 that followed changed everything.

From that point, it was country first, or what was left of the country. Women stepped into the power vacuum created by social upheaval, spurred on by their grasp of urgency.

This was hardly the time for women to fill the streets, demonstrating for their rights. Instead, with few exceptions, the abandonment of Rwanda by the rest of the world lent great appeal to the notion of elevating the women-empowering ideals of yore. How redemptive to reach back into the annals of a powerful queen mother, a fearless (if disguised) female warrior, and a pioneering cabinet member from three decades before.

But that was then. How can the country now move beyond the empowering ideals of yore?

ODA: The way forward is hand in hand. Give a hand and
get a hand.

ALPHONSINE N.'s beauty academy has a purpose greater than training a
cohort of young people to be skilled in manicure, massage, and braiding—
although generating a team of dependable stylists to staff her chain of
salons is an added benefit. The students in their white lab coats share
creative tips and mingle around the haircutting stations. They're all here
to learn a trade they hope will earn them consistent work or, in some
cases, work they can at last feel proud to do.

A number of the students have prostituted themselves. Alphonsine
has set up a program they can participate in confidentially not only to
learn the skills to work in a salon but also to receive counseling and
mentoring to help them stay off the streets. She visited places in the
capital where men were buying the bodies of women and girls, and she
encouraged them to come to her academy. *You need to listen to them carefully, slowly. And then step by step, you try to understand how they came to
that situation.*

*They show you what they want to achieve. They have ambition! Most peo-
ple think they don't, but they do.*

Several of Alphonsine's enterprises have a social bent to them, even
if she sees herself foremost as a standard businessperson. She made her
foray into industry by investing in a beauty salon (or "saloon," as it's typically spelled and pronounced in Rwanda). Soon she amassed a network
of salons and a commercial property. She rents out the storefronts and
puts her beauty academy in the back.

Alphonsine's latest venture is an affordable housing development. She relishes her status as a rare woman in business. *You know why I want to do this new project? Well, one reason . . . only men are building houses! Only men take on these big projects.*

Whether with vulnerable students at her academy or over tea with fledgling entrepreneurs, Alphonsine carves out time for mentorship.

Most of the younger ladies are really serious, and they look to us as role models. They come to my office to discuss my experience. I take them through what I've been doing, and I coach them on how they should behave if they want to achieve, if they want to go further.

Even tomorrow, I have an appointment with a girl who wants to establish a hair salon. I can guess she'll want to know the challenges I've faced in my business, and what solutions I've found. Most of them see me on TV or read about me in newspapers. I don't know where they get my phone number! But I'm really, really happy to share my experience with them.

Then a deft nod to her housing project: *We show them that we can do big things, like men. It's not a competition, just making our contribution to the economy, and to the nation. We're just helping to try and solve problems, because problems are always there, and we should be part of those bringing solutions.*

Mentorship is at the crux of sustaining and building on the work of activists over the past twenty years. But few formal programs coordinate these exchanges, and women in the vanguard often express disappointment about the lack of continuity or about not finding time to form relationships with those who could follow their lead.

LOUISE says women need to proactively cultivate the next generation by modeling the roles and also speaking out about what it took to get there. *We should share our experiences much more and talk about the hardships we've lived. We can be candid about the difficulties women face in school or in the workplace, and keep giving them that message of strength. They can't give up!*

She adds a typical Louise elixir of logic and will. *Women have to keep going, to a point where they feel like they're almost there, and it makes no sense to turn back.*

On the other hand, veterans suffer the classic angst of social movements. They question their impact and worry that young women today

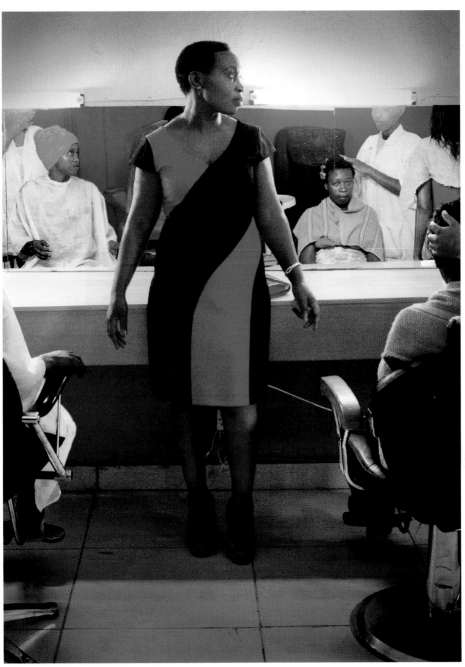

Entrepreneur Alphonsine Niyigena.

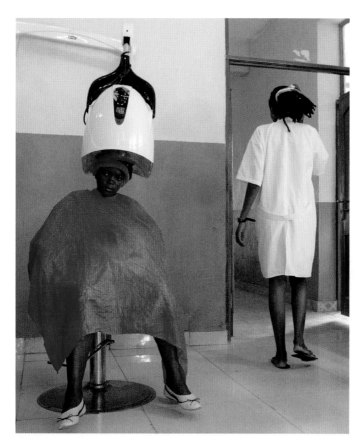

Students at Alphonsine's Universal Beauty Academy practice new skills on each other first.

don't appreciate the sacrifices or won't feel the necessity of continuing their struggle.

JUSTINE M. is concerned that she sees energy among her peers flagging. *Building the next generation isn't forgotten, but it's not sustainable, especially when you're talking about high-quality activism: the real women who would not be scared to be called feminists. Rwanda's feminists. Fearless women who call corruption "corruption" and don't sugarcoat it by calling it something else. Very few are left.*

She mentions several women and then struggles to come up with other names. *So, you know, there is a generation gap—no question about it. Women today are in school, but they have zero idea how we fought for affirmative action.*

Artist Carole Karemera.

Today we have women ambassadors! Before Beijing, before our movement, our rules said there could be no female ambassador. The law we changed in 1998 stated that, in order to be an ambassador, you need the permission from your husband. Can you imagine! It discriminated against a woman (a) who was not married, (b) a widow, or (c) married to a jealous husband. . . .

Tell me, how many men would give consent for his wife to become an ambassador, since an ambassador's spouse is not supposed to work? You're supposed to be a stay-at-home and support your partner. In my Rwandan culture, a man would never consent to be a stay-home dad and support you. So that was clear discrimination, and we argued for the transitional parliament to change those laws.

We did the frontline activism, but we forgot to build the next generation. That's the key. When Inyumba was appointed minister, she was not quite thirty! But if you ask a thirty-year-old today who isn't part of the government, who isn't part of anything, most will just tell you, "Oh, I believe women deserve their rights. Blah blah blah blah." But if you ask them, "Tell me a bit about how women's voices in Rwanda came to be heard," they have no clue. They don't know the history or why it's important.

First of all, we don't document very well. But it's more. The challenges were so immense when this got started. We didn't have time to build the front line and then go back and build the incoming generation.

•   •   •

Justine M. may be right. Many women like her ponder their seasoned sense of purpose and in candid moments admit to feeling the movement lacks direction. Being among the first to chart this pursuit was energizing in part because it required them to band together, to claim a common vision, to look beyond differences. Outcomes were unknown, and that itself was exhilarating.

But the lament is far from the minds of young women emerging from the nurturance their foremothers fostered. They've come of age in a different era, with different stories and mores governing how they see their place in society.

Like the generation before her, **CAROLE** held images of Rwanda in her mind's eye, painted by her mother. Carole had been born in Belgium and saw herself as both European and Rwandese. *The Rwandese part of me* *was really idealized.* She had only seen the country of her parents' birth through a plane window when flying to visit her grandfather in Burundi.

In 1994, we saw the images of Rwanda right in our living room, so suddenly it was the right time to discuss why we were born outside of the country. And the images were really violent, so it forced my mother and my aunties to talk about our history. Even if we were born refugees, we were never taught to hate at all. So we said, "Okay, can you now explain this country of milk and honey?"

Two years after that conversation, Carole packed a duffel bag and flew to Rwanda.

When I went back—or went for the first time—it was a journey to discover my country for myself, on my own terms. It was difficult to talk about everything with my mom, and my father and sister had barely escaped the genocide. Carole wasn't going to talk about the terrors to family members just after their brush with death. *Everyone was in shock. So I said none of them could come with me.*

I refused to go to memorial sites. Actually, there weren't even memorial sites yet. . . . I just wanted to see the beauty of my country. It was quite dangerous at that time, but I knew some people who could tell me, "Okay, you can take that road today but maybe not tomorrow."

She spent the whole six weeks moving around, hitching rides or piling into crowded minibuses. *I used to say "I'm Rwandan," but now my feet know what that means. I know how the hills are.* Often she walked alongside women returning from the fields and crossed from village to village by foot. The sight of her—with her dancer body and shorn hair—sparked curiosity, she remembers with a smile. *I was so full of muscles. There was this idea like, "Is she a girl? A man?"*

I was visiting all parts of my country, except for the West, where my father was from. I said, "This part I can only visit with him, but the rest I can do by myself."

Carole was finishing her degree in Belgium but found time each year to spend in her true country. *I joined a group of African writers from the diaspora. This was 1998 and the first time that I sat with the survivors, with killers, visited the sites where massacres had taken place. And it was like . . . whoa. Hell. This was where it becomes really difficult to confront being Rwandan. But I was—how can I say?—lucky enough to have a medium to absorb*

Skulls, each once full of life, of those who perished at one massacre site.

and process it. Through my art. I could have discussions with those writers, philosophers, to try and understand and explain.

That time in Rwanda was very difficult, because you could feel the energy of the people who left, of the people who passed away, and at the same time the energy of the living. People were crying in the morning and then laughing in the afternoon when they discovered someone else was alive. I felt like, I'm just a girl. What can I do here? I don't know how to build houses. I don't have health diplomas—the things people needed at that time.

Everyone was traumatized. No one was talking about what they felt. As an artist, I thought, this is a bomb that will have to go off one day. The culture is to be introverted, reserved. And I said, "This can't work forever." In my mind, art would have something to do with how we would cope. But no one had time to think about this then. They needed to eat. They needed HIV drugs. So I just took this all in.

I went back to Belgium, and I wasn't sure I wanted ever to go back to Rwanda. As a student in Europe, you learn about the genocides—the Jewish, the Armenian. You learn about the mechanisms of genocide. I said to my mother, *"But I don't understand how we . . . we have the same language, the same culture, so how come . . ."* She hesitates over her words. *It was really hard for me to stand up and . . . be proud to be Rwandan.*

Carole not only visited again, she moved back. She drew on her background as a dancer and actress and worked with other artists to test out some projects they felt could be helpful and sensitive. They set up a library bus and toured the country visiting elementary schools. They helped local artists build art centers. Carole played the lead role in the HBO production *Sometimes in April*, the first major film about the genocide produced in the country, with an almost entirely Rwandan cast and crew.

She's particularly fond of one project that encouraged people to sift through their full range of memories, not only concentrating on 1994. *I'd say, "Okay, if you could keep only one memory, and after that we erase all the others, which would you choose?" And everyone would laugh! Only one memory? Then they're smiling and thinking, " . . . only one?" An hour before they're just sitting distracted, but when you talk about life memories and ask them to search their minds, they're like, "Wow."*

One woman shared that her most important memory was when she was living with thirteen family members in one small house. She said, "I was fifteen years old, and I was complaining, 'I have no space!' But now I realize that was the most beautiful moment in my life. Of the fourteen of us, just four are remaining. But when I think about being crowded like that, feeling each other, breathing together . . ."

You realized that the neighbors you targeted or the person in prison—you had some good memories of them. It was like placing your bets on life and not thinking only about death.

The young Rwandans coming back are motivated by duty, curiosity, and a desire to contribute to the new era of their homeland. Some want to take up the mantel of women's rights activists but with a modern twist and coach young female entrepreneurs, technology specialists, or artists. Others, like Carole, are compelled to delve deeper into the haunting effects of the genocide and bring out stories even from that time that offer hope and a way forward.

I met a young girl who was completely beside herself because she'd just realized that her father did the budget for the genocide. She was twenty-six, and she felt like, "That's impossible. Not my dad." So there are different ways of reacting. It's difficult to reject your family. But if you're lucky enough, you're surrounded by people who will take you as yourself. The message is: "You are not your parents. They'll remain your parents whatever you do in life, but you can act and make different choices."

•   •   •

A year before her death, Gender Minister **INYUMBA** appealed to women with her famous soft-spoken intensity, squarely placing the onus for empowerment on them: *Now that you have the government that advocates for you, develop self-confidence and use the available opportunities to raise your value as we fight to develop our country.*

Developing their country, in the broadest sense of the phrase, requires women to step forward, juggling competing demands in a society that strongly values them as homemakers, even as it increasingly welcomes their input in political and social matters.

Twenty-four-year-old **NADINE** could allay some of Justine M.'s concerns about the "blah, blah, blah" younger generation. The responsibility to push the movement forward falls not just to the early generation of women leaders. Nadine has taken the call to heart and is already recruiting her peers to engage—with the example she sets, but also tough love.

My friends, even my siblings, I know they look up to me. They say, "We didn't even recognize you!" "Nadine, you're so busy now! You're a professional lady, and you're not giving us a lot of time."

You know, sometimes when you're a teenager, there's no plan. Your friends just come to you and you sit and talk, and sometimes I'm like, "You know, I'm going to give you twenty minutes, then I'm going to read my book, or I'm going to work on something." And they're like, "Why?" I say, "Because we're only talking, and I'm looking for something that can help me more in my future. I'm trying to develop my skills and my personality, and I'm trying to become someone really. . . . I like you so much, so I will give you some time, but not all of it. And you should do the same. You should have some schedule in your life." I mean, I didn't have these ideas, but I learned them.

Far from questioning the lasting purpose of the women's movement, Nadine draws passion from believing that her generation will preserve a legacy set in motion by heroes.

Aloisea Inyumba started when there were very few women in leadership. But those leaders are getting older, so you have to think, who is the future Aloisea Inyumba?

That's, like, my dream. We're still young. We can do as much as she did. Or even more.

Genocide has no silver lining. That idea itself is an outrage to our sensibilities. When writing about even moderate opportunities in the wake of mass violence, the scope of tragedy must not be obscured.

In Rwanda, that scope was notorious: nearly one million people killed between April and July 1994. With a UN peacekeeping mission already on the ground as the tempest brewed, the depth of calamity might have been mitigated. But by either willful disregard or pledges of ignorance, this small country became an infamy borne by the international community as well as the perpetrators.

Now, more than two decades later, the end of this account can turn to the informed community writ large, those men and women who may directly or indirectly influence how countries progress toward fair representation of all citizens.

Some of you are preachers, professors, or pundits looking for the ingredients of meaningful democracy, not simply a recipe replete with lofty words. Others are women, like me, who have too often let obstacles define our way. These stories and analyses light the path that we call our future.

Many of us are parents, focused on a new generation. I hope that as you've taken in these stories, you've felt a push to pull your daughters into leadership. Perhaps you'll see in those daughters and their daughters flourishing hope for a more stable, less violent world.

And so we emerge, different from when we began some 350 pages ago. And hopefully that difference is akin to lessons (a banal word that seems obscenely light) that we can recite to ourselves over and over, as we develop new habits of mind and habits of heart.

Try as we may to not make the same mistakes, we'll never get it right. But we don't have to get it as wrong as in Rwanda. As I said in the introduction, no two countries have the same combination of insights or experiences. Obviously they all have talented and trained women leaders. But in addition, countries of every size, political structure, and economic status join Rwanda with breakthrough advances. As we learn from them all, here are four thoughts—actually only fleeting mentions of thoughts, since each is worth its own tome.

1. Elevate Women throughout All Sectors of Society

"How did we do it? How were we able to pull it off?" Those who ask, in marveling at our success, underestimate the power of women. Women working objectively for a common cause and toward a common goal.

—Ellen Johnson Sirleaf, the president of Liberia, as guest of President Kagame at a regional women's conference organized by Aloisea Inyumba

In Rwanda, both male and female members of Parliament say that women were more likely to prioritize education, health, children, and basic needs. But outside that country, as all manner of researchers have examined whether women as a group are more honest than men as a group, many of their findings suggest that this folk wisdom is generally true: women have an abundance of these and other positive qualities— although there are always factors that play against each other. (For example, being more empathic makes it harder for women to compete against others for public office.) Still, these characteristically feminine attributes are essential in countries that we hold up as modern beacons for the world in which we want to live.

The value of elevating women is not a matter of conjecture. For decades, a litany of research has rolled in. Across Moscow, Dubai, and New York, women are more trustworthy than men. Fortune 500 companies with more women on their boards have a stronger bottom line. And Bangladeshi women repay loans at a much higher rate than men.[1] U.K. female politicians have stronger constituent relationships; in the United States they cosponsor more bills across party divides. In India they fund more water infrastructure for the community.[2]

Involved in policy making from the ground up.

And so elevating women is not simply about fairness or rights, but a matter of life and death: Yes, globally violence against women correlates with countries going to war. But in addition, their education leads to fewer children (and less strain on the environment), and it's the most important factor in child malnutrition. One statistic is particularly stunning: the World Bank says that in Brazil income to a woman, compared to income to a man, impacts child survival by 20 percent.[3]

It's possible to keep a psychological distance from these statistics. Legislators may assign staffers to examine the paradox that high child mortality leads to larger families. Environmentalists may get lost in the weeds of the relationship between family size and deforestation. But for the woman holding her dying child, the mental anguish and physical toll of her grief are the stuff of poetry and prayer, which reach far beyond pencils and paper—in a space called soul.

That is the "why" of women's advancement. But what of the "how"? Where's a model that can lead us forward?

Simply put, strong women in policy making means stronger policies for women. In 2016, the United States, ninety-fifth in the world in the number of women in parliament, is hardly a paragon; actually, there's no state that comes close to matching Rwanda's 64 percent. The largest gap between any two countries in the world is between Rwanda and the next in line, Bolivia, with a parliament that's 53 percent female.[4]

In addition to other outstanding levels of representation (e.g., approximately half the Supreme Court judges and half the cabinet), women make up 20 percent of the Rwandan National Police.[5] And despite all the population's discrepancies in the rights and literacy of men and women, the 2015 Global Gender Gap Index of the World Economic Forum ranked the nation sixth out of 142 in gender equality. (The United States is twenty-eighth.)

How have other countries surpassed the United States so dramatically? Certainly the lauded leadership pipeline is important, but from my experience in partisan politics its consequence is overrated. In fact, rarely do people speak of a pipeline when discussing men's strong numbers in the public sphere: more often than women, men target the position they want and just go after it.

So rather than look elsewhere for keys to the global advancement of women, it makes more sense to flip back to part II, which lays out ten basic elements that unexpectedly merged to support women's upsurge in Rwanda. The model found there—a trend line from high political offices to low—is so counterintuitive to Americans that it's hard for us to wrap our minds around it. These women were in high positions *before* they held a large number of local offices. It took hands-on mentoring, as women appointed by the top leadership or elected to high positions returned to their villages to convince local constituents that politics isn't just a man's sphere. The equivalent would be U.S. Congresswomen going back to their home districts with such focused energy that they doubled the number of female mayors in one election.

That dynamic of high-echelon leaders enticing upward movement from the bottom of the power pyramid reflected both necessity and a strong value of the Rwandan Patriotic Front. But it has been a clear emphasis of the president himself, whose pull from the top has been incalculably powerful. I left a great many more references to his encouragement in my video files than I included in this book.

Another key element in women's surge is probably linked to how particularly relational they are. That's the power of role models: it's striking how often the names of Inyumba and a few others are invoked by women and girls urban or rural, across years, and throughout provinces.

Still on the relational proclivity of women, much more than men, they advance in groups. There must be trailblazers, of course. But the courage and comfort women draw from companionship is probably why in Rwanda (and elsewhere) they rarely are consumed with pushing themselves as individuals into the limelight. Men, when asked why they want to be in top political positions, are more likely to note their own forceful competencies and successes; women usually talk about how they can help their nation by shaping policies that promote businesses, education, health care, fair wages—and, if necessary, by actually running for office themselves.

And finally, women bring into public policy and society writ large an important balance of perspectives and styles. With a career that spans the apex of academia as well as the security sector, Joseph Nye's voice carries extraordinary gravitas as he reaches beyond the gender differences debate to apply his own conclusion: "In the past, when women fought their way to the top of organizations, they often had to adopt a 'masculine style,' violating the social norm of female 'niceness.' Now, however, with the information revolution and democratization demanding more participatory leadership, the 'feminine style' is becoming a path to more effective leadership. In order to lead successfully, men will not only have to value this style in their women colleagues, but will also have to master the same skills."[6]

Professor Nye's words are directly applicable to Rwanda, where women from base to crest have powered their country's progress. In the words of **MARIE**, former senator and president of the women's caucus: *Our country is in a difficult position. But when women, with one voice, say, "We want things to change for the better," it's possible. It's possible.*

2. Open Your Thinking about the Meaning of Security

> Over the long sweep of history, women have been and will be a pacifying force. Traditional war is a man's game: tribal women never band together to raid neighboring villages.
>
> —Steven Pinker, Harvard professor and author of *The Better Angels of Our Nature: Why Violence Has Declined*

Despite how the military and law enforcement establishments may claim the word, "security" is broader than we've imagined, in plot and among players. The relatively new notion of human security includes food, health care, and shelter, but also emotional ties. Figuring out what we need, and how to ensure we have it, is the work of scientists and politicians, but also teachers, doctors, and counselors. Watchful mothers; nurturing fathers; doting brothers; protective sisters. These supporting cast members rarely are listed in the drama of history. But those without family or friend testify to pain so great that they may end the ache by ending their lives—an act as deadly as any other battle.

Unlike bombs, bullets, and barbed wire, human security is more compatible with humanity, and with human beings, for that matter. To wit, a Kenyan parent asked me, "What difference is it if my daughter is shot, or if she's gang-raped coming home from school and dies of AIDS? She's dead."

Rwandans have figured out a model that's rare in a world awash with weapons. A decade ago, parliamentarian **AGNES** said to me, *Sometimes people define peace in terms of war, but it's more. For the long term, we have stable institutions, our political parties are working, we have elections. We also have investments, a strong economy as a solution to poverty. We know how to build effective programs at the local, regional, or African levels. These are strong pillars of peace.*

Going further, a new paradigm of security has required a new nomenclature. The words "peace process" have long referred to talks happening at a formal negotiating table. But the process of making peace is much more nuanced. Foreign policy experts have tuned in to this complexity, now using jargon like "first track" (the formal meetings), "second track" (behind the scenes), and "third track" (the overall environment) to indicate whether the action is taking place at the negotiating table, between

Presiding over a session of Parliament.

negotiators in a hotel corridor tête-à-tête, or influenced by a report on the evening news.

Another turning point in the security paradigm has become deciding whether the goal is to end war or build peace. The difference is profound. Ending war is about fighters putting down their arms. Building peace requires citizens to extend their arms. Empirical analysis of eight decades of international crises shows that mediation may result in short-term stability—a cessation of hostilities—but the cost is frequently long-term peace.[7] That's because ending war, with fighters stashing their Kalashnikovs under the table and dividing up the lumber, the diamonds, and the oil, doesn't make space for new players with new ideas. Yet lasting peace relies on as many stakeholders as possible—universities, religious groups, government ministries, businesses, media outlets, parliaments, victims' associations, youth groups—in fact, the more the better. Those organized groups (and visionary individuals) will find their own, often unintentional, ways of building connections over the chasm of the conflict. Parliaments will fund reparations, businesses will exchange products, youth groups will stage hip-hop concerts, and so on.

These three shifts in the definition of security—extending to general well-being, recognizing multiple levels of influence, and expanding to positive forces from across society—have just started to acknowledge the potential of having women as major contributors. Data from a wide range of postconflict settings demonstrate that women's participation transforms structures, methods, and outcomes of peace processes writ large. From the earliest days picking up the remnants of Rwandan society, to designing foundational documents like the 2003 constitution, to organizing laddered women's councils across the country, women have been a steadying weight.

Those of us who work worldwide can imagine Agnes's words coming out of the mouths of our brave and wise friends in Guatemala, Myanmar, Libya, or Kosovo. But from concept to deed, we've seen in this book how women's groups have carried out values of the ruling Rwandan Patriotic Front and other progressive political parties, going to extraordinary lengths to secure a full, lasting peace. They've sat together weaving baskets, building trust as they've told each other their stories. They've cooked for prisoners who attacked them, meals to be delivered to the jails by the wives with whom they now worship. They've started enterprises, intentionally hiring across ethnic lines and social strata.

My choosing those examples is no surprise, since women's leadership is my particular foreign policy area. But this theme goes beyond my personal interest. We must account for women's impact on stability to have a security paradigm rooted in reality.

Their impact is often marked by inclusiveness. Perhaps that's because women have firsthand experience being excluded. Whatever the reason, they bring into decision making other stakeholders, often minorities who might otherwise become spoilers. Whether in negotiated agreements, seminal political structures, or postconflict reconstruction plans, when women are central, the process includes wide-ranging popular priorities (such as human rights or anticorruption laws). As they organize the new peace, women address the cause-and-effect loop of conflict.

More and more individual studies are creating a fuller picture. For example, we see from 182 negotiations that a peace agreement is 35 percent more likely to last for fifteen years if women participate in its creation.[8] Another study of forty peace processes, from Indonesia to Yemen, concludes that "when women's groups have influenced a peace process, a peace agreement was almost always reached and the agreement was more likely to be implemented. When women's groups had little or no influence on the process, the chance of reaching an agreement was considerably lower."[9]

To those who disagree with Professor Pinker's premise that females are less prone to group violence than males, even if women don't have that virtue, they are perceived that way—and public perception counts. (Among 64,000 people surveyed in thirteen nations by authors of *The Athena Doctrine*, a 2013 best-seller, two-thirds feel the world would be a better place if men acted more like women.) In negotiations, credibility comes from not being seen as full party to the conflict. Here women have an advantage, generally eschewing violence. But they're critical to the next stage too, since the ultimate success of an agreement depends on its being accepted in day-to-day life, and women are, for the most part, not only keepers of the house but also keepers of the community.

With a policy picture this blindingly obvious, how is it possible that more than two decades later (from 1992), a mere 9 percent of negotiating team members and a minuscule 2 percent of the actual mediators have been women?[10]

Perhaps the problem is that a more complex process (with representatives from 51 percent of the population) is messier and more unpredictable. It's also possible that our problem is the lens through which we look at security. One of my great failures as a diplomat was as U.S. ambassador to Austria hosting fourteen days of negotiations between two of the warring parties in Bosnia. Until we were all at the White House for the signing of the agreement, and I looked around the auditorium at a sea of gray suits, I was unnervingly unaware that the teams were 100 percent male.

Or perhaps we think that the problems women face (often on behalf of the entire community) can be relegated to a lower tier of priorities while men work on the supposedly hard issues. The engagement of women—who often have a strong sense of what is needed to find common ground, as well as a pragmatic willingness to compromise—has almost always been ignored. Here's another possibility for their exclusion that carries a punch: when I asked a UN official why there were no women in the negotiations going on across Africa, he replied that the warlords refused to have females on their teams. They were afraid the women would compromise. The irony wasn't lost on either of us.

As I finish writing this epilogue, horrific wars are raging in Syria and South Sudan. Their social structures and governance systems are broken. There, and in virtually every other conflict zone in the world, women like those in Rwanda have been tested. They are strong, wise, and willing.

In Rwanda, serving on the constitutional drafting committee was a key political boon. However, despite seventeen more years of global wisdom from which to learn, in Egypt, after the Tahrir Square revolution, men's 94 percent majority on the drafting committee spelled a key political disaster.[11]

Of course this isn't about Rwanda and Egypt. At the end of the American Revolution, Abigail Adams famously urged her husband John to "remember the ladies" as he played a major part drafting the U.S. Constitution.[12] Since postconflict is usually preconflict, we can wonder how the U.S. Constitution might be different had John's memory been better. Had half the drafters been women, might they have given themselves the vote, instead of having to wait 150 years? Since we know that women tend to look out for other excluded groups, might they have insisted on voting rights for all adults, including black people? Or perhaps directly abolished slavery, saving the country from a civil war, the greatest horror of its history?

However appealing the dream, traditional security is an entrenched sphere, and it's hard for women to break in. Including them is a matter of political and social will, but the more that women use their leadership in government to insert themselves into peace processes, the more the security culture will change, and the more other women will want to follow.

Unlike many of their predecessors, most of today's women leaders have grown into power since the UN conference in Beijing, which I've referred to before, and will again. They bring an acute awareness of themselves as female, with an alternative to a brawnier style of governance. The question is whether policy makers will respond to their ideas with a paternalistic sigh, like the general with whom I met at the end of the initial U.S. "shock and awe" bombing of Baghdad. When I urged that he broaden his search for "future leaders of Iraq," which had yielded hundreds of men and only seven women, he said patiently, "Madame Ambassador, thank you so much for your time. And let me assure you, we'll address women's issues after we get the place secure." I wondered which women's issues he was talking about. Breast cancer? I was talking about security.

3. Outsiders, Show Up

> PATRICIA: Of course to sustain the social sector, we need economic development. You know, we don't have donors who will remain forever to hand us checks.

Back in 2002, Patricia's wariness was prescient. Rwandan women are now known globally for their high achievements, even though the nuts and bolts of their scaffolding have not been obvious. Their climb has been paradoxical: isolation made them strong, and strength now attracts partners.

That puzzle is a fascinating element in Rwanda's recent history as success has bred success. President Kagame doesn't hesitate to point out the inconsistency of current outsider helpers, closing a speech at the African Economic Conference by saying, "Official development assistance may be scarce, and its efficiency regressive. The case for weaning ourselves off aid is strong enough, and this reality should spur us into fast-tracking appropriate plans towards this end."[13] It's a theme he repeats frequently, often linking his warning to the abject failure of the world to intervene in the genocide. In a head-turning twist, his assertion that he is determined to make his nation independent of international assistance (such as that of the UN) has been an implicit attraction to smaller assistance providers.

That self-reliant, pragmatic, and enterprising tone brings in outsiders who believe they will be able to conduct business straightforwardly instead of under the table. "Many Chinese and Western corporations invest in Africa for access to sub-soil assets, cheap labor and government favors," says Michael Fairbanks, presidential advisor and chairman of the board of the Akilah Institute for Women. "But those who invest in Rwanda do so because the government is competent; the private sector is lauded; and because public and private sector leaders have a shared progressive vision. They believe, for example, that the only investments with the possibility of infinite returns are investments in women."[14]

There are hundreds of examples of outside businesses, philanthropists, and NGOs drawn to Rwanda because of the country's combination of needs and possibilities.

Earlier, when we described Janet and Joy working with widows and other vulnerable women to produce stunning jewelry carried by Macy's and other retail outlets (from Neiman Marcus to the U.S. Holocaust Museum), we didn't say that a primary partner has been activist Mary Fisher, who showed by example the kind of fulfilling life a person with HIV/AIDS can live and inspired many of the Gahaya Links entrepreneurs to start treatment. There's also Michael Ruettgers, former head of data storage giant EMC Corporation, who helped densely populated Rwanda develop technology as a trade not dependent on land. And investor Bobby Sager, an energetic and influential Young Presidents Organization activist, has brought his family philanthropy and the attention of many other entrepreneurs into the country to support small, innovative NGOs.

Similarly, when we write about the public health successes overseen by Minister of Health Agnes Binagwaho, we should be mindful of hospitals and clinics funded in part by USAID (the U.S. foreign aid agency), as well as the extensive network of Partners in Health. That organization is the child of world-renowned physician Paul Farmer, who brings in medical specialists from abroad but also engages more than 7,000 Rwandan community health workers in his web of care, to serve some 800,000 patients.[15] Dr. Farmer put Rwanda at the top of the list of countries in which his organization has been on the ground, in large part because of the responsiveness of the government. He says succinctly, "We get more done in Rwanda than anywhere else in the world." (He even moved his family to Kigali for nearly a decade.) Former U.S. president Bill Clinton

Computer lab at the Akilah Institute, Rwanda's first women's college.

says his own work to end HIV/AIDS could have been a much greater success if other state leaders had responded like Kagame.

Our Institute for Inclusive Security is one of several invited by parliamentarians and government officials to offer expertise to a ravaged public-sector system. Law schools from Oxford, Stanford, Harvard, and other world-class universities have contributed to the crafting of the new constitution and the evaluation of the gacaca justice system, as well as a host of other broad or discrete projects.

Myriad education entrepreneurs have created opportunities for women and girls. The Maranyundo Girls School grew out of one of Inyumba's Boston visits, where she and Sister Ann Fox inspired local philanthropists to imagine and help create the high-achieving middle school. Similarly, the Akilah Institute for Women, the country's first women's college, was the shared vision of dedicated, young, and energetic Elizabeth Dearborn-Hughes and key Rwandan advisors, who together recognized the need to encourage and provide an avenue for young women to study beyond high school.

The return of talented Rwandans to their homeland is astounding, especially considering that many returnees were born in exile. That's in no small part due to Inyumba's ongoing work with the diaspora before, during, and after the genocide. She was often at his side as President Kagame traveled abroad, the two of them encouraging the diaspora to be part of the rebuilding. Even with her death, his constant efforts continue to pay off; formally and informally, there are now a host of opportunities for young Rwandans, spurred by organizations like Bridge2Rwanda, which sponsors new university scholarships annually for the country's next generation of leaders.

Obviously, few of us are moving to Rwanda to start a school. Few will host President Kagame's entourage for anything like a technology charrette to analyze how his nation might expand exports. But historic change happens less in grand sweeps than in small gestures. Anyone fortunate enough to be living nearer a bookstore than a bomb shelter can share the story of Rwanda's women with those worldwide who stare into broken mirrors and see broken families and broken dreams. Their spirits are not broken. Like the women of Rwanda, they must rise.

4. Remember, Make Room

For Rwandan women leaders, taking opportunities (often made possible by the hosts) to attend international conferences has come with a price as the leaders have been pulled from their posts at extremely fragile times. But those gatherings have also had enduring payoffs.

In the first postgenocide years, invitations flooded in, so much so that the women had to get permission from the top to leave the country. That said, in addition to outside contacts that led to more help for their nation, seeing themselves through others' eyes, and in a different context, was important to their personal power.

In particular, a delegation of courageous activists made the long journey to the UN's Fourth World Conference on Women: Action for Equality, Development, and Peace (which we referenced in earlier chapters).

They and Bosnian women who had suffered the unimaginable campaign of rape as a weapon of war became the focus of outrage, sparking urgent declarations calling for change. That said, the UN moves at glacial speed. It took an absurd thirteen years for the Security Council to unanimously pass Resolution 1820, which asserts that "rape and other forms of sexual violence can constitute war crimes, crimes against humanity or a constitutive act with respect to genocide."

Perhaps the most important part of Beijing was not the words on paper, but the extent to which the enormous gathering was galvanizing. **JUSTINE M.** says, *I remember vividly—Beijing was a trigger. It was 1995, one year after the genocide. We were looking left and right—no stable institutions. Nobody to hire you—or even fire you! No clear structure where you fit in.*

At home we had, I don't know, probably half a million widows. Two million orphans hanging around in orphanages, churches . . . we didn't know where to start, but we needed to do something. The conference was a stepping-stone, because we came back with a uniting cause. That solidarity was the entry point to the development you see in this country. We had our great, great women like the late Minister Inyumba, the late Veneranda Nzambazamariya, the late Judith Kanakuze, to name a few. But most importantly we had the will and determination to speak for women's rights. The public sector was working collectively with civil society. We would meet to talk about issues and solutions—until 4 AM. We'd just stand up—cry or sing or clap or jump—to get more energy. Then we'd sit again.

I was the first student of gender studies. When I came back from Beijing, I had a big task, in collaboration with Pro-Femmes and Réseau des Femmes: Go into the community—rural areas, the grass roots. Explain to women what gender is and how it can help them.

I traveled the entire country. Some women were building their own houses. My role was to tell them that they weren't alone. "Women around the world are trying to make a difference," I said, "and this is a part of them making a difference."

I'm not sure I was explaining the right thing—but whatever it was, it was very, very inspirational; I think I gained more than they gained from me. They actually named me "Gender"! As I passed by, they'd call out, "Gender! Gender!"

When they returned, women were able to base their advocacy on for-

Yes, and yes again as Inyumba encourages women to step forward.

mal declarations and resolutions from that meeting, including the provision in the Beijing platform supporting a 30 percent quota for women in decision-making positions. But the change wasn't theoretical. As Justine says, *Most of the first bunch of women in the Parliament were Beijing women.* Today's world record for women in parliament was born in Beijing, because someone insisted on making room.

· · ·

There are millions of women who, like their sisters in Rwanda, find their lives turned inside out by fighting all around them and atrocities perpetrated on them. They've begun our interviews with phrases like, "I never in my wildest dreams imagined that our community . . ." or "I was the high school principal, and my husband was the sports reporter for the paper; we were normal, everyday citizens . . ." or "I hope nobody, even the people who did this to my family, ever has to go through what we experienced." As they've told it, the shooting started, prayers became war whoops, and residents were suddenly refugees without address or identity.

I said at the beginning of this epilogue that we can learn from countries of every size, every political structure, and every economic status. Inclusive Security works with bold women in more than forty conflicts who are putting their lives on the line as they create new ways of thinking about peace and stability. Those leaders (including delegations from Rwanda) have not only learned from each other about causes and cures of war. Even more important, they tell me, has been the moment they discovered they're not alone. I hope they're finding those moments inside these pages.

In Libya, for example, Dr. Alaa Murabit and her colleagues at the Voice of Libyan Women walk into schools and workplaces, but also the homes of extremists. Sitting down with people who feel backed into a corner, they draw from every aspect of their culture, including, of course, religion. But at a wider level, they're creating innovative education and media campaigns to mold a more open society.

Pakistan's Professor Mossarat Qadeem has a decade of experience deradicalizing extremists by working with legislators, religious leaders, and teachers to talk young men out of suicide attacks. She has taken that challenge to mothers, helping them bring their own sons out of radical groups, and ferreting out jobs to replace the income their young men lose when they defect.

To end the Troubles, the cross-sectarian Northern Ireland Women's Coalition entered parliamentary elections just because only heads of sizable parties would be invited to the peace talks. When extremists broke the cease-fire, Protestant Monica McWilliams and Catholic May Blood dragged the hard-liners back to the negotiating table. The two were alone in insisting that compensation for victims of violence, reintegration of political prisoners, and joint education for Catholic and Protestant youth were addressed in the final agreement—issues crucial after three decades of conflict.

For too long, Luz Mendez was the only woman (out of thirty seats) in talks that ended thirty-six years of war in Guatemala. Now, leaders of the women's movement had someone with whom to connect. Together, they pushed until the peace accords included pioneering standards for women's rights.

It turns out that that Guatemalan experience has been replicated in war zones across the world, since women seem to be particularly adept at mobilizing coalitions. In the Philippines, it was the government and Islamic women—on opposing negotiating teams—who continually pushed for a broader base of support across religious, indigenous, and youth groups. They united to persuade the public to compromise, and when violence threatened to derail the talks, they went into the streets, pressuring spoilers back to the table.

Rwanda, Libya, Pakistan, Northern Ireland, Guatemala, the Philippines—in countless places over countless years, where women have been given an inch, they've taken peace forward by a mile.

Chaos Cracks Open Culture

> When society requires to be rebuilt, there is no use in attempting to rebuild it on the old plan. No great improvements in the lot of mankind are possible until a great change takes place in the fundamental constitution of their modes of thought.
>
> —**John Stuart Mill, *Autobiography***

Disruption—whether in nature or man-made—often provokes a reordering, permanently or temporarily. Massive social unrest, war, or groundbreaking innovation can dismantle a power structure, disturbing ingrained, seemingly fixed expectations about who has authority or influence once the tumult subsides. For better or worse, a backlash toward established ways can result. In some cases, an unexpected legacy of positive growth takes root.

With Rwanda, we see an extreme example: a horrific political and social breakdown with 10 percent of the population dead in one hundred days, a slaughter by farmers, teachers, priests, and others, directed by local officials.

But the memory of how wrong we got it in Rwanda is a dogged reminder of how hard we must work to get it right elsewhere. Vital lessons are buried in the aftermath of the catastrophe. Word is now spreading that another story is emerging from the loss, abandonment, and utter devastation derived from blindness to the humanity of neighbors, in the house next door, or the humanity of neighbors across the world. This may be the most dramatic example in history of women's resilient leadership as, encouraged from the top, they have put their shoulders to the wheel to rebuild their country from the top echelons of the government to the smallest village council.

In Rwanda, chaos cracked open the culture. Stepping back, the most unexpected and counterintuitive recommendation to policy makers is that we look for opportunities in disruption. The possibilities may range from the release of political prisoners to reorganization of government departments to new laws enshrining rights. Bedlam creates needs that allow the emergence of fresh players, who may be constructive or destructive. At those times, from the inside or the outside, we can weigh in to support the positive.

More narrowly, if we believe women are a stabilizing force, we must find ways to advance their power in rebuilding—immediately after the collapse of systems, traditions, and expectations, as well as beyond. As I've already noted, immediately postgenocide the population had a significant majority of females, due to death, imprisonment of men, and the flight of fighters into neighboring countries. But even when the gender proportions equalized as Rwandan men and women long in exile returned to their homeland, soldiers returned from Congo, and prisoners were released from jails, women didn't relinquish their clout.

A great many of Rwanda's recent policies carry a gender overtone. The country has made a name for itself with its hard-line anticorruption stance, a position that tends to favor women in public perception. Widespread citizen participation (by women as well as men) reinforces the concept of common good. Progressive gender roles and rights, enshrined in law and ardently promoted by civil society and government, prioritize the safety of women and increasingly promote their contributions on a footing equal to men. Emphasis on environmental protection, such as the now-famous plastic bag ban, sets a forward-looking tone of nurturing and preserving finite resources for future generations. Programs promoting equitable education emphasize the worth of girls while they elevate care for children. Prohibition of ethnic identification is designed to advance united national allegiance (a worthy if arduous aspiration), which projects the perceived feminine value of reconciliation.

A new generation is rising for whom the 1994 genocide is a part of history, not of memory.

All that said, will the gains women have made, and key male leaders have advocated, endure beyond the current blend of public sector and social circumstances? Have the changes permeated deeply enough into the society—not just its elites and those in power—to withstand political shifts and the ascension of new players, who may or may not share current leaders' proactive inclusion of women?

Twenty years offers a positive trajectory, but the legacy of this postgenocide period is constantly evolving and will ride on the ability of leaders—women and men—to bolster the stake Rwandans across the country have in enduring stability and meaningful reunification. But as the foundation, *the participation of women is transforming the new democracies. It's the key, it's the key. Every bright leader and bright nation will invest in their women,* **INYUMBA** said to me.

Stars may align, and we may help align them, creating a saving opportunity: Social turbulence, political expediency, progressive thinking, and courageous organizing may usher in an era of women's leadership. A time marked by anxiety, despair, and pessimism may become an occasion for redemptive hope.

Introduction

1. Nicole Hogg, "Women's Participation in the Rwandan Genocide: Mothers or Monsters?," *International Review of the Red Cross* 92 (March 2010): 69–102.

2. Joseph Nye, "When Women Lead," Project Syndicate, February 8, 2012, http://www.project-syndicate.org/commentary/when-women-lead.

3. Another notable exception in addition to Hogg, "Women's Participation in the Rwandan Genocide," is African Rights, *Rwanda Not So Innocent* (London: African Rights, 1995).

4. Central Intelligence Agency, "Africa: Rwanda," in *The World Factbook*, 2013, https://www.cia.gov/library/publications/the-world-factbook/geos/rw.html.

1. Foremothers

Epigraph: Peace Uwineza and Elizabeth Pearson, "Sustaining Women's Gains in Rwanda: The Influence of Indigenous Culture and Post-genocide Politics" (Washington, DC: Institute for Inclusive Security, 2009), 8.

1. The National Gender Policy (Kigali: Government of Rwanda, 2004).

2. The Pressure Builds

1. Valerie M. Hudson, Bonnie Ballif-Spanvill, Mary Caprioli, and Chad F. Emmett, *Sex and World Peace* (New York: Columbia University Press, 2012).

2. Intertwined with ethnic motivations for the genocide was a backlash against women's expanding roles in pregenocide Rwanda. As anthropologist Christopher Taylor wrote in his seminal work on the sexual dynamics of the violence: "To many Rwandans gender relations in the 1980s and 1990s were falling into a state of decadence as more women attained positions of prominence in economic and public life, and as more of them exercised their personal preferences in their private lives." Taylor found that representations of women, especially in the vulgar cartoons published in extremist newspapers in the years leading up to the genocide, "foreshadowed the degree of sadism perpetrated by extremists on the bodies of their victims." Christopher Taylor, *Sacrifice as Terror: The Rwandan Genocide of 1994* (New York: Bloomsbury, 1999), 157.

5. Genocide

1. Christopher Taylor, *Sacrifice as Terror: The Rwandan Genocide of 1994* (New York: Bloomsbury, 1999).

2. Details of the Pauline Nyiramasuhuko case from Mark A. Drumbl, "'She Makes Me Ashamed to Be a Woman': The Genocide Conviction of Pauline Nyiramasuhuko, 2011," *Michigan Journal of International Law* 34, no. 3 (2013): 559–603, Washington and Lee Legal Studies Paper no. 2012-32.

6. Immediate Aftermath

1. Atle Dyregrov, Leila Gupta, Rolf Gjestad, and Eugenie Mukanoheli, "Trauma Exposure and Psychological Reactions to Genocide among Rwandan Children," *Journal of Traumatic Stress* 13, no. 1 (2000): 3–21.

Part II. The Path to Public Leadership

1. Rwandan Ministry of Social Affairs, 2007 census, as described in "Census: Rwanda Genocide Survivors Estimated to Be 300,000," Hirondelle News Agency, August 28, 2008, http://www.hirondellenews.com/ictr-rwanda/412-rwanda-political-and-social-issues /22237-en-en-280808-rwandagenocide-census-rwanda-genocide-survivors-estimated -to-be-3000001128811288.

2. Heidy Rombouts, "Women and Reparations in Rwanda: A Long Path to Travel," in *What Happened to the Women?*, ed. Ruth Rubio-Marín (New York: Social Science Research Council, 2006), 208.

7. Community Training Ground

1. Patrick E. Tyler, "Hillary Clinton, in China, Details Abuse of Women," *New York Times*, September 6, 1995.

8. A Pull from the Top

1. Paul Kagame, remarks in a Q&A following a speech at Brandeis University, Boston, April 23, 2014.

11. Caucus Crucible

1. Helle Schwartz, "Women's Representation in the Rwandan Parliament—An Analysis of Variations in the Representation of Women's Interests Caused by Gender and Quota" (Gothenburg University, 2004).

14. The Quota

1. Roster of Rwandan members of Parliament, Parliamentary Library, Kigali.

2. Aili Marie Tripp, "The Changing Face of Africa's Legislatures: Women and Quotas,"

in *The Implementation of Quotas: African Experiences*, ed. Julie Ballington (Stockholm: International Institute for Democracy and Electoral Assistance, 2004), 72–77.

3. Prior to administrative restructuring of the country.

15. Pioneering in Parliament

1. Elizabeth Powley, "Defending Children's Rights: The Legislative Priorities of Rwandan Women Parliamentarians," Institute for Inclusive Security, April 2008, https://www.inclusivesecurity.org/publication/defending-childrens-rights-the-legislative-priorities-of-rwandan-women-parliamentarians/.

2. Powley, "Defending Children's Rights."

3. Helle Schwartz, "Women's Representation in the Rwandan Parliament—An Analysis of Variations in the Representation of Women's Interests Caused by Gender and Quota" (Gothenburg University, 2004).

Part III. Bending toward Reconciliation

1. "Imagine Coexistence: Assessing Refugee Reintegration Efforts in Divided Communities," Fletcher School of Law and Diplomacy, 2002, http://heller.brandeis.edu/coexistence/pdfs/democracy/imagine.pdf.

2. From Elizabeth Powley, "Strengthening Governance: The Role of Women in Rwanda's Transition: A Summary," United Nations, Office of the Special Adviser on Gender Issues, 2004, http://iknowpolitics.org/sites/default/files/strengthening20governance20-20the20role20of20women20in20rwanda27s20tra.pdf.

18. Bringing Them Home

1. For more details on ingando, including descriptions of typical activities presented at the camps, segments of the population required or encouraged to attend, the history of the concept, and the effect on promoting fence mending and furthering state authority, see Andrea Purdekova, "Rwanda's Ingando Camps: Liminality and the Reproduction of Power," Working Paper no. 80, Refugee Studies Center, University of Oxford, 2011.

19. Rethinking Rape

1. The 1996 Genocide Law created special chambers within the existing courts to focus on crimes connected to the genocide. Subsequent laws, in 2000 and 2004, refined the process. The new legal code distinguished between three categories of perpetrators based on varying degrees of responsibility, and confessions could result in lighter sentences. Category 1 included masterminds of genocide, including those who committed sexual torture; Category 2 pertained to people who intentionally or unintentionally killed or who injured with the intent to kill, as well as crimes committed to physically harm someone but without the intention to kill; and Category 3 was for those accused of looting and other property crimes committed during the genocide.

2. Report on the situation of human rights in Rwanda, UN Commission on Human Rights, E/CN.4/1996/68, January 29, 1996.

3. Court documents, judgment of case ICTR-96-4-T, *The prosecutor v. Jean-Paul Akayesu*, http://jrad.unmict.org/webdrawer/webdrawer.dll/webdrawer/search/rec&sm_ncontents =ictr-96-4&sortd1=rs_datecreated&count&template=reclist.

4. Amelia French, "Women Break Their Silence over the Rape of Rwanda," *Independent*, November 9, 1997, http://www.independent.co.uk/news/women-break-their-silence-over -the-rape-of-rwanda-1293264.html.

5. Akayesu sentence, transcript, *Prosecutor v. Akayesu*, Case No. ICTR-96-4, Sentence, October 2, 1998, University of Minnesota Human Rights Library, http://www1.umn.edu /humanrts/instree/ICTR/AKAYESU_ICTR-96-4/Sentence_ICTR-96-4-T.html.

6. Navanethem Pillay, Judicial Archives of the International Criminal Tribunal for Rwanda, October 2, 1998, http://www.un.org/en/preventgenocide/rwanda/resources/pod casts.shtml.

20. To Testify

1. Del Ponte was also pressing for the International Criminal Tribunal for Rwanda to prosecute crimes committed by the RPF and had been spearheading a secret investigation along these lines, pitting her against both the Rwandan government and its allies. She described this ultimately unsuccessful effort in her book, *The Hunt: Me and My War Criminals* (2008). "Carla Del Ponte Tells of Her Attempts to Investigate RPF in Her New Book," Hirondelle News Agency, April 2, 2008, http://www.hirondellenews.com /ictr-rwanda/407-collaboration-with-states/collaboration-with-states-rwanda/21710-en -en-020408-ictrrwanda-carla-del-ponte-tells-of-her-attempts-to-investigate-rpf-in-her -new-book1076110761.

2. Human Rights Watch, *Shattered Lives: Sexual Violence during the Rwandan Genocide and Its Aftermath* (New York: Human Rights Watch, 1996).

3. Binaifer Nowrojee, "Your Justice Is Too Slow: Will the ICTR Fail Rwanda's Rape Victims?," United Nations Research Institute for Social Development, November 2005, 3.

4. SEVOTA is an acronym for Solidarité pour l'Epanouissement des Veuves et des Orphelins visant le Travail et l'Auto-promotion (Solidarity for the Blooming of the Widows and the Orphans Aiming at Work and Self-Promotion).

21. Off the Sidelines

1. Paul Behrens and Ralph Henham, eds., *The Criminal Law of Genocide: International, Comparative and Contextual Aspects* (New York: Routledge, 2007).

2. Human Rights Watch, *Shattered Lives: Sexual Violence during the Rwandan Genocide and Its Aftermath* (New York: Human Rights Watch, 1996).

3. Here again it's important to note that crimes committed by the RPF do not fall under the remit of gacaca, creating tension among people who alleged harm at the hands of these soldiers.

23. Risk and Resignation

1. Hollie Nyseth Brehm, Christopher Uggen, and Jean-Damascéne Gasanabo, "Genocide, Justice, and Rwanda's Gacaca Courts," *Journal of Contemporary Criminal Justice* 30, no. 3 (2014): 333–52.

2. The case of Asiel Simbarikure (2009) came before the community of Busoro, where he had served as a local government administrator, in 1994.

25. Safety: A New Language

1. Elizabeth Pearson and Elizabeth Powley, *Demonstrating Legislative Leadership: The Introduction of Rwanda's Gender-Based Violence Bill* (Washington, DC: Inclusive Security, 2008), 18, https://www.inclusivesecurity.org/wp-content/uploads/2012/08/1078 _rwanda_demonstrating_legislative_leadership_updated_6_20_08.pdf.

2. Human Rights Watch, *Struggling to Survive: Barriers to Justice for Rape Victims in Rwanda* (New York: Human Rights Watch, 2004).

3. Faith Mukakalisa, 2006, quoted in Pearson and Powley, *Demonstrating Legislative Leadership*.

4. Aimable Nibishaka, 2006, quoted in Pearson and Powley, *Demonstrating Legislative Leadership*.

26. Challenging Changes

1. Quoted in Jeanne Izabiliza, "The Role of Women in Reconstruction: Experience of Rwanda," paper presented at Consultation on Empowering Women in the Great Lakes Region: Violence, Peace and Women's Leadership, Addis Ababa, Ethiopia, May 30–June 1, 2005, http://genderandsecurity.org/projects-resources/research/role-women-reconstruction -experience-rwanda.

2. Jane M. Umutoni, "Nurturing Women's Entrepreneurship and Promoting Reconciliation in Post-conflict Rwanda: Buranga Women's Cooperative" (master's thesis, Centre for Gender Culture and Development, Faculty of Social Sciences, Kigali Institute of Education, 2011).

28. Health Means Whole

1. *Amarira y'umugabo atemba munda.*

2. Neal Emery, "Rwanda's Historic Health Recovery: What the U.S. Might Learn," *Atlantic*, February 20, 2013, http://www.theatlantic.com/health/archive/2013/02/rwandas-historic-health-recovery-what-the-us-might-learn/273226/; and "Vital Signs: HIV Prevention through Care and Treatment—United States," *Morbidity and Mortality Weekly Report* 60, no. 47 (2011): 1618–23, http://www.cdc.gov/mmwr/preview/mmwrhtml/mm6047a4 .htm.

31. Little Ones

1. Atle Dyregrov, Leila Gupta, Rolf Gjestad, and Eugenie Mukanoheli, "Trauma Exposure and Psychological Reactions to Genocide among Rwandan Children," *Journal of Traumatic Stress* 13, no. 1 (2000): 3–21.

32. Reading Rights

1. Law on the Prevention and Punishment of Gender-Based Violence, no. 59/2008, *Official Gazette* of the Republic of Rwanda, October 9, 2008.

2. "Education," UNICEF Rwanda, accessed August 10, 2016, http://www.unicef.org /rwanda/education.html; "Millennium Development Goals Rwanda, Final Progress Report: 2013," UNDP Rwanda, December 2014, http://www.rw.undp.org/content/dam /rwanda/docs/Research%20and%20publications/Millenium%20development%20goals /UNDP_RW_MDGR%20Rwanda_31_03_2015.pdf.

33. Solidarity and Sisterhood

1. Justine Uvuza, "Hidden Inequalities: Rwandan Female Politicians' Experiences of Balancing Family and Political Responsibilities" (PhD diss., Newcastle University, 2014).

35. Sowing Confidence

1. Personal interview with researcher Felix Muramutsa, 2016: "Families realized that this is a problem that you can't hide. With the law, people could see that people were being punished. The law didn't create new cases but instead raised hidden cases that were happening. People saw that keeping a secret would support the rapist. Of course it's still a long process, and we still hear about the cases where people are ashamed and don't want to speak about it. We're still figuring out the confidentiality issues, like how to handle pregnancy and abortion in the case of attack."

2. 1988 Family Code of the Republic of Rwanda, cited in Justine Uvuza, "Hidden Inequalities: Rwandan Female Politicians' Experiences of Balancing Family and Political Responsibilities" (PhD diss., Newcastle University, 2014).

37. Planting Deep

1. Education statistics from the National Institute of Statistics of Rwanda bear out Zaina Nyiramatama's observation: the 2012 literacy rate was 65 percent for women, 72 percent for men. From Fourth Population and Housing Census in Rwanda, conducted in August 2012, http://statistics.gov.rw/node/1086.

Epilogue

1. Lois Joy, Nancy M. Carter, Harvey M. Wagner, and Sriram Narayanan, "The Bottom Line: Corporate Performance and Women's Representation on Boards," *Catalyst*, October 2007; Bert D'Espallier, Isabelle Guerin, and Roy Mersland, "Women and Repayment in Microfinance: A Global Analysis," *World Development* 39, no. 5 (May 2011): 758–72.

2. Sarah F. Anzia and Christopher R. Berry, "The Jackie (and Jill) Robinson Effect: Why Do Congresswomen Outperform Congressmen?," *American Journal of Political Science* 55 (2011): 478–93; Raghabendra Chattopadhyay and Esther Duflo, "Women as Policy Makers: Evidence from a Randomized Policy Experiment in India," *Econometrica* 72, no. 5 (September 2004): 1409–43.

3. World Bank, "Issue Brief: The World Bank and Gender Equality," Washington, DC, 2009.

4. Interparliamentary Union, "Women in National Parliaments," December 2016, ipu .org/wmn-e/classif.htm.

5. "Women Constitute 20 Per Cent of Rwanda's Police," Together Rwanda, March 13, 2014, http://www.togetherrwanda.com/2014/03/women-constitute-20-per-cent-of-rwandas -police/.

6. Joseph Nye, "When Women Lead," Project Syndicate, February 2012.

7. Marie O'Reilly, Andrea Ó Súilleabháin, and Thania Paffenholz, *Reimagining Peacemaking: Women's Roles in Peace Processes* (New York: International Peace Institute, 2015), 3, citing Kyle Beardsley, "Agreement without Peace? International Mediation and Time Inconsistency Problems," *American Journal of Political Science* 52, no. 4 (October 2008): 723–40; Kyle Beardsley, *The Mediation Dilemma* (Ithaca, NY: Cornell University Press, 2011).

8. Research by Laurel Stone, published in O'Reilly, Ó Súilleabháin, and Paffenholz, *Reimagining Peacemaking*, 12–13.

9. Based on a comparative case study of forty peace and transition processes carried out by Thania Paffenholz at the Graduate Institute in Geneva. See O'Reilly, Ó Súilleabháin, and Paffenholz, *Reimagining Peacemaking*.

10. Pablo Castillo Diaz and Simon Tordjman, "Women's Participation in Peace Negotiations: Connections between Presence and Influence," New York, UN Women, October 2012.

11. Mohamed Al Agati with Noov Senari, "Women and Equal Citizenship: Analysis of the New Constitution of Egypt," Arab Forum for Citizenship in Transition, December 2012.

12. Letter from Abigail Adams to John Adams, Braintree, March 31, 1776.

13. Speech by President Paul Kagame of Rwanda, at the opening of the 2012 African Economic Conference, October 30, 2012, http://www.afdb.org/fileadmin/uploads/afdb /Documents/Generic-Documents/Kigali-Rwanda%20-%2030%20October%202012%20 -%20Speech%20by%20H.E.%20Paul%20Kagame-President%20of%20the%20 Republic%20of%20Rwanda%20at%20the%20Opening%20of%20the%202012%20 African%20Economic%20Conference.pdf.

14. Personal interview.

15. Partners in Health, Rwanda country page, http://www.pih.org/rwanda.

INDEX

constitutional reform: early initiatives in, 129–34; gender quotas and, 141–45; women's leadership in, 135–39

Coomaraswamy, Radhika, 189–90

cooperative enterprises, women's development of, 239–41

countrywide women's councils, 114–21

culture in Rwanda: deference to authority in, 95; gender and family in, 27–32; stoicism in, 251–56; women's role in, 13, 15, 24–32, 163–64, 293–98

Cynazaire, Aloysie, xix, 202

Dearborn-Hughes, Elizabeth, 370

Del Ponte, Carla, 194, 380n1

development assistance for Rwanda, 366–67

division of labor, gender and, 24

domestic violence: legislation against, 229–34; protection for women from, 258, 260–64

Dusabimana, Josephine, xxiv, 63–66, 295

Duterimbere (Go Forward), 40, 87–88

economic policies: women entrepreneurs and, 242–50; women's advocacy for, 366–67; women's economic cooperatives and, 237–41

education: children's right to, 278–87; gender and, 16–17, 30–32, 39–41, 280, 282, 331–35; for girls, 16–17, 32, 39–41, 280, 282–87, 291–92, 331–35; government positions and requirements for, 152

elections in postgenocide Rwanda: political strategies of women in, 151–59; women's leadership in, 116–21, 142–43, 331–44

entrepreneurship of Rwandan women, 242–50, 306–13, 345–55, 367–69

ethnic identity: colonialism and, 26, 34–36; in exiled communities, 44–51; genocide in Rwanda and role of, 9–12;

post-independence ethnic violence, 44; potter community, 324–26; women's power and, 38–43

evangelical congregations, postgenocide growth of, 239–41

exiled communities, women's leadership in, 44–51, 98

Facing History and Ourselves, 22

Fairbanks, Michael, 368

Family Code, 312

family structure: children's rights and, 279–87; genocide and destruction of, 85–86; reproductive rights advocacy and, 260–64; in Rwandan culture, 27–32, 293–98

Farmer, Paul, 368–69

Fisher, Mary, 368

Forces Démocratiques pour la Libération du Rwanda (FDLR), 176–81

Forum for African Women Educationalists (FAWE), 282

Forum of Rwandan Women Parliamentarians (FFRP), 125–28, 186–88

Fourth World Conference on Women, 91, 370–72

Fox, Sister Ann, 369

Frankl, Victor, 33

gacaca proceedings: genocide trials and, 200–205; perpetrator-victim dynamics during, 211–18; rape victims' participation in, 206–10; security risks for witnesses in, 211–18

Gahaya Links, 308–13, 368

Gakuba, Jeanne d'Arc, xxiii, 114, 118–21, 320–21

Gasamerga, Wellars, xxvii, 149

Gasana, Emmanuel, xxii, 302–4

Gasinzigwa, Oda, xxvi, 154–56, 345

gender: constitutional equalization reforms and, 135–39; cultural contexts of, 24–32, 377n2; education and, xxvi,